YOU ARE
WHAT YOU
WRITE

YOU ARE
WHAT YOU
RITE

BY

Huntington Hartford

Collier Books
A Division of Macmillan Publishing Co., Inc.
New York

Macmillan Publishing Co., Inc.
866 Third Avenue, New York, N.Y. 10022
Collier Macmillan Canada, Ltd.

You Are What You Write is published in a hardcover edition by Macmillan
Publishing Co., Inc.

Library of Congress Catalog Number: 72-91262

First Collier Books Edition 1976

Printed in the United States of America

TO
AGNES HARDECKER
AND
MARIE RICCI

The skeptics are all those who have stood aloof, which is reminiscent of the story told of Charles Lamb, who was said to have declared his aversion for a stranger. "But you don't know him," pleaded his interlocutor, "let me introduce you." "No, no," objected the essayist. "If I should know him, I'm apt to like him."

—*Graphology—a Handbook* by Henry A. Rand

Acknowledgments

Like any student of so large a field, I have incurred many obligations to the work of my colleagues and predecessors all of which I hope are acknowledged in their proper places in the text. But I would like here to express my particular gratitude to several people whose help in preparing this book was invaluable. The first and foremost is Miss Marie Ricci, my secretary, and the staff at the office, without whom, I must declare over their protests, there would be no book at all. With the persistence of a combination of Madame Curie and Sherlock Holmes, Miss Ricci not only put my research into intelligible form but followed to the bitter end all those trails of acknowledgment and bibliography (and whatever else Macmillan and I left for her to do) which insured a publishing date within the foreseeable future. Next is Mr. Collin Weber who managed to find time between his medical studies and his honeymoon to take the heterogeneous material with which I provided him and painstakingly put it into categories out of which I could ultimately produce chapters. Thirdly, there is Timothy Dickinson who in his own words "plowed through the typescript" with amazing erudition and indefatigable energy before my editors were confronted with it, leaving them with little to correct except in the area of punctuation. If you are writing a book, whoever you are, Timothy Dickinson is a must! Finally, my very deepest gratitude to Ulrich Sonnemann for permitting me to quote him so extensively throughout. Dr. Sonnemann is certainly one of the world's greatest graphologists (and sociologists as well) and let us hope that he returns soon from Munich to his second home in the United States for an extended stay—graphology needs him here.

I am also deeply grateful to the following individuals:

To Alfred Kanfer for the invaluable time and cooperation he gave me in working out my chapter on Cancer.

To Dr. H. Houston Merritt, Dean Emeritus and Vice-President Emeritus, Faculty of Medicine, Columbia University College of Physicians and Surgeons, for the warm sympathy and interest which he showed in writing the Foreword to my book.

To Thea Stein Lewinson and Dr. Joseph Zubin for their inspiring study of rhythm in handwriting, upon which so much of my chapter on the subject has been based.

To George A. Mapp and John P. Kernan for the gracious permission to use their unique material in my chapter on Business.

To *Playboy* magazine and Daniel S. Anthony for use of the title, which was first suggested to me, by the way, by my good friend Cathy Warren of *Vogue* magazine. (Mr. and Mrs. Anthony have increased Klara Roman's original three courses at the New School for Social Research to a three-year program in Graphology—six semester courses which include Graphology IV, "Handwriting Analysis in Business and the Professions," and Graphology VI, "The Psychopathology of Handwriting.")

To Mrs. Carlton Cole, my literary agent, whose frequent calls urging me on kept me in a state of healthy panic.

To Mrs. Kate A. Wolff (widow of Werner Wolff, who wrote "Diagrams of the Unconscious").

To Rose Wolfson, Ph.D.

To Herry O. Teltscher, Ph.D.

To The Pierpont Morgan Library; The New York Public Library (Manuscript Division, and Henry W. and Albert A. Berg Collection); Frederick Ungar Publishing Co., Inc. for permission to reproduce illustrations from their publications including Klara Roman's *Encyclopedia of the Written Word*; Dr. Jan Van Loewen Ltd. for use of pages from *Time Remembered* by Jean Anouilh translated by Patricia Moyes.

Finally I wish to express gratitude to all those who have permitted me to reproduce illustrations.

Contents

HEALTH, CRIME, BUSINESS

EXAMPLES

APPENDICES

Foreword

The title of Mr. Hartford's book is *You Are What You Write.* This might seem to imply that your writing controls your character and your destiny. I would like to paraphrase this statement with the words "you write what you are."

Mr. Hartford also notes that the medical profession has for many years been greatly interested in handwriting. His statement that "handwriting is brainwriting" is true and very significant.

Handwriting is controlled by muscles innervated by nerves arising from the ventral horn cells of the spinal cord. The flow of stimuli to the cells in the spinal cord is regulated mainly by the motor centers in the cortex of the dominant cerebral hemisphere. These impulses are integrated and modified by stimuli from nerve centers at the base of the brain (basal ganglia), the cerebellum, and other subcortical centers. Disturbances of these centers which produce changes in handwriting have been the chief interest of the neurologist. The neurologist can understand how injury to the basal ganglia in Parkinson's disease influences the size and shape of the letters and the flow of the script as the result of rigidity and tremor of the muscles. Similarly he can readily recognize that reduplication or omission of the loops in the formation of "M" or "W" accompanied by misspelling and tremor is evidence of disease of the frontal lobes by general paresis. He can understand how disease of the primary controlling centers of the brain can influence handwriting, but it is difficult for him to see how disease in other organs—cancer of the intestines, for instance—can recognizably influence the script.

Psychologists and psychiatrists have concerned themselves with the effect of diseases of "mind" on the script.

The graphologist takes both of these factors into consideration, but emphasizes the role of personality in the development of a handwriting which is characteristic for each individual.

The physician is likely to neglect the role of the great masses of the cerebral cortex which are concerned with the synthesis of and elaboration of information received from the external world and from the body itself. These so-called association areas are concerned with thoughts, intellect, and emotion. They control the formation of the individual as a whole, which is best described by the term "personality."

It is perhaps the role these centers play in the handwriting that is not understood by the physician. He can readily recognize the changes due to disturbances of or faulty control of the major projection centers (motor cortex, basal ganglia, and cerebellum), but he is not able to recognize the role of the association areas in the elements of the script which are of great interest to the graphologist. The physician is not aware of the importance of such factors as rhythm, pressure, beginning strokes and the like either because he is not trained to recognize them or because he considers them too erudite to be evaluated accurately.

The graphologist thinks these characteristics of the script to be of paramount importance. He considers them to be the manifestation of a myriad of factors which have played a role in the evolution of the individual and of great value in recognizing the subject as a distinct and unique personality.

A more complete knowledge of the relationship of the primary projection centers and the association areas of the cortex should be the goal of both the physician and the graphologist alike.

It is to be hoped that a study of this book by physicians and graphologists will lead to this goal.

H. HOUSTON MERRITT, M.D.
Henry L. and Lucy Moses Professor Emeritus of Neurology, Dean Emeritus and Vice-President Emeritus, Faculty of Medicine, Columbia University College of Physicians and Surgeons

INTRODUCTORY

Is Graphology a Science?

Is graphology a science? The answer, in my opinion, is another question: Is there a sound in the forest when no one is there to hear it? The famous psychologist Alfred Binet called graphology "the science of the future," and unfortunately "the future," though getting a bit closer, has not quite arrived. For many years the high priests of graphology have been blowing their rams' horns before the impregnable walls of the medical profession, which in spite of a few cracks have yet to come tumbling down like the walls of Jericho.

Many people take astrology more seriously than graphology as a gauge of personality, and I am myself always curious to find out the sign under which someone was born. But of course the total personality is made up not only of the date of birth but of heredity, environment, and even daily moods. The picture that handwriting draws includes all these. If one looks up the article "Handwriting" in the *Encyclopedia Britannica*, one indeed finds a serious and thorough section by Joseph Zubin, a professor of psychology at Columbia University, and Rose Wolfson on graphology. If the claims of graphology could be scientifically validated, says Zubin, handwriting would offer the most accessible means of evaluating the personality of both patients and normal people. But the statistical method which he and Thea Lewinson (a graphologist educated in Berlin) present for our approval is too technical to have been completely accepted by subsequent graphologists. Sometimes the very scholars who are most capable of reaching the ear of the medical profession make such a thorough and elaborate case in dealing with our questionable subject (which at best, like psychology itself, bears the stigma of being an art as well as a science) that the true significance of their message is in danger of being ignored.

There is a story about three people from different nations who were asked to write a book about the elephant. The Frenchman wrote *Sex and the Elephant*, the Englishman *Hunting the Elephant with Gun and Camera in India*, and the German turned out *An Introduction to the Study of the Elephant* in six volumes. Werner Wolff devoted the entire first half of his exhaustive and thoroughly commendable book *Diagrams of the Unconscious* (subtitled "Handwriting and Personality in Measurement, Experiment and Analysis") to establishing "a scientific basis for a positive relationship between graphic movement [handwriting] and processes which involve that psychological factor which we call 'personality.'" He spent 177 pages, in other words, in an introduction to his subject to assure its being taken seriously. See how insecure we graphologists are! On the other hand, of course, graphologists with little or no scientific background—of whom there are hundreds, including myself—anxious to reach the general public and perhaps make a few dollars from their chosen profession or hobby (and I won't exclude myself here either), often write in too subjective and arbitrary a manner for serious consideration. Some of the columnists and authors of do-it-yourself books (with tracing paper to give your temperature on the "love register") continue to give a meaning to every letter and every curlicue of the script in the tradition of the nineteenth century French founder of graphology, Abbé Michon, in spite of the general acceptance by serious graphologists of the Gestalt theory. Others, like M. N. Bunker, the founder of the International Graphoanalysis Society, give lip service to science without following its methods. "The system of handwriting analysis known as Graphoanalysis is not to be confused," says Mr. Bunker, "with outdated graphology." He tells us that it is "exact, scientific" and "used throughout the civilized world for pleasure and profit." The subtitle of his first chapter affords us a further description of his method: "Grapho Analysis gives you protection from chiselers, thieves, heartbreak and murderers. . . ." How much more can you ask?

But in spite of Mr. Bunker's attack on it, graphology has not been without supporters in the world of science throughout the years. One of the first was Adelle Land, instructor at the University of Buffalo, who wrote a monograph on the subject in 1924. She dismisses palmistry and phrenology as incapable of quantitative results or even detailed observation, claiming that there is little relation between the thoughts and emotions and cruder aspects of the external organism such as, for example, a large and bulging forehead. She finds intelligence tests themselves "too simple" (for all their complexity) to reproduce the nuances of human nature in the manner that the tone of a voice or the expression or an eye can do, but finds in handwriting a record of the personality in which these rapid and fleeting nuances can be permanently captured. Later in 1933 the famous psychologists Gordon W. Allport and Philip E. Vernon agreed with Continental psychologists in seeing in graphic movements the quintessence of expression. "Handwriting provides material that is less artificial than tests," they said, "and more convenient for analysis; and since it can be studied at leisure, it is superior to facial expression, gesture, and gait, which are so fleeting and difficult to record. . . . No one who has considered carefully the experimental and theoretical work on handwriting seems to deny the *a priori* case for graphology." Allport and Vernon found an alert and sympathetic interest in the subject in Europe, symbolized by societies and journals in Germany, France, and Holland. There, scientific graphology and clinical practice traveled hand

in hand. They found the prevailing attitude among American
psychologists, on the other hand, one of skepticism and mistrust;
it was customary here, they said, to find graphology contemptu-
ously dismissed along with phrenology and palmistry, or deplored
as a public menace of the "gold brick" variety. As a consequence,
they concluded, very few psychologists in this country studied
graphology's methods or claims seriously; one of them called it
"a tissue of exaggerations."

Handwriting, of course, has long been used for purposes of
identification, but the profession of authentication lives in a
world of its own with great disdain for its poor but proud cousin.
But from time to time in recent years, graphology in America
has received a polite nod from the Olympus of MDs and PhDs.
There is the work, of course, of Lewinson and Zubin done at
Columbia University. There is Dr. William Perl, practicing at
the prison at Fort Leavenworth, who comments that he analyzes
the handwriting of every prisoner as part of his routine evaluation. There is Dr. Hector Ritey, Diplomate in Psychiatry of the
American Board of Psychiatry and Neurology, who wrote that
"handwriting analysis has a definite advantage over every other
projective technique, inasmuch as the patient is completely unaware of the fact that he is undergoing a test while writing." (He
is concentrating, that is, unlike the patient taking the Rorschach
and TAT tests, rather on what he is writing than how. The extent to which the "how" becomes automatic is the yardstick to
the discerning graphologist of the authenticity of his science and
its claim to the subtitle of "brainwriting.")

I have spent many years asking men, women, and children
for specimens of their writing. Some graphologists feel that writing can never be analyzed on request in this manner, but I disagree. I always ask my victims to write variations on the sentence
"I am walking down the street to get the horse and buggy out
of the old carriage house." I don't remember how the sentence
started, but I know that its purpose, like the one about the
quick brown fox and the lazy dog, has been to include as many
letters as possible of the alphabet and particularly the ones that
interest me most. Because I want the writing to be as close to

automatic and unselfconscious as possible, there are certain other requests I make of the writer. I ask him to use a pen or pencil, whichever is most natural to him, for in that way pressure would be most truly reflected. (No ballpoints.) I ask him to sit comfortably and to write on an even surface. I tell him not to worry about spelling, which would break his concentration. I ask him to write rather fast and informally, as if he were dashing off a letter to an old friend or taking down notes at a lecture (cases in which he would give least thought to how his writing looks, so long as it is legible). Finally, I ask him to write the specimen two or three times, because I find that the last specimen is often more mature and interesting than the first. Occasionally people balk at doing this, asking why one specimen should not be enough. Very occasionally someone refuses to write, and I am reminded of an old friend from Salt Lake City who would turn purple in the face denying it when I told him that his handwriting showed signs of obstinacy.

Is "writing to order" truly automatic? Is it "brainwriting"? I have found that when I ask people to write they divide into two groups—the believers and the disbelievers. If I may be permitted a highly subjective opinion, it seems to me that the believers are generally more imaginative; they feel the value of graphology though knowing little about it. The disbelievers have varying ways of telling you that you cannot analyze their writing. "I never write—I always use a typewriter," they say, or "I write badly" (to a graphologist there is no such thing as "bad" writing—the "worst" is sometimes the best), or "You can't read my writing, because I write in several different ways" (simply betraying their immaturity), or "It's not really my writing, because I copied the writing of a friend I admired in school." The truth of the latter case, of course, is that we all learn somewhere, and it is those things that make an impression that we retain. If someone sees a Greek "d," for example, and uses it the rest of his or her life, it is because a natural affinity for it exists. Perhaps it is to avoid such personal reactions that graphologists prefer previously written script. But such script has other problems. One must be told the age and sex of the writer (neither indicated through the script), the speed of the writing, which is difficult to ascertain at second hand, and of course the circumstances under which it was written. Was it written calmly or under emotional strain? Was the person addressed a friend or a stranger? And the graphologist analyzing a specimen from the past also needs sufficient material, enough variety of letters, and a signature. Two other factors must always be taken into consideration in analyzing writing, whether present or past: the educational level and the native language. Like school copy, both tend to have less influence on the writing of the intelligent person as he matures (witness the writing of Lincoln), but the influence remains strong in the writing of the less intelligent.

by the people, for the people, shall not perish from the earth.

Abraham Lincoln.

November 19, 1863.

Abraham Lincoln *

The late Klara Roman in her posthumously published *Encyclopedia of the Written Word* presented what she called an "overall concept" of graphology, and she enumerated three principles: that handwriting is unique and never duplicated—like a face, it retains its essential characteristics throughout the years; that it is continually in the process of change, reflecting the growth and aging of the writer and the effects of crucial events; and third, like speech, voice, gesture and so forth, that it retains its consistency of expression. There is a dichotomy in the stock arguments that handwriting can be changed at will on the one hand or remains always the same on the other that goes to the heart of the value of graphology. Of course neither is true. At

* From *Encyclopedia of the Written Word* by Klara G. Roman. Reprinted by permission of Frederick Ungar Publishing Co., Inc., New York.

the same time, if handwriting did not change and if it did not also remain consistent, there could be no scientific analysis of it. It changes superficially with moods. June Downey, of the University of Wyoming, made a study of signatures in this regard many years ago. It is the opinion, however, of H. J. Jacoby that a momentary mood cannot fundamentally alter the forms of a letter in a person's handwriting, commenting that only in cases of psychosis had he found changes sufficient to place the identity of the writer in doubt. It changes in youth, it changes with old age; and of course it changes with ill-health. But these are not arbitrary changes made at will; they are generally gradual and from the inside out. Werner Wolff, as I have said, wrote half a book attempting to prove that handwriting is made up of "diagrams of the unconscious," and to whatever degree the unconscious is consistent throughout our life, so is our writing. Further proof may be seen in cases given by Robert Saudek of the writing of men blinded in war who many years later wrote with an identical script. And the consistency of the signatures of such famous

Napoleon in victory *

Napoleon in defeat *

* From *Handwriting—A Key to Personality* by Klara G. Roman. Reprinted by permission of Pantheon Books, Inc., New York.

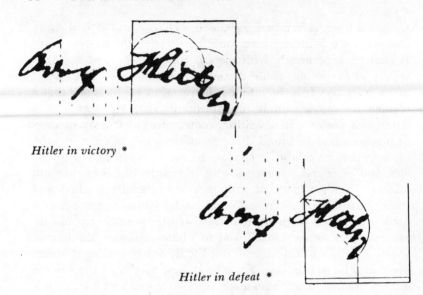

Hitler in victory *

Hitler in defeat *

and notorious men as Napoleon and Hitler, penned in victory and defeat over a period of years, is illuminating.

Saudek was a noted German graphologist writing in England during the Twenties. The first chapter of his book *The Psychology of Handwriting* is entitled "Common Objections Raised against Graphology," where he lists and refutes six objections.

The first objection is that handwriting is not connected with the character of the writer, but depends exclusively on the muscular constitution of the hand. To prove in reply that it is primarily the personality which controls writing, directing the hand, Saudek points out the following: that the mood, the person addressed, and the state of health all influence writing; that writing with a different hand, as in the case of Nelson after he lost his arm, or writing with the mouth or even with the foot, are believed to have little ultimate effect on the writing; and finally, that when hypnotized, one writes according to the character sug-

* From *Diagrams of the Unconscious* by Werner Wolff, Ph.D. Reprinted by permission of Grune & Stratton, Inc., New York and Mrs. Kate A. Wolff.

Writing of Admiral Nelson after he lost his arm *

gested by the hypnotizer. (Jacoby describes how it was suggested to a young student in a condition of light hypnosis that he was a young girl and then that he was an anarchist but though when he was called upon to write in these states his script altered— not, Jacoby says, in such a way as to correspond to the writing of actual anarchists—the fundamentals of his writing remained quite consistent.)

Jacoby's own example—a student
Natural handwriting †

Under hypnosis—
as a young girl †

Under hypnosis—as an anarchist †

* From *Autographic Mirror* Volume 1.

† From *Analysis of Handwriting* by H. J. Jacoby. Reprinted by permission of George Allen & Unwin, Ltd., London.

Second objection: that writing materials (pen, pencil, paper) are more decisive for handwriting than the character and momentary mood of the writer. But, taking into account the mechanical circumstances under which the specimen is written, the quality of the paper, the nature of the pencil or pen and ink, the manner in which the pencil or pen is held, the angle to the writing surface, once again it is something more fundamental than the muscles which is seen to predominate.

Objection number three: that handwriting is the result of school teaching and thus children write a similar hand without possessing a similar character. In reply Saudek refers to the experiment of the influential Jules Crépieux-Jamin, the pupil of Abbé Michon, with a group of children of the same age, in the same class, and with the same writing teacher, who of course wrote entirely differently. He claims that while the characters of children are less developed than those of adults, important personal characteristics are revealed in no less a degree. (I would not go quite so far, because the most critical characteristics, I believe, do not appear until puberty or later.)

Objection number four: members of the same profession frequently write a similar hand without possessing similar characters. Refutation: it is only to non-graphologists, says Saudek, that the handwriting of the same profession appears very similar. "In the whole living human race there are not two individuals who have the same handwriting, just as there are not two identical oak leaves in existence." (Nor two doctors, may I add, with good handwriting!)

Fifth objection: handwriting is not dependent on character, since it would otherwise remain unchanged. The answer here, of course, is that writing changes gradually along with the character over a period of years and superficially with moods. Sixth and last objection: handwriting cannot reflect character, as it is capable of arbitrary modification. This is, however, true only in a very restricted sense. In the case of thousands of forgeries examined, features of the writing which were altered were almost invariably graphologically irrelevant but often striking to the unpracticed observer. The pen was held differently, the slant or size changed, flourishes added or eliminated. The changes were crude and exaggerated and obvious to the expert. That anyone should disguise his handwriting systematically in a long manuscript, says Saudek, so that nothing of his own character should be revealed is theoretically impossible. I would like to make a concluding observation of my own, as I have to do every now and then to ensure having this book published. (I tried very hard at my first meeting with my publisher to convince them to let me edit instead of write a book, but no go.) Imitation, it is said, is the sincerest form of flattery, and there are indeed one or two graphological signs, I hate to admit, which are much too easy to imitate. If you ever run across my former secretary, Barbara Solier, and notice the Greek "d"s and the figure-8 "g"s in her script, just take a look at the writing of her ex-boss!

Almost all graphologists agree that age and sex cannot be determined from writing (Ulrich Sonnemann and others include handedness), though many of them have found minor exceptions to the rule. Crépieux-Jamin stated that "there will always be examples of effeminate men and virile women; the former will employ the feminine and the latter a masculine type of handwriting. It is the psychological and not the physiological personality which is revealed in handwriting." Alfred Binet, the "founder" of intelligence testing, went far toward proving the latter statement in a study regarding intelligence and character that he made at the request of Crépieux-Jamin in 1906. He was much more successful in his correlations of intelligence than of character, but he concluded that neither age nor sex could be positively indentified through handwriting. Dr. Ludwig Klages, his contemporary, was an early maverick on the subject, claiming that the writing of males was more "connected" than that of females, reminding us of the feminine intuition of which we speak today which may be indicated by broken letters. Gordon Allport stated that most graphologists indeed insist on being told the sex and age of the writers before they undertake an analysis, since they are unable to deduce them. Louise Rice, the founder of the American Graphological Society, claimed that "every graphologist has realized that sex simply does not exist" (mean-

(1850)

Miss Stevens

I should like to enquire of you the reasons why you as a teacher and of course over me only a scholar should treat me in such an unhumane manner as to send me out of the class for laughing a little too loud which I can assure you I am perfectly unable to control and which no punishment will cure me of. You cannot deny that I have not tried to behave better in class lately. If I wanted I could sit still (without saying a word) in a corner and suppose all the class were to do it would not you think that all the class were very stupid indeed and you would have to do all the talking the scholars saying nothing. If I cannot be treated well I would rather than be treated as I have been I shall next term go into E III which recites to Miss Torrey or else omit History & Grammar all together. I do not say this hastily in anger but you cannot say but what I have said it a great while and I think that upon reflection you cannot say but what I have been treated unjustly. I hope before the term ends we shall be on better terms than at present. Going into E III is a long contemplated step. Please give me your opinions?

J. Pierpont Morgan

J. P. MORGAN. *Extraordinary maturity of J. P. Morgan in his early teens. Note the good rhythm and elimination of unnecessary strokes, the strong "t" bars and the figure-8 "g"s.* *

---

ing "does not show") in handwriting; she goes on to say later that "another thing that cannot be expressed in handwriting is age." She points out that the writing of the little Josef Hofmann, the great pianist, could easily have been taken for that of a grown man—and similarly, I might add, the writing of the young J. P. Morgan. Yet she somewhat contradicts herself regarding sex when she claims that women have a more decided rhythm than men, calling this the only graphological sex distinction.

Approaching the present, Klara Roman agrees with Crépieux-Jamin in her description of men with delicate body contours and feminine traits and women with athletic muscular development and low-pitched voices whose writings would be difficult to identify. Sonnemann, who considers information concerning age and sex a standard requirement for graphological practice, enters a dissenting opinion on the subject of age. Though age can rarely be ascertained during the years of maturity, he sees frequent exceptions in the cases of young and old. Articulation of writing as a task, he says, presents the child with an obstacle which tends to slow down the speed and to increase the pressure of his writing (as opposed to that of most adults, except the immature ones with the same handicaps). He also finds a tendency to contraction, a greater disconnectedness, and something he calls "meagerness" in the writing of old age. He finds a tendency toward contraction in masculine writing and toward release in feminine, but of course this is no guarantee of the actual sex of the writer. Finally there is Alfred Mendel, the Viennese graphologist, who shows us a beautiful example of an alternating downstroke and upstroke in the logo of Brooks Brothers, and claims that the stable axis, as he calls the downstroke, is confirmed in his experience as the masculine symbol in writing. Proving—or disproving—that remarkable statement should be an intriguing bit of research.

Logo of Brooks Brothers

How can graphological findings be given scientific validity? In the opinion of Ulrich Sonnemann, "The only possible criterion of indisputable relevance for the objectification of personality descriptions is the recognizability of the described subject's identity by persons who know him well. The only sound solution, then, appears to be matching experiments, in which a group of personality descriptions derived on the basis of 'blind' graphological analysis are plotted against the group of the subjects described and in which the 'judges'—who have to be thoroughly acquainted with the personality of each of them—are asked to determine the identity of the subject of each of these descriptions. Such matching experiments can and should be tightly controlled. They can and should be subjected to the most rigorous statistical analysis. Yet, in order also to answer the question of the reliability of the method as such—i.e., independently of the individual graphological worker—such experiments would have to involve a larger number of psychologists thoroughly trained in the graphological method. At the present time, no such group appears to exist in this country. That the day may not be distant when it will not only exist but when its skills—in education, in social work, in vocational guidance, and, most of all, in psychiatry and clinical psychology—will finally have proved themselves beyond doubt is the author's hope and confident expectation."

The History of Writing

Klara Roman, whom I knew slightly and some of my associates knew better in life, is beginning to communicate with me a lot more clearly now that she has gone. A particularly belated communication, too, since her most important book, *The Encyclopedia of the Written Word,* came out not only posthumously but in fact just a few months ago after I had finished almost all my own research, forcing me to retrace my steps in more than a few places. One of the most interesting and erudite parts of her book is the series of sections on the history of writing, starting with alphabetic forms and passing through such scripts as cuneiform and hieroglyphic to a discussion of the instruments and the origins of writing—out of which, I gratefully acknowledge, much of this chapter is drawn. Few graphologists have given serious attention to such information.

Prehistoric cave paintings, says Miss Roman, suggest that knowledge and familiarity with some tools and materials of writing preceded the formulation of any system of communication by signs or symbols. The earliest known writing materials were hard substances: stone, bone, ivory, metal, or wood. The Ten Commandments were said to have been inscribed by Moses on two tablets of stone; and the laws of the Twelve Tables of the Romans were graven in brass. North American Indians used the wampum belt to commemorate their treaties and bargains. The first attempts to express ideas graphically belong more to the history of art than of writing; the ideas of writing and drawing were identical in prehistoric Egypt and early Greece, and for a time the two functions may have gone hand in hand. In the very earliest stages of writing, a picture as exemplified by the pictograms of Oriental script stood literally for the object it

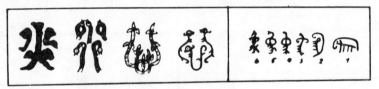

Pictograms of Oriental script *

represented. Eventually pictures began to represent not only the original subject, not only the sun, for example, but bright, light, and day, and finally to be associated with the original sound of the word it stood for. There was thus a transition from the pictogram through the abstract ideogram to the phonogram, or sound sign. All three usually coexisted in the same system, as in Chinese writing today and as was true of the last stages of the great ancient systems of Egyptian hieroglyphics and Babylonian cuneiform—the resulting confusion contributing to their demise.

Bright	Obstructed	Forest	To see	To sit	Emperor
明	閑	林	見	坐	皇

Ideograms †

* From *Diagrams of the Unconscious* by Werner Wolff, Ph.D. Reprinted by permission of Grune & Stratton, Inc., New York and Mrs. Kate A. Wolff.

† Reprinted by courtesy of The American Museum of Natural History, New York.

Hieroglyphics *

Cuneiform *

Hieroglyphic and cuneiform writing, going as far back as 3,000 years B.C., contained the seeds not only of our Western alphabets but of Arabic, Russian, Indian, Mongolian, and many others. The word "cuneiform" was derived from the Latin *cuneus*, meaning "wedge," and *forma*, meaning "form," and for thousands of years writing was accomplished by the Sumerians and their neighbors—the Babylonians, Assyrians, Hittites, and Persians—by impressing soft clay in the form of a tablet with a wedge-shaped stylus and then baking it. In the eighth century B.C. there was a library of 20,000 clay tablets in Nineveh.

While the Sumerians were learning to use the wedge-shaped stylus, the Egyptians were already writing on papyrus from reeds of the same name that grew along the banks of the Nile,

* From *Encyclopedia of the Written Word* by Klara G. Roman. Reprinted by permission of Frederick Ungar Publishing Co., Inc., New York.

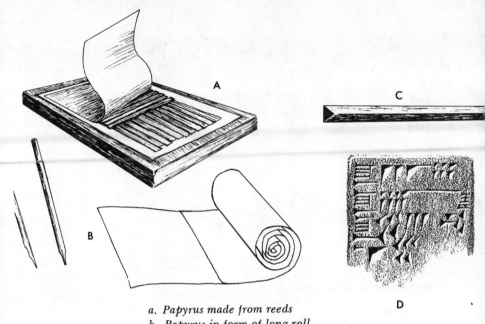

a. *Papyrus made from reeds*
b. *Papyrus in form of long roll*
b. *Reed pen*
c. *Wedge-shaped stylus*
d. *Impression of writing on baked clay* *

using the sharpened end of the reed as a pen. By the beginning of the Christian era, papyrus was the most popular writing material in the Western world. Finally, becoming scarce and expensive, in its own turn it was replaced by parchment. Probably developed in ancient Greece, parchment prepared from the skin of sheep, goats, and calves offered a better surface for writing than papyrus and was likely to last longer. The reed pen continued as the writing instrument until the advent of the quill pen, made from the feathers of geese and turkeys and known as early as the seventh century A.D. The last great advance in writing materials was the advent of paper. Not introduced into Europe until the eleventh century, it had been used in China for over a thousand years. It was the broad-edged or square-cut pen (either reed or quill) with its alternate thick and thin strokes, together

* From *Lettering* by Charles R. Anderson, © 1969 by Litton Educational Publishing, Inc. Reprinted by permission of Van Nostrand Reinhold Company.

Parchment *

with the smooth writing surface of parchment and paper, that made the curves of Roman and later cursive writing possible. Certainly it is true that the histories of the alphabet, of language, of the style of letters created, and of the finesse and mobility of writing instruments, were a continuously interacting process. It was both the search for new techniques and the accident of finding them which has created our modern scripts—and our language.

The origin of the alphabet was probably around 1800 B.C. and the numerous Semitic prototype scripts were gradually channeled into two main streams—the Phoenician and the Aramaic. From the Aramaic derived the Arabic and Hebrew scripts. Persian,

* Reprinted by permission of The Pierpont Morgan Library, New York (M. 710, fol. 191v).

Turkish, Mongolian, and to some extent Brahman scripts were adapted from the Aramaic. Northern Arabic writing did not develop till around the sixth century A.D., since the tent-dwelling Bedouins preserved their ancient poetry through oral tradition only. The written language was crystallized in the Holy Writ of Islam, the Koran, the first book in Arabic, and in spreading the word of the Moslem religion, Arabic became one of the chief languages of the world. Arabic, of course, runs from right to left, has only seventeen letters for expressing twenty-eight consonants, and has no vowels, which explains the accompanying dots and dashes which give tone and vowel value to the words. The phonetic value of letters of the Hebrew script has endured

الحمد لله وحده والصلاة والسلام على

رسول الله،

امي الحنون،

انني وصلت الى امريكا نهارا الاربعاء الاخير

واستقبلت من طرف بسيد ابراهيم موسى

استقبالا حارا. وزرت نيويورك العظيمة

مع هذه المرأة يعني سيد ابراهيم موسى.

والسلام.

Arabic writing *

* From *Encyclopedia of the Written Word* by Klara G. Roman. Reprinted by permission of Frederick Ungar Publishing Co., Inc., New York.

The Hebrew script *

for almost four thousand years, due to reverence for Biblical
books and the Talmud. It is still inscribed in the difficult path
from right to left, though the rebellious individual letters are
often traced with the contrary and forward motion.

The Phoenician ancestor of the ancient Semitic scripts, according to Roman, seems to have had the most direct lineal
bearing on the modern alphabet. After being carried to Asia
Minor and elsewhere, the Phoenician alphabet was admired and
adopted by the Greeks, who with an alphabet of ultimately
twenty-four letters, including vowels and definite symbols for
consonants, provided a true phonetic alphabet suitable for all

* From *Alphabets & Ornaments* by Ernest Lehner. (Dover Publications,
Inc.)

The Phoenician script *

the Indo-European languages. The Phoenician script was changed
in direction from leftward to rightward, and more cursive forms
were developed for writing on parchment, papyrus, wax, and
other soft materials. The change was slow and gradual, and
during the transition period the Greeks wrote one line from left
to right and the next from right to left: "backward and forward,
as the ox plows." Centuries after the change Germanic tribes

* Reprinted by permission of Musee du Bardo, Tunisie.

were still writing from right to left. The Roman alphabet, whose
capital letters were to remain the classic models of Western writing up to the present, emerged by way of the Etruscan from the
Greek; and a rightward cursive script, looking not too different
from the modern, became the everyday correspondence-hand of

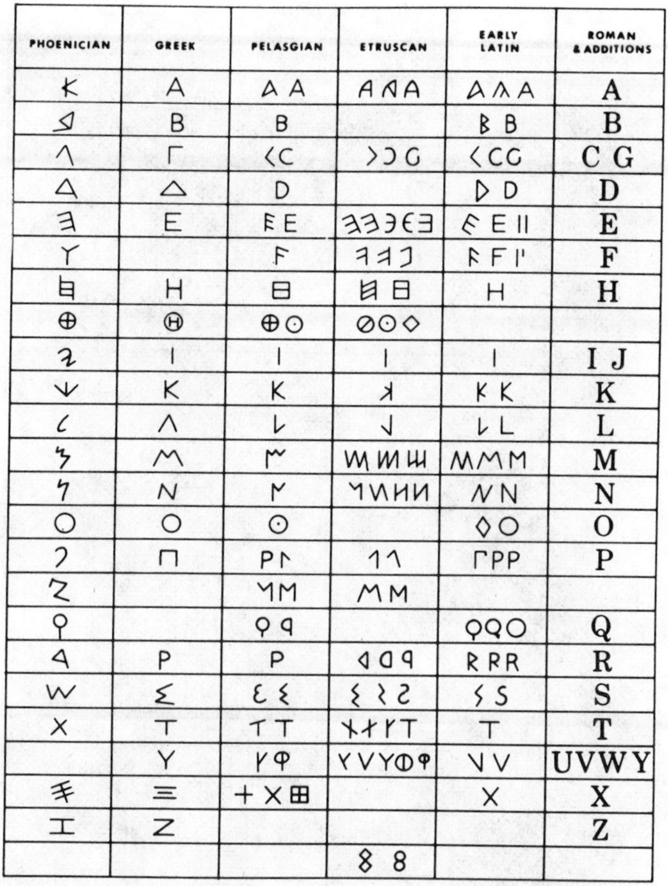

PHOENICIAN	GREEK	PELASGIAN	ETRUSCAN	EARLY LATIN	ROMAN & ADDITIONS
Қ	A	Λ Λ	Λ ΛΛ	Λ ΛΛ	A
◁	B	B		ଅ B	B
Λ	Γ	ᐸC	ᐳϽG	ᐸCG	C G
△	△	D		ᐅ D	D
∃	E	Ⅎ E	ⅎ⅃∃⅁	Ɛ E ‖	E
Υ		Ⅎ	⅂⅂⅃	Ⅎ FⅠᐟ	F
�

目 | H | ⊟ | ⊟ ⊟ | H | H |
⊕	⊕	⊕⊙	⊘⊙◇		
ﻭ	Ⅰ	Ⅰ	Ⅰ	Ⅰ	I J
↓	K	K	⅄	K K	K
ᒪ	Λ	Ⅼ	⅃	Ⅼ L	L
Ꝝ	M	ᒼ	ᙢ ᙢ ᙁ	ΛⅢ ΛⅢ ΛⅢ	M
ꟻ	N	ᖾ	ꟼᐱᕁᕁ	Λ N	N
○	O	⊙		◇ O	O
ꟼ	Π	Pↂ	↿↿	�lᒣꟼꟼ	P
⟨		ꟻM	MM		
ꝯ		ꝯ ꝯ		ꝯꝯꝊ	Q
ᐊ	P	P	ᐊꝺᐊ	R RR	R
W	Ƹ	ƐƷ	ᔓᔕ	ᔕ S	S
X	T	ᴛᴛ	⟊⟊ᴛᴛ	ᴛ	T
	Υ	ᴦΦ	ᴦᴠᴦᴠⵁΦ	ᴠᴠ	UVWY
ꘌ	Ξ	⛉Ⅹ⊞		Ⅹ	X
Ⅱ	Z				Z
			8 8		

Development of Roman alphabet *

* From *Lettering* by Charles R. Anderson, © 1969 by Litton Educational
Publishing, Inc. Reprinted by permission of Van Nostrand Reinhold Company.

the Romans. Roman writing disappeared for a while in early Britain but returned to the scene via the teaching of Irish monks by missionaries and via such manuscripts as the famous Book of Kells, the pride and joy of Dublin.

Book of Kells *

* Reprinted by permission of The Board of Trinity College, Dublin.

Copyists of ancient times were called calligraphers, and the preparation of ornate and elaborate manuscripts was done almost solely by the priestly castes and professional scribes, who in ancient Greece and Rome were held in the highest esteem. With the breakup of the Roman empire, calligraphy withdrew to the cloisters and monasteries, where the finest manuscripts were prepared and great libraries were built. The medieval church was the principal vehicle of literacy; the memory of its near monopoly is perpetuated by the interlocking meanings of such words as "clergy," "clerical," "clerk," and "clerisy." It was an exemplary test of the Jesuit rule of obedience that if a member of the Society should receive a command while writing, he must act upon it without even completing the letter of the alphabet he had begun. It was not until the beginning of the eighteenth century, with the rise of English commerce, that English calligraphy became prominent. An even, flowing hand for business correspondence called the "round hand" was developed at this time for everyday use. In 1766 a book was published entitled *A Treatise on the Art of Writing, in Which Rules are Laid Down for Writing All the Hands Now in Use with Propriety and Elegance.* Script writing was later introduced into English elementary schools, deriving from the Roman characters. A system has been in use in France and the convent schools of

Spencerian method *

* From *Encyclopedia of the Written Word* by Klara G. Roman. Reprinted by permission of Frederick Ungar Publishing Co., Inc., New York.

the Sacred Heart that was particularly arbitrary and conventional, and in our own country a system called the Spencerian, which was taught in public schools during the late nineteenth century with various later copies of it, including the Palmer method.

It was this "veritable Prussian-American drill," as Robert Saudek called it, which Saudek accused of "contaminating" the art of writing "by the most terrible, the most prosaic and unimaginative word of our modern vocabulary, by the word efficiency." He found an analogy in England in the physical education of upper-class English society in which an upright position was cultivated from infancy to old age and one could mistake a lady of seventy for one of twenty-five. "Not dissimilar conditions prevail in regard to writing," he claimed. In my opinion this was a poor analogy, for American writing from George Washington on has always been identified with a forward-leaning slant, and even the "efficiency" of the Spencerian and Palmer methods was forward-leaning. Besides that, Saudek himself points out it was in England as far back as 1887 that the first series of *Copybooks for Upright Penmanship* appeared, and soon afterward the conservative upright writing became the fashion in all English schools. So much so, in fact, that the English medical profession joined the movement, and dire warnings were afoot that if one did not sit in the correct position while writing, one was in serious danger of myopia and no less than curvature of the spine! An Englishman who wrote at that time with a pronounced

Palmer method *

* From *Encyclopedia of the Written Word* by Klara G. Roman. Reprinted by permission of Frederick Ungar Publishing Co., Inc., New York.

slant, in fact, must be considered, according to Saudek, to have possessed "lack of discipline, hastiness, impatience, feminism" and all kinds of horrendous faults. Despite reading his chapter on the history of graphology three or four times, I have never quite been able to figure out whether or not he blamed all this on the Americans!

With the advent of the typewriter and the pressures on time of modern business and the professions—resulting, for example, in the notoriously indecipherable writing of doctors—calligraphy today has become almost a lost art. The need for speed—at the root of all cursive writing—has overcome the demand for that elegance and beauty which at one time saved many invaluable manuscripts from destruction by the barbarians simply as works of art, though they neither understood nor cared about the content. Cursive script is to calligraphy, it has been said, what dialect is to educated speech. Throughout history there has been a conflict between the demand for legibility and permanence on the one hand and speed on the other, between the so-called "book hands" of official documents and the "pen hands." As one author put it, today a dozen tailors in Paris dictate the female fashions; the guild of teachers of calligraphy used to dictate how a nation was to write.

Book hand *

Pen hand †

* From *Autographic Mirror* Volume 1.
† From *Universal Manuscript.*

mm   summer

nn   running

The school-copy *

When children throughout the centuries have been taught to write, then, they have traditionally been taught in a formalized style which had nothing to do with the individual personality of the child or the science of graphology. Not only has personality been ignored, but until a few years ago it was often damaged, as was the case until all too recently when children who were naturally left-handed were forced to conform to the standard pattern and write with their right hand, frequently causing stuttering and other nervous disorders. Graphology has been almost entirely unknown to those who taught the art of writing, and concepts of penmanship were promoted by handwriting teachers in accordance with varying national school patterns. But to some extent each child individualizes his outlines from the very start of writing, and teachers even in infant schools have no difficulty in distinguishing between the work of different pupils. The graphic personality begins early. Werner Wolff once played three pieces of phonograph music to children in a nursery school—a march, a waltz, and a cowboy song—and the children were asked to draw how the music sounded. The infants identified the marches with angles, the waltzes with curves, and the cowboy songs with scenes from nature.

In general the modern school pattern starts to be departed from at puberty, and the rapidity and completeness with which the real personality is superimposed on it over the following years is the indicator of maturity. An adult today who writes exactly as the school taught him might be considered extremely rigid and suffering perhaps from an inferiority complex which he seeks to hide, or perhaps an actual intention to deceive; there may be even more serious pathological implications. The vestiges of the school copy which sometimes remain through life are the subjects of a great deal of the basic discussion of this

---

* From *Encyclopedia of the Written Word* by Klara G. Roman. Reprinted by permission of Frederick Ungar Publishing Co., Inc., New York.

book. The rounded handwriting sometimes characteristic of rather old-fashioned and reactionary people, for example, and the "arcades" which often accompany it are typical of school copy, as are the unnecessary beginning strokes about which I write later in my chapter on speed and Appendix C.

But apart from the obvious advantages in neatness which are constantly stressed by pen and pencil companies in crusades for better penmanship, the school copy is by no means an entirely negative influence. Much of the crudity and awkwardness in communication which we frequently see in the writing of the illiterate and uneducated is improved by it. There is also a consistency which by way of the eventual "essential letter form," or average letter, of which the graphologists speak, may become the building blocks of character and intelligence in handwriting. The school copy is in a sense the right wing, the Establishment, of writing. It has a perfection about it, limited though it is, the admiration for which may provide adolescents with some of that therapy which we discuss in Chapter 3 in regard to the work of Paul de Sainte Colombe and Raymond Trillat. We see it in typography, in advertisements, everywhere we go. To paraphrase W. C. Fields, anyone who hates the scribbling of kids can't be all bad!

Handwriting or Brainwriting?

Of all the feats of muscular coordination of which human beings are capable, says one author, the highly organized process of writing is the most intricate and therefore perhaps the most revealing. Moreover, it supplies a permanent, objective pattern which can be studied repeatedly and at leisure. To what extent is it purely muscular and not psychological? The layman sometimes believes that writing depends exclusively on the physical movement of the hand, which is obviously untrue, or the writing materials used. But certainly there are physical factors to be taken into consideration by the graphologist.

H. J. Jacoby has an excellent paragraph on the physical factors which limit, influence, or distort the smooth transition of thought to paper.

Before the graphologist starts to analyze somebody's handwriting, he has to ascertain the influences which are to be

attributed to the writing organ (hand, foot, mouth, etc.)
and to those parts of the cerebrum which are participating in
the act of writing. Other facts to be considered are: influence
of the writing surface (smooth, rough, porous, presence of

Holding a quill pen *

* Engraving by George Bickham from *The Universal Penman*, Dover Pictorial Archives, Dover Publications, Inc., New York.

ligneous fibre, greasy, chemically treated, paper, or parchment, etc.); influence of writing instruments (quill pen, pencil, copying pencil, chalk, carbon, fountain pen, stylograph, and various other types of pens—fine or broad nib, hard or soft pen, fuzzy nib, clean, rusty or dirty pen, fluid or thick ink, fresh ink, old and jellied ink, copying ink, China ink, etc.); influences of the hold of the pen (vertical, horizontal, close to the nib, etc.); influences of the size of the writing surface (folio, postcard, entries in guest-books, visiting cards, etc.) and its position on the writing desk (slanting position, parallel line to the writing desk, change of position whilst writing); influences of the writing support (smooth or uneven); of the lighting conditions (glaring, dazzling, dim light); influence of external conditions (traveling train or other vehicles, at the post office, on unstable desk); influences of a personal nature (notes entered in great haste into a diary, the so-called "private shorthand," writing with unfamiliar writing material, in a great hurry, with unusual care, writing in the case of blindness, extreme shortsightedness, under the influence of alcohol, fever, illnesses).

Robert Saudek has further elaborated on the importance of certain physical factors in evaluating slant: "If the arm is held too close to the body, if the thumb is held too stiffly, if the end of the finger is too far from the point of the pen, if the paper is held in a wrong position, if the characters are given a wrong direction, then the pupil, instead of writing upright, will write slanting." It is also said that the writing of illiterate people sometimes shows an uphill tendency, the arm being held in such a way that the center of motion is so far to the right that as the hand moves along it is inevitably held above the general line of writing. (This of course relates to the basic line.)

As far as the instrument is concerned, Raymond Trillat, in *Expérience de Graphothérapie en Psychopédagogie,* comments on the historical progression in the refinement and accuracy of instruments of writing. Charcoal was used by prehistoric man to make drawings in his cave, a stylet was the instrument used for cuneiform writing and for engraving on wax. Then writing became more delicate, reaching extreme daintiness in Chinese writing with the use of a paintbrush; in European writing this evolution occurred through the use of the goose feather. During the early nineteenth century the appearance of the steel pen was revolutionary because of its lasting flexibility and subtlety, and later the advantage of the fountain pen was discovered with its regularly flowing ink which insured an evenness of line. And finally today, many writers are tempted to use the ballpoint (which is often convenient but which neither Trillat nor I myself prefer because of its rather crude and unreliable nature). The pen, it has been said, is like a cutting needle which transforms the essence of music into the wax of a master record. On the writing paper, as on the phonograph record, an underlying motive is reproduced. They both must be "played back" to reveal their hidden content.

The pen, then, is an extension of the body and functions with it. But the fact that the pen is selected for psychological as well as physical reasons (my mother, for example, used a stub point in her later years, when her physical strength was less but her involvement with material things and her abounding energy were much greater) points to the predominance of the psychological in the writing process. In some cases the relative importance of the two is in doubt. Is the illegibility or the hesitation caused by a writer's being unfamiliar with the language, or by poor spelling, or by a psychological or merely a mechanical problem? How important is his familiarity with the writing process, as indicated for example by the time he takes to adjust his pen to the paper whenever he commences to write (or at the beginning of each word, which involves the beginning strokes of which I speak elsewhere)? And what about the factor of heredity? There have been excellent studies of the factors governing the inheritance of stature, eye color, and other physical traits, while accurate studies upon the inheritance of mental and moral traits are still lacking, as June Downey observed many years ago. Darwin made a classic observation about the similarity of handwriting of fathers and sons, but he never pursued the question of

Handwriting of father, Joseph Chamberlain, and his two sons *

innate determination versus choice, nor how much of that inheritance he considered purely physical.

In spite of all these external factors influencing the character
of the writing, the consensus among graphologists is that handwriting is "brainwriting" and that, for example, those who have
lost an arm, like Lord Nelson, have reverted to the same characteristics with one hand as they showed with the other. In the
most comprehensive book ever written on graphology, *Diagrams
of the Unconscious*, Professor Werner Wolff summed up this
point of view:

Graphic patterns cannot be explained by environmental conditions influencing the act of writing, such as quality of paper
and pen, position and circumstances of writing. The form of
graphic patterns cannot be considered only a product of learning and of cultural stereotypes, because graphic forms determine each other in a unique configuration, characteristic of

* From *Handwriting—A Key to Personality* by Klara G. Roman. Reprinted
by permission of Pantheon Books, Inc., New York.

the individual. We have demonstrated by measurements that size, form, and position of graphic patterns originate neither in chance nor in conscious intention, but that they reflect unconscious principles of organization. Thus, graphic movements are "diagrams of the unconscious." Since these unconscious patterns are modified by psychosomatic changes of the organism, such as elations, depressions, and seizures, graphic movements are evidenced as a reflection of psychosomatic processes.

If graphology can be used to diagnose personality disorders, can it be used as a therapeutic tool? The term "graphotherapy" came into use around 1930, but the technique had been demonstrated in 1908 to the Paris Academy of Medicine. Its efficacy was tested clinically at the Sorbonne between 1929 and 1931 by two eminent French scientists, Dr. Pierre Janet and Professor Charles Henry. Dealing principally with alcoholics and "problem" children, the experiments confirmed that the system, intelligently and conscientiously applied, gives excellent results.

What is graphotherapy? To quote Raymond Trillat, who during the Fifties had great success in clearing up mental disturbances in children by changing their handwriting, "If you can study someone's handwriting and deduce ideas about his character, why can't you reverse the process? By modifying his handwriting, perhaps you can modify his personality." Graphotherapy received little attention in America until 1956, when *Time* magazine published an article on Trillat and his work. Said *Time*: "When he first began his experiments with children, Trillat found that many of their inner problems showed up clearly in their writing. The introverts had difficulty connecting their letters; the timid tended to squeeze all theirs together. Gradually, Trillat concocted a set of corrective exercises designed to give children a sense of 'continuity, creation, and equilibrium.' In overcoming a defect in any one of these elements, said he, a child must first develop a feeling for rhythm, melody, and harmony." Paul de Sainte Colombe, who styles himself a psycho-graphologist, has carried on the work of Trillat and other graphotherapists up to the present with writing and teaching.

Samples of Trillat's corrective exercises *

Both men emphasize, as Sainte Colombe puts it, that "the elemental personality must always be respected." They oppose the use of "script" and other artificial styles as damaging to the personality. They are opposed to changing a left-handed person into a right-handed one. To quote Trillat, "It is very dangerous to attempt certain graphic changes such as forcing a nervous person to write in a soft graph or even just to try to strengthen the slant of the handwriting, because these changes would totally disregard the writer's graphic personality. . . . This is like creating a mask and having the subject act a part for which he is not equipped."

In dealing with a child, according to Trillat, one ought to say, "I am going to ask you to make a great effort: give me two minutes of your time every morning." This makes such effort

* From *Expérience De Graphothérapie en Psychopédagogie* by Raymond Trillat. Reprinted by permission of Vigot Frères, Paris.

fun. Trillat never wished to tire the child, and for that reason he rarely asked him or her to write more than two lines. On the other hand he felt it was important to establish a time to perform the exercise—gradually changing the writing—and to adhere to it, and indispensable that the work be carried out in the morning before regular work is started. The mind is thus refreshed after a night's sleep and more receptive. The treatment ordinarily lasts from six to eight months but sometimes takes longer.

Before treatment it is essential to study the writing seriously to discover deficiencies or graphic problems. Subject matter should be selected with particular concern for the child's interests and emotions. Attention should be given to the words and letters used, and if a child has trouble with certain words, they should not be passed over until the difficulty has been resolved. At the beginning of the exercise all letters should be continuously connected. It is of great importance, also, to round all the movements. Any angular gesture, says Trillat, has deep repercussions on the child's psyche. This is particularly pertinent to stuttering, which is graphically visible in "the shaky, mended, hesitant, broken, patched-up appearance" of the writing. Relaxation is emphasized by coordinating the breathing with the regular rhythm of the writing. Correct position is essential during all these exercises. The feet must rest flat, the shoulders must be supported by the opposite elbow and forearm on the table.

In the course of this treatment, three difficulties may occur—with the child himself, from ill-will, laziness, absence of mind; with the parents, who may be excessively impatient for results or else may oppose the whole program; and finally with the school. In any case it is of supreme importance to establish an atmosphere of confidence, according to Trillat, between the child and the handwriting teacher, in order that he may neither rebel nor be discouraged. A tall order for any teacher!

Trillat cites some interesting examples of problems in handedness which he claims to have cured by his therapy. He would first give what he called his "test for checking of laterality." He would ask the subject several times to pick up something; he would play ball with him; he would ask him to shuffle and cut a pack of cards; he would ask him to kick a football, or hop about on one foot. In this way he found out whether the child was truly left-handed or merely copying someone he admired. One little girl, for example, became left-handed to attract the attention of her left-handed father in an attempt to get closer to him when an unwanted little brother was born. As she was not naturally left-handed, over a period of time her right hand was "reeducated." Another child, a boy, was really left-handed but refused to use this hand for fear of being ridiculed by his schoolmates; since he started by himself to use his right hand, he was educated to use it without further problems. In the case of another left-handed child, his right hand could not be educated, but since the position of his left hand was so bad that it was causing a visual defect, the position was corrected and he learned to write comfortably with his left hand.

Most of the available research on the subject of left-handedness seems to have been done in New York, at the New School for Social Research, by Ulrich Sonnemann, who was an associate professor there, and particularly by the late Klara Roman, whose work I greatly admire (despite her belief to the contrary). Sonnemann feels that all truly wide handwriting has a tendency to broaden, and all truly narrow writing to tighten, their letter forms relative to their connections, but that the exception in the latter case is the writing of the left-hander whose narrowness, being less psychological than physiological, fails to tighten up and may thus reveal a clue to its left-handed origin. However, he still feels that information concerning handedness is a third necessary datum in addition to those of age and sex.

Paul Broca, who in 1860 began to establish the location of specific functions within the brain, defined the phenomenon of handedness in these words: "We are right-handed because we are left-brained." Most people, their ancestors having started off thousand of years ago using the right side of their bodies—and particularly their right hands—have sensory and motor abilities, says Roman, such as speech, writing, and reading, located in the left side of the brain. What happens to the relatively few individuals whose motor abilities originate in the right side of the

Leonardo's diaries. Mirror writing, like Arabic, is easier for left-handers *

brain and are thus left-handed by nature? Like all minorities, they are under pressure no matter which path they follow. In my own case, as was customary in the earlier part of the century when the problem was still unrecognized, I was forced to change to writing with my right hand and became a classic exemplar of the consequent stuttering, inhibitions, and hypertension. The only natural way for a left-hander to write is a complete reversal of the conventional way—that is, mirror-writing, proceeding from right to left, as in the famous instance of Leonardo's diaries. But since this is psychologically fine but unintelligible, most left-handed children are taught to write today in the conventional manner but with their left hands. Even with this method there may still be traces of inhibition which are inseparable from the unnatural rightward movement of the arm. (Where right-handers tend to prefer garlands, according to Roman and Sonnemann, left-handers prefer arcades, which are known to be a secretive characteristic; and it is interesting to note that Mahatma Gandhi is said to have written official papers with his right hand but private papers with his left.)

Roman made a study of the handwriting of 283 pairs of identical twins. In observing their behavior and attitudes, she found a strong tendency for the twins to be the mirror image of their partners, one emphasizing the right, the other the left side in posture, movement, writing habits, etc. This tendency coincided with a fairly equal division between the partners in regard to handedness and to leftward and rightward slant, which she as-

* From *Handwriting—A Key to Personality* by Klara G. Roman. Reprinted by permission of Pantheon Books, Inc., New York.

Gandhi—right hand and left *

sociated with their opposing characters. Here again we find a tendency toward inhibition on the part of the left-handed partner. In one case two identical twin girls were asked to write with the paper placed in a straight position before them. When the left-handed girl found that her writing was extremely backhand due to her inability to compensate her leftward trend by turning the paper, she began to cry. Her writing truly represented a graphic pattern which was "a diagram of the unconscious," a unique configuration characteristic of one particular individual which originated neither in chance or in conscious intention.

* From *Diagrams of the Unconscious* by Werner Wolff, Ph.D. Reprinted by permission of Grune & Stratton, Inc., New York and Mrs. Kate A. Wolff.

The Beginning of Graphology

The underground science of graphology has shown its head from time to time throughout history in chance remarks by famous people which have been preserved down to the present. Aristotle wrote, "Just as all men do not have the same speech-sounds, neither do they all have the same writing." The historian of the first twelve Caesars, Suetonius, analyzed the writing of the Emperor Augustus: "He does not separate the words," he said, "nor carry over to the next line any excess letters." Which sounds like a man whose mind ruled his heart, which was certainly true of Augustus. Nero once commented that he did not trust a man in court because "his handwriting showed him treacherous." A fine one to talk! The eleventh-century Chinese painter and philosopher Kuo Jo Hsu said, "Handwriting can infallibly show whether it comes from a person who is noble-minded, or from one who is vulgar." And of course the observation that personality is revealed in physical movements is as old as the Bible itself, as Werner Wolff points out. Proverbs VI, 12-13, says "a

43

naughty person, a wicked man, walketh with a froward mouth. He winketh with his eyes, he speaketh with his feet, he teacheth with his fingers. . . ."

In modern times famous people have not been entirely unaware of the overtones of personality in handwriting. Gainsborough, while painting a portrait, would keep a letter written by his model before him on the easel. Edgar Allan Poe engaged in a sort of intuitive graphology, possessing a collection of autographs. Leibnitz wrote that "the handwriting nearly always expresses in one way or another the natural temperament, unless it be that of a writing master, whose writing lacks spontaneity." Disraeli wrote that "handwriting bears an analogy to the character of the writer, as all voluntary actions are characteristics." And Stefan Zweig said, "A man may lie, simulate, disown himself, but in one thing man is inseparably attached to the innermost truth of his nature—in his handwriting. Handwriting . . . is as unique as his personality." Other amateur graphologists were Dumas *père*, Zola, George Sand, Madame de Staël, Browning, Verlaine, Alphonse Daudet, Gogol, Chekhov, Einstein, and Thomas Mann.

Perhaps the two most famous cases in modern history of curiosity about handwriting are those of Goethe and his friend Johann Lavater in Germany and of Walter Scott in Scotland. Says Crépieux-Jamin of the former: ". . . in a letter he [Goethe] wrote to Lavater, he speaks of the study of handwriting as a known fact; 'There does not exist the shadow of a doubt that handwriting has its analogies with the character and with the human mind, and that it can afford at least a presentiment of the kind of feeling or of the mode of action, inasmuch as we must also admit a certain harmony with the personality, not only in the features and in the general conformation of a man, but also in the facial expression, the voice, and in the movements of the body.' Goethe goes on to point out," says Crépieux-Jamin, "the difficulty of systematizing the facts, assures Lavater of his interest in such researches, and advises him to continue the collection of data upon the subject. The letter was the cause of Lavater's observations upon handwriting. He was then engaged in his great work upon physiognomy and all that touched upon the external manifestation of a man's personality interested him. Following the advice of his friend, he collected autographs, and he devoted several pages of his book to the study of handwriting." (In his own day, Lavater was best known as a mystic and philosopher, but he has been better remembered since his death for the work on physiognomy. Unfortunately that work has come in for its share of criticism, the *Encyclopedia Britannica* stating that "it left the science of physiognomy as desultory and unscientific as it found it." What would the *Encyclopedia* have commented if he had tackled graphology as his *chef d'oeuvre!*) Crépieux-Jamin continues:

> Lavater refers to the variation often seen in the same person's handwriting, and says, truly enough, that so far from being an argument against the truth of graphology, it is a proof in its favor, as showing the effect of this or that mood upon our handwriting. He refers also to the difference in handwriting according to nationality, just as there are national traits of physiognomy; and we may here point out this variation is to be expected, for if one nation is characterized by, say, more thrift than another, or by greater excitability, a graphologist would find the signs of thrift or of excitability more frequently shown in the handwriting of that nation than in the handwriting of a nation not having these characteristic traits so generally diffused among its members.
>
> Lavater concluded with these words. "Another idea which I leave for the consideration of those who may be, as I am, impressed with it: I notice in the majority of cases an admirable analogy between the manner of speech, the gait, and the handwriting."

Walter Scott, whose shorthand of genius in the constant omission of "i" dots belies theories about such omission meaning a bad memory, had the following to say about handwriting in 1827 in his novel *Chronicles Of The Canongate*. Describing the impression he received when reading a manuscript written fifty or sixty years before he was born, he wrote:

There was something in this conclusion which at first reading piqued me extremely, and I was so unnatural as to curse
the whole concern as poor, bald, pitiful trash, in which a silly
old man was saying a great deal about nothing at all. Nay my
first impression was to thrust it into the fire. . . . A little reflection made me ashamed of this feeling of impatience, and
as I looked at the even, concise yet tremulous hand in which
the manuscript was written, I could not help thinking, according to an opinion I have heard seriously maintained, that
something of a man's character may be conjectured from his
handwriting. That neat but crowded and constrained small
hand argued a man of good conscience, well-regulated passions, and to use his own phrase, an upright life; but it also
indicated narrowness of spirit, inveterate prejudice, and hinted
at some degree of intolerance which, though not natural to the
disposition, had arisen out of a limited education. . . . Then
the flourished capital letters which ornamented the commence-
ment of each paragraph, and the names of his family and of
his ancestors whenever these occurred in the page, do they
not express forcibly the pride and sense of importance with
which the author undertook and accomplished his task? I persuaded myself the whole was so complete a portrait of the
man, that it would not have been a more undutiful act to
have defaced his picture, or even to have disturbed his bones
in his coffin, than to destroy his manuscript.

And what a complete portrait of another man, the great and
good Walter Scott.

The letter forms which have descended to us, as Louise Rice
put it, through the many avenues—from the early cuneiform or
angular to the later cursive or curving, through Babylon and
Egypt, Crete, the Hittite culture, Phoenicia, Greece, and Rome—
belong to all the Western world. Each modern country imparts
its own national twist but not so much as to prevent analysis
by a trained graphologist. Even Hebrew, Arabic, and Turkish
scripts, having started at the same source many centuries ago,

have not been so remotely different from Western writing—when one becomes used to reading from right to left—as to be entirely analysis-proof. Chinese or Japanese writing, of course, with their pictographs written from top to bottom, is totally outside the scope of European or American graphology, in spite of the Chinese saying that "he whose writing leans to the right is as a reed bent by the wind of love." (The upright Chinese writing, in fact, does not lean at all!)

Because of the variations by each country on the original theme, nationality is to some extent disclosed in handwriting, though not *race*. It is where a person was brought up, not where he was born, that one sees in his writing. If one wishes to analyze a specimen, it is important to know whether or not it has been written in the writer's native language; if the writer has been taught to write a second language during his adult life, the script will usually be too stilted to analyze. According to Louise Rice and Dorothy Sara, her faithful disciple, Spanish and Italian writing is characterized by flowing capitals indicating gaiety and a love of beauty; French by meticulous letter forms showing logic and fine sensibilities, and by the prominence of the letter "m"; German by its intricate, angular letter forms (and incidentally the preference for dominating capitals which characterizes German nouns); and Russian by its overornamented

Spanish writing *

* From *Handbook of Facsimiles of Famous Personages*, Karl Geigy (ed.). (Rudolf Geigy Pub., Basle, Switzerland)

Certamente derivata da un esemplare greco dell'aureo periodo fidiano del IV. secolo. In conclusione opera di estrema rarità e grande importanza

Italian writing

La bague de Monsieur sera prête très prochainement et je pense faire l'envoi de ces deux pièces dans quelques jours.

Avec toutes mes excuses pour ce retard, je vous prie d'agréer — Madame, mes respectueuses salutations

*French writing ***

Entschuldigen Sie bitte, dass ich Deutsch schreibe, ich muss es. Mit freundlichen Grüssen und vorzüglicher Hochachtung

German writing

capitals, long connecting strokes, and sprawling rhythm, pointing to talkativeness and an outgoing personality. No better national picture exists in handwriting, says Miss Rice, than that afforded by the typical Russian script. And of course she and Miss Sara and many other writers have had a great deal to say on the subject of English and American writing, the latter, incidentally, not too different from Russian.

* From *Précis de Graphologie Pratique* by Docteur Camille Streletski. Reprinted by permission of Vigot Frères, Paris.

Russian writing—Rasputin *

To Louise Rice during the Twenties it is the "hustling go-getter" whose writing is most typical of the American, with its wide letters, rapid rhythm, and forward-leaning slant which she identifies with what she calls the vital or "salesman" type. This is the type that might best confirm the conclusion that the English-speaking peoples are "on an ego trip" when, unlike all other nations, they refer to themselves with the capital letter "I" and to all others whom they address with the small letter. In any case, according to Miss Rice and others, American writing has been primarily known for its variety and individuality of expression, and perhaps it was as an antidote to this excessive freedom that the Spencerian and Palmer methods were imposed on American writing during the late nineteenth century.

In the early seventeenth century Camillo Baldi, an Italian physician, wrote "a small treatise with a long title," as Dorothy Sara puts it, on handwriting analysis, and wandering magicians went from castle to castle practicing the new art. But it was not

* From *Collecting Autographs and Manuscripts* by Charles Hamilton. Copyright 1961 by the University of Oklahoma Press. Reprinted by permission of the publisher.

until the nineteenth century that a group of French church-men—which included the Bishop of Amiens, the Archbishop of Cambrai, and the Abbé Louis Flandrin—held discussions on a subject to which either the Abbé Flandrin or his pupil the Abbé Jean-Hyppolite Michon gave the name "graphology." Michon generally shares the credit for putting the discipline on a system-atic basis with his own pupil Crépieux-Jamin and the German Ludwig Klages, who between them fitted isolated signs to char-acter traits. For forty years he collected thousands of handwriting specimens and studied them, and in 1871 he founded the Society of Graphology in Paris, of which Henri Bergson later became honorary president. According to Saudek, Michon possessed an extraordinary gift of observation and was a born empiricist; but he was branded by later graphologists, as Roman says, as a mere "interpreter of signs." The fixed signs of Michon, it is true, were so numerous and arbitrary that they invariably contradicted one another unless some coordinating factor was introduced, and he made no effort to resolve the contradiction by a more general theory of personality as did his pupil Crépieux-Jamin. At the same time, wherever there is serious study of graphology, much of the credit must be given to the debate between the atomistic theory of fixed signs of Michon and the holistic theory of Crépieux-Jamin: between nineteenth-century absolutism, one might say, and turn-of-the-century relativity (by which no one sign can be interpreted without its being related to others).

Fixed signs of Michon. Dot "like comet lost in space" held by Michon to indicate very occasional attacks of a cerebral disorder. *

Signs of obstinacy—Michon *

* From *Système de Graphologie* by Jean-Hippolyte Michon. (Librairie Marpon et Flammarion, Paris)

Jules Crépieux-Jamin is considered the most important French graphologist. According to Saudek, he was unsurpassed as a practical worker, endowed with a faculty of sympathetic penetration and an innate talent for judging handwriting. Although he was not a scientist in the modern sense of the word, his "rich, expressive, and plastic terminology," as Saudek called it, spread his influence far and wide. Most of the work of Louise Rice, who founded the American Graphological Society in 1927, was based on Crépieux-Jamin's. Saudek has a way of speaking in superlatives which are often no more scientific than the object of his praise or blame, and no sooner has he given Crépieux-Jamin credit for "demolishing" Michon's "untenable" theory of definite signs than he turns around and demolishes his hero by stating that "on the ruins of the old system he destroyed he reared but a new edifice of crooked construction." (In trying to understand Crépieux-Jamin I tend to agree!) While Saudek praises Crépieux-Jamin for recognizing that the lack of a sign was not necessarily indicative of the converse characteristic on the part of the writer, and that a definite style could only be termed characteristic when constantly recurring and in varied forms, he assails him for believing that every symptom that proves the same trait of character emphasizes that trait.

Crépieux-Jamin divides the physical aspects of handwriting into six components: pressure and speed (which he combines), form, dimension, direction, activity, and order. Within each genus there are many species representing the details of handwriting, such as whether or not it is ascending or descending, connected or disconnected, etc. The intensification and combinations resulting from coordinating these characteristics with each personality brings about the so-called theory of resultants for which Crépieux-Jamin is known. He tells us that "for example we may find a handwriting which is rapid, a sign of activity, and which also ascends, another sign of activity; the resultant meaning is thereby reinforced, and we obtain *ardent activity*." The theory of psychology which finally emerges does not impress Saudek, though he admires the virtuosity of its expression, because in his opinion it makes assumptions not yet accepted and oversimplifies the problem (he calls it the "multiplication table of the primitives of psychology"). He does approve, however, of the great importance that Crépieux-Jamin places on first ascertaining, by means of his theory, the intellectual superiority or inferiority of his subject before going on to analyze the writing. No individual signs can be truly evaluated, the Frenchman claims, without a correct estimate of this standard, anticipating the Gestalt theory of the Germans.

In the late 1890s Crépieux-Jamin persuaded the famous psychologist Alfred Binet to interest himself in handwriting, and it was the positive results of the latter's investigation at the Sorbonne, suggesting that there was a definite correlation between specific handwriting signs and honesty and intelligence, that inspired Binet to call graphology "the science of the future."

Wherever graphology is today recognized as a science, however, the credit for its origin is generally given to the German philosopher Ludwig Klages. Klages first proclaimed his new theories of graphology in a publication called *Monthly Journal* over several years at the beginning of the twentieth century and subsequently wrote five books on the subject, which to Saudek in the Twenties contained "most of what is worth knowing about theoretical graphology." Klages postulates two forces within man—the "mind" which binds and inhibits him and the "soul" which frees and develops him creatively. He argues that these two forces are always dynamically at variance and are "actualized" in man's expressive movements, such as walk, speech, gesture, writing, etc. It is in handwriting, where the movements between the two forces are captured and recorded, that they are most accessible for study and interpretation. On these principles, according to Lewinson and Zubin, Klages founded a new system of graphology. "This system," they say, "provided the basis for a synthesis which the graphologists before Klages had been striving for, namely, to perceive the 'Gestalt' or totality of a given handwriting sample, and at the same time to differentiate the individual elements creating the specific 'Gestalt' effect."

By "soul," according to Rose Wolfson, Klages means a cosmic life force that flows through all the phenomena of the world, through man, animals, seasons, wind, rain, mountains. Klages

Gabriele d'Annunzio

dal Benàco, 1921.

Rhythm in the writing of d'Annunzio *

calls the unobstructed and natural tempo of this force "rhythm" and the effort to regulate and demark it "measure." Mind is measure, the wish to regulate, control, and inhibit, and resides in the tendencies toward contraction. Soul is rhythm, the wish to expand, the power to integrate control and go beyond it, and resides in the tendency toward release. (A small, self-conscious handwriting might be considered contracted, a flowing writing, released.) Klages describes rhythm as an "indefinable something" that can only be understood intuitively and identifies it with a "wholesome personality." Fast writing he associates with a natural, spontaneous rhythm as opposed to the often artificial character of slow writing. All releasing tendencies, however, were to Klages not necessarily rhythmic ones. One had to take into account the "form level" of the writing—presumably the aesthetic and intellectual qualities—and the dynamic relationship between the contracting and releasing tendencies, in search of which he established tables wherein he hoped to provide objective criteria.

Lewinson and Zubin hold that Klages' tables suffer from a logical fallacy which prevent them from being used for a purely objective rating of rhythm. After having discussed the subjective evaluation of harmony and regularity as the chief qualities of rhythm, Klages also included these same two factors in his list of contraction-release indices which are supposed to be an objective tool for judging it. In other words, to the factors that make possible an objective evaluation of rhythm, he adds the intuitive qualities of rhythm itself. So far as Klages utilizes the concepts of contraction and release and of rhythmic balance as

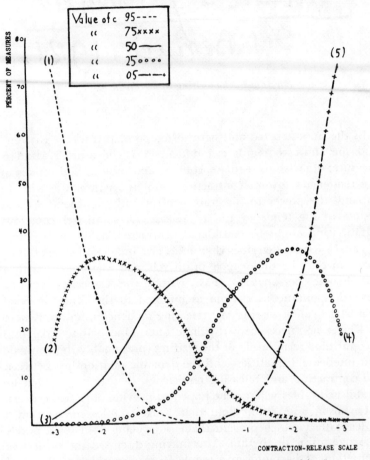

Distribution of expected proportionate frequencies for the contraction-release scale for five values of the strength of the contraction tendency (c=95, 75, 50, 25, and 05)

Contraction-Release Scales of Lewinson and Zubin *

a norm, Lewinson and Zubin agree with him and use his theory of graphology as a basis for their own theory twenty years later. Where they part company with him is regarding the definition of "good rhythm," and in an attempt to find a scientific answer to this question they provide scales of contraction and release in which the degree of rhythm present in each writing element

* From *Handwriting Analysis* by Thea Stein Lewinson and Joseph Zubin. Reprinted by permission of the authors.

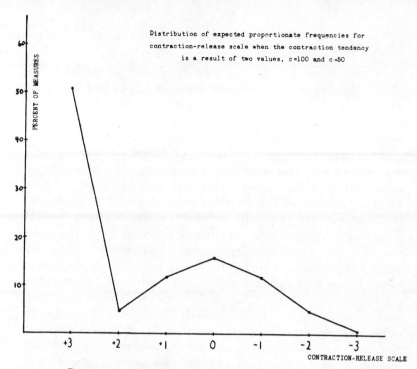

Contraction-Release Scales of Lewinson and Zubin *

can be judged, with rhythmic balance in the middle. Unlike Klages, who tends to find his "rhythmic balance" nearer to release than to contraction, Lewinson and Zubin find as much fault with the absence of control in extreme release as they do with the absence of spontaneity in extreme contraction. In measuring three dimensions of writing in geometrical and quantitative terms, the vertical, the horizontal, and depth or pressure, they were able to obtain a reasonable assessment of the degree of rhythm. In assessing the *quality* of a script, however, in terms of their so-called "essential letter form," they were, in my opinion, not so successful. But more of that in my chapter on rhythm.

According to Roman, Klages was antagonistic toward experimental psychology and claimed that graphology should be dealt with as a science apart, by "psychologically-minded" persons. (A

* From *Handwriting Analysis* by Thea Stein Lewinson and Joseph Zubin. Reprinted by permission of the authors.

little more than kin, and less than kind!) He persuaded many other graphologists not to participate in clinical and experimental work, implying that once his own experiments had been completed no more were needed. The result was that cooperation between graphology and medicine ceased for a considerable time.

One cannot conclude a discussion of Klages without saying a word about Dr. Max Pulver, a professor at the University of Zurich, whose work, though in German and not translated into English, still lives in the annals of graphology. In giving a symbolic meaning to the writing space, Pulver extended Klages' graphological system into the area of psychoanalysis. His addition of a third dimension, depth, to the usual ones of height and width was the basis for part of the theory of Lewinson and Zubin. Depth he equated with pressure, which symbolically represented the individual's libido or instinctive biological functioning. He referred to movements in the breadth dimension as symbolically either moving away from or toward the environment, and he theorized that movements in the vertical dimension symbolically referred to the individual's rational coordination. I will have more to say on Pulver, especially in regard to his doctrine of "zones," in Chapter 12.

PERSONALITY

Rhythm

Rhythm is the broad pattern of natural repetition and variation, as graphologist Daniel Anthony, of the New School for Social Research, puts it, found in the ebb and flow of the handwriting. Normal pressure calls for an emphasis on the downstrokes and a release on the upstrokes. This periodic tension-relaxation mechanism should be regular and automatic, and is a major criterion in the assessment of rhythm. According to Lewinson and Zubin, if the handwriting is rhythmically balanced, then the personality is also balanced and well adjusted. Extremely

Excellent rhythm of a friend in the Philippines

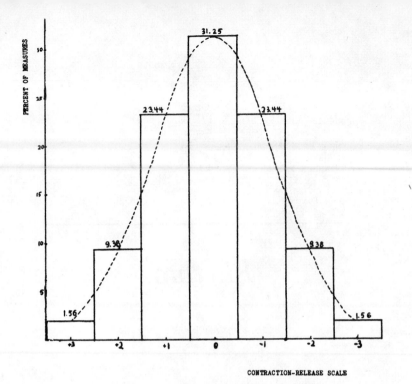

Bell-shaped graph *

contracted writing is theorized to be so rigid and hemmed in by emotional control that the writer is unable to function smoothly, while one whose writing is released and loose may lack such control. Most of us can be classified somewhere between the extremes, the curve forming a symmetrical bell-shaped graph. Ideal rhythm, of course, like the free swing of a golf stroke which is neither cramped on the one hand nor out of control on the other, is at the peak.

Long before I was intimidated by the intellectual world into a reasonable facsimile of scientific conformity (because of which, you may notice, I try to give credit in this book to those scholars whose works I borrow from), I had a nice little theory about rhythm. Moss Hart once said to me at a cocktail party before the opening of a new musical he directed called *My Fair Lady* —I wondered what he was so pleased about!—that he and I had

* From *Handwriting Analysis* by Thea Stein Lewinson and Joseph Zubin. Reprinted by permission of the authors.

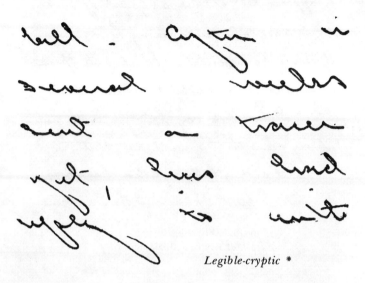

Legible-cryptic *

"held up pretty well over the years." So, I believe, has my theory, which includes four tests for good rhythm: it cannot be too rounded, it cannot be too angular, it must retain its legibility and correct formation of letters—but in the face of speed, and ideally it ought to approach that kind of individuality which Louise Rice dubbed legible-cryptic, meaning that the writer has invented forms of the alphabet which do not correspond exactly to the known forms but which are strictly adhered to in the writing.

Does this theory hold up in modern graphology? Somehow it does. Regarding rounded and angular writing, it is interesting that on the contraction and release scale of Lewinson and Zubin in which ideal rhythm (and good emotional adjustment) is found in the middle, both the extreme amplification of rounded writing and the oversimplification of angular writing are found at the ends. On the dichotomy of legibility and speed, the comments of

* From *Character Reading From Handwriting* by Louise Rice. Copyright, 1927, by Frederick A. Stokes Company. Reprinted by courtesy of J. B. Lippincott Company.

Woodrow Wilson's writing.
Excellent rhythm plus *originality* *

Klara Roman are worth repeating. "The graphologist must ascertain," says she, "whether it is precision or speed which tends to be modified or lost when the writer is in a hurry. . . . In a well-adjusted person, control and concentration usually serve to maintain a steady pace in spite of the presence of possible distracting stimuli. . . ." In other words, both precision and speed are retained. Finally, we come to the subject of originality of letter forms. To Crépieux-Jamin, handwriting which was harmonious, meaning among other things "graceful and original," was the chief graphic sign of superiority of character. To Saudek, writing in England many years later, a prime criterion for determining the quality of handwriting is the degree of originality in the form of the letters. And Sonnemann concludes in his book *Handwriting Analysis*, written while he taught at the New School for Social Research in New York, that of three global considerations of the level of form quality in writing, the first is to be defined as the combined degree of aesthetic balance and of originality of form.

* From *The Papers of Woodrow Wilson, 1896–1898,* ed. by Arthur S. Link, Vol. 10 (Copyright © 1971 by Princeton University Press). Reprinted by permission of Princeton University Press.

Thea Stein Lewinson and Dr. Joseph Zubin collaborated in 1942 in advancing a theory of graphology which, it was hoped, might "serve as a stimulus for the scientific study of a subject in which there has been a great deal of loose thinking." In the following summary of their theory I will borrow freely from the authors themselves and from George Mapp's interpretation of their statements. The method of Lewinson and Zubin presented in their book *Handwriting Analysis* is based on the work of Ludwig Klages in its use of the concepts of contraction and release of the graphic factors and the concept of rhythmic balance as a norm. However, it departs from Klages' theory of rhythm with the premise that rhythm is the midpoint between contraction and release—i.e., rhythmic balance is the central point between the contracting and releasing tendencies, balanced handwriting movement lying in the middle. To Klages, as I have said, there was a simple dichotomy between the plus of rhythm and the minus of regularity, the natural life flow versus something which he called "consciousness" but which he equated with introspective attitudes which could better be defined as self-consciousness. The true consciousness of external awareness, as

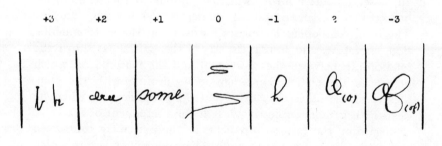

Contour of letters

+3   +2   +1   0   -1   ?   -3

Seven-point continuum *

* From *Handwriting Analysis* by Thea Stein Lewinson and Joseph Zubin. Reprinted by permission of the authors.

Sonnemann agrees, qualifies and conditions rather than impedes a spontaneous flow of feeling and emotion.

In preparing an objective scale for estimating the degree of rhythm present, Lewinson and Zubin proceeded as follows. First, the intuitive evaluation of the total handwriting sample was replaced by a minute analysis of the individual letters or parts of letters, and each of these elements was measured or rated. Second, the resulting measures and ratings were referred to a seven-point continuum of contraction–rhythm–release in order that the status of a given individual on the continuum could be determined. Lewinson and Zubin analyze handwriting into a total of twenty-two factors. These twenty-two factors are distributed into four components, or dimensions, of height, width, depth (which is pressure), and form. Height means primarily the height of the three zones, middle, lower, and upper, and is supposed to show the relationship between the intellectual, emotional, and instinctual tendencies (a theory of Pulver's with which I disagree, as I explain in Chapter 12). Width deals with the breadth of the letters, distance between words, slant, and so forth, and shows the relationship between the individual and his environment. Depth, the dimension from the front to the back of the writing, refers to the degree and control of pressure and symbolizes the instinctual sphere. Form, which cannot be measured mathematically, is rated, or judged, on the basis of an "essential letter form" which is similar to the school copy but created by superimposing numerous handwriting samples. The form component comprises the contour, shape, ornamentation, curvature, and similar aspects of the writing. It shows the relationship between the individual and the material on which he works, the elaboration when he is dealing with the complexity of the objective world, and the simplification when he deals with it more subjectively. It is the component of art.

Regarding the form component, at the extremely contracted end of the seven-point continuum one finds either letters which are very narrow—with the "air" pressed out of them—or a variety of curlicues, flourishes, ornaments, and distortions which indicate high tension. At the other end, that of extreme release, one finds

Note the sinuous stroke in the last word, "remain." *

either letters "blown up" to the point where almost all detail is lost or else a breakdown of formality and form itself in the sinuous, wavy stroke that graphology calls a thread. Sonnemann sees a desire to "slip through" life somehow as being reflected in the progressive shrinking of the concluding letters of words. "This 'secondary thread' writer," he explains, "evidently is dominated by the experience of having to get ahead in this dimension (the middle zone) somehow and no matter how, having, in that process, to maintain his ego regardlessly and at any price. This implies that his leading motivation is drive for self-preservation operating at the expense of all others: continuously fleeing rightward and avoiding commitments on its way." Visions of Bunyan's Pilgrim fleeing with his hands over his ears to avoid hearing the pleas of his wife and children!

The chapter which is essentially the last in Lewinson and Zubin's book is entitled "The 'Working Hypotheses' for Explaining the Graphological Factors." While there is a footnote on the opening page in which Dr. Zubin gracefully disclaims co-authorship here, bowing to Mrs. Lewinson's experience, on the third page Mrs. Lewinson apologizes for what she herself admits to be the lack of scientific evidence to test the validity of her interpretations. Why all this scholarly hedging after having come so far? The "working hypotheses" which Mrs. Lewinson describes, though obviously derived from the Gestalt theory of Klages and Pulver (the global and holistic approach), have a certain naïveté

* From *Graphology A Handbook* by Henry A. Rand. Reprinted by permission of Sci-Art Publishers, Cambridge, Massachusetts.

about them which in my opinion may have given Lewinson and Zubin a bit of concern. Remember the Abbé Michon, in one sense the real founder of the science of graphology, and at the same time the whipping boy for generations of future scholars to whom the oversimplified one-to-one conclusion that a weak "t" bar implies procrastination, regardless of the Gestalt of the writing, is a mortal sin. Try as I can to read otherwise in Mrs. Lewinson's chapter, the height of the middle zone can only denote the degree of self-importance; the direction of the lines, nature of mood; the distance between lines, sense of proportion; the breadth of the letters, strength of self-confidence; the direction of the slant, attitude toward environment; the left-right tendency, introversion-extroversion; the depth of pressure, energy; the contour of the form, degree of creativeness. These conclusions, little modified by qualifying factors, have a certain dogmatism about them which could be considered inappropriate to so speculative a subject; on the other hand, such dogmatism can also be looked on as the potential certainty which lights up the eyes of all researchers in science. In any case, Mrs. Lewinson should be honored rather than criticized for the rather simple, direct nature of these hypotheses. Let us congratulate her for attempting to give more scientific credibility to conclusions which have been the intuitive heritage of graphology from almost the beginning.

I have one quarrel with Mrs. Lewinson, however, regarding her definition of rhythm, and that lies in her inclusion of originality of form—inspired perhaps by the "form level" of Klages— as an essential part of it. It is Mrs. Lewinson's intention to find a royal road to the understanding of graphology through one aspect of writing—rhythm. No one can deny that the first three of her four components—height, width, and depth—relate directly to rhythm. No one can even argue that both the complexity of the contraction end and the simplification of the release end are not directly dependent on the shape, if not the originality, of letters. At this point we are so close to identifying good rhythm with good writing that we can almost consider it a foregone conclusion. And yet ought the quality of a script to be judged by rhythm only?

In my own definition of rhythm years ago I discussed the angular versus the rounded, speed versus precision of lettering. But when I came to the last part of my definition, the "legible-cryptic," I consciously hesitated and finally added it as a sparkling afterthought. Mrs. Lewinson bases her "form component" on an essential letter form with an analogy to the school copy whose chief virtue is the fact that it has neither too much form nor too little. In my opinion all the immature beginning strokes discussed later in Chapter 7 and Appendix C will not necessarily drop out just at the top of her scale, nor will the beautiful shorthand of "legible-cryptic" necessarily find its peak there. I believe it is easier to judge originality and style by a separate standard. And there is much rhythm of limited beauty which might tend to look too good on the Lewinson scale. This is the rhythm of the charming but superficial "nice guys," the high-IQ-boy-wonders who never fulfill their apparent potential, as well as the "what-makes-Sammy-run's" and the con artists. Those with such rhythm often manage to juggle their way through life with amazing dexterity. But in this century of high-pressure salesmen I do not like to see a standard which might tend to glorify them at the possible expense of more creative people.

Connective Forms

After working on this book for a couple of months, I began to find that there were several writers to whom I kept turning back, and most of all to Sonnemann. I believe that there is nothing more interesting in his book *Handwriting Analysis* than his dis-

Angular writing *

*From *Guide to Personality Through Your Handwriting* by Irene Marcuse, Ph.D. Reprinted by permission of Arc Books, Inc., New York.

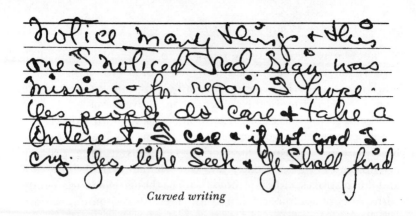

Curved writing

Curved writing of a drug addict *

cussion of the angular and the curved, perhaps nothing more interesting in all graphological literature. The words themselves and their implications, as he says, are well enough known to require little comment. The two qualities can be said to involve, he tells us, "the totality of our reality experience." The more complex phenomena combine them: with angular lightning you have curved clouds, with male you have female; you have Prussian marches and love songs, may I add, and war and peace. When the straight line turns at an angle it is on the side of firmness, hardness, finality, of pushing, aiming, hitting; when a line turns by curving it is on the side of reconciliation, softness, compromising, joining, embracing (with emphasis on the sensuous and the physical). Sonnemann quotes Klages to the effect that

* From the files of The Handwriting Institute, Inc., New York.

the angular movement suggests a goal to be reached rather than a need for combining and uniting, and of course both are essential in our daily experience. Symbols of this dichotomy are seen in handwriting in the angles of connective forms on the one hand and in the curves of garlands and arcades on the other.

Sonnemann then goes on to seek an even wider and more basic category to cover angularity. He finds it in a primary orientation toward violence, allowing in handwriting only up-and-down strokes, either-or moves which, though made frequently with patience and moderation, constitute a succession of decisions which never lose sight of ultimate goals. He then speaks of the physiological side of this orientation. The performance of straight and sharply terminated movements of the fingers, he says, requires a counterimpulse. The necessity to control this recoil is basic to all coordinated volitional movement, he continues, but the manner of conducting this control is characterologically revealing. When the reflex is mastered by utilizing it, without any attempt at suppression, in its natural force and approximately in its given direction, the writer is strongly inclined to become as fully as possible absorbed in his actions and interests, inclined to "do a thing for its own sake." A propensity on his part to extreme and rapid changes is thus indicated—which implies a predisposition, with a minimum of inner conflict, for the self-steering of creative thought. A further conclusion about such angularity, says Sonnemann, is its inherent moralism—not in the sense of high or low level, good or poor script, but simply that the inner experiences of the angle writer are articulated according to an imperative need to say "yes" or "no," ruling out the easy evasion of a middle road. Believing, however, that really great and creative rhythm is rarely seen except in the harmony of the angular with the rounded, I would like to leave an extra last word on the subject to Daniel Anthony in his *Psychogram*. "Angularity in low form level scripts," says he, "is a mark of oppression, dogmatism, cynicism, or tyranny. It can also manifest the kind of rigidity and inflexibility which results from anxiety, inhibition, repression, and fear. This low form level angled writer (with little style and character in the script) usually spends

Dan Anthony's example of angularity—low level *

too much of his time resolving his emotional problems which result from his frustration-aggression cycle."

The ultimate contrast to the angle, of course, is the curve, and the curves by which letters are made and connected are called arcades and garlands. To Sonnemann, the arcade is not entirely a curve, and he goes so far as to assert that "the nearest relative of the angle among the other forms of binding is clearly the arcade." The arcade, if not an angle, certainly cannot be written with the flowing ease o fthe garland; where the garland, converting the copybook arcade "m" and "n" into "w" and "u," acquires its impetus from the force of gravity of the arm in starting the letter downward in a fast, natural movement, the arcade starts forward and upward in a clockwise direction, slow and controlled.

According to Klara Roman, the terms "arcade" and "garland" were first employed in the sixteenth century by the writing masters of Nuremberg. To Roman, the form of the arcade suggests a bridge, a ceiling, a hut on the ground, and, she claims, is often found in the writing of architects and sculptors. The idea of enclosure with the world shut out and only the façade shown is, of course, a corollary. To return to Sonnemann, the arcade is an obstacle surmounted, a position secured; it is a

* Reprinted by permission of Daniel Anthony.

gesture of ruling and of fencing-in; it is the arch symbolic of the power of the Roman Empire, and it is the drawing of a circle beyond which, one might say, intruders are held at bay in the battle of the individual with himself. It is the ego. Where the arcade closes off, the garland opens up; where the arcade rules, says Sonnemann, the garland submits. In the arcade, the position of rest is at the bottom; in the garland, it is "suspended in air." The garland writer is at home at the bottom of the concave, *within* the world; the arcade writer's home is a place of security *from it.* It is characteristic of the more socially oriented garland (according to Sonnemann) that it is used more frequently by women than men. The arcade is frequently cast as the villain of connecting signs. To Daniel Anthony, it is merely oriented to self, protective, conforming, and conventional. But to many graphologists those who take the slow, laborious path of writing their ovals in a clockwise direction betray a secretiveness which sometimes borders on deceit. Saudek goes so far as to say that all writing in which we discover arcades is the reflection of "internal mendacity." He declares that arcades never occur in isolation and finds confirmation in other features indicating insincerity.

My beloved mother's writing;
"m" and "n" into "w" and "u" and continuous series of garlands

To Crépieux-Jamin the curve is an aesthetic sign of the highest order, associated with gentleness and imagination and the harmony of graceful writing, and the typical curve, of course, is the garland. It is said by most graphologists to reveal cordiality, an obliging nature, spontaneity. Because they are more easily produced, Saudek claims, garlands transform school copies into softer and more flexible forms, and are the embodiment of aversion to harshness and abruptness. They are generally regarded as signs, he says, of "benevolence, conciliation, amiability, and sensitivity." But there is also a minority report on garlands. The pleasure-loving writer whom Dorothy Sara describes is also a lover of luxury and perhaps idleness. He is often an imitator rather than an innovator, with a stronger desire to be the center of attention than to create. The stroke of the garland which ends in a rounded upward sweep at the end of a word is a sign perhaps of ambition but also of immaturity. And the rounded writing which is large and almost machinelike in its regularity, giving us, according to Louise Rice, the seemingly mild person who is really "set" in opinions, can be composed of garlands as well as of arcades. My beloved mother, who found a combination of finality and love an irresistible formula by which to guide her son, wrote with a continuous series of garlands that looked like an exercise in perpetual motion. I myself have sometimes won-

Rounded upward sweep

dered about the accepted interpretation of garlands. With their initial downward stroke, their counterclockwise motion, their unfinished endings and even their Greek "d's," are they really the sign of the extrovert as we are always told? Who decides whether they are centrifugal as presumed or centripetal like arcades? There is a saying that the extrovert strikes his match outward and the introvert inward; certainly the primary force of the garland is downward, in the direction of the self rather than otherwise. In any case, the roundness of both arcade and garland is as much of an extreme at one end of the scale as the

The great rhythm of a great man *

* From *Experiments with Handwriting* by Robert Saudek. Reprinted by permission of Dr. A. Saudek.

Disconnected writing *

angle is at the other, and I am firmly of the opinion that it requires an inspired combination of both, seasoned with a dash of
speed without loss of accuracy, to produce the finest rhythm.

In speaking about connective forms, it would be a grave omission not to say a few words on the subject of the presence or
omission of the actual links between letters, the connecting
strokes. Generally speaking, as Louise Rice puts it, the element
of logic is superseded by intuition in proportion to the number
of words whose letters are disconnected. According to De Witt B.
Lucas, "broken words . . . clearly indicate the graphic sign for
intuition—people who 'know without knowing how they know.' "
School-copy, on the other hand, prescribes connection. Insistence
upon the connection of letters carried into adult life can mean
either a slavish adherence to the school-copy or a compulsive
desire to follow one letter with the next with the least chance of
the mind of either the writer or the reader going astray. The
most extreme example of the latter is where not only letters but
words themselves are frequently connected, as in the cases of
Walter Scott and Somerset Maugham, said to be characteristic of
writers. The great concentration of such writers means, as Lucas
puts it, that they think, plan, act, and execute according to their

* From *Encyclopedia of the Written Word* by Klara G. Roman. Reprinted
by permission of the Frederick Ungar Publishing Co., Inc., New York.

His love had turned for a moment to migrant bird that happens on a ship to ocean and for a little while folds its tired wings .

W. Somerset Maugham

Connected letters *

preconceived and established ideas and do not raise pen from paper until each word is and often several words are written. Gibbon composed by the paragraph, and, according to Ben Jonson, Shakespeare "scarce blotted a line."

Most graphologists have had something to say on the subject of connecting strokes. Klages contended that connectedness, as reflecting a logical cast of mind, is a masculine trait, while disconnectedness, associated with intuition, is a feminine one. June Downey commented that connected script seems to be the product of the practical, organizing type of mind, broken script of the intuitive, original, fertile type. To Sonnemann the tendency of disconnectedness is to isolate, enclose, collect, conserve, fence off; of connectedness, to bind, mix, bring together, arrange. Dorothy Sara warns us of the danger of confusing the broken letters of intuition with the more formal ones of printing. People who write their letters in Gothic type, such as designers, print elaborately to attain physical beauty, while engineers print simply for mathematical precision, but neither do so essentially out of intuition. Perhaps the most famous example in the annals of disconnected writing is that of Leonardo da Vinci, and everything that is said about such writing seems to be illustrated in his script: the feminine intuition, if you like, the feeling for

* From *Handwriting Tells*, copyright © 1936, 1959, 1969 by Nadya Olyanova, reprinted by permission of the publishers, The Bobbs-Merrill Company, Inc. and Peter Owen Ltd.

Please to accept my warm greetings & thoughts for the New year; & I hope it will be a very happy one for you.

Gothic script

physical form of the designer and the architect, and the precision of the engineer. But the creator of *The Last Supper* was also a great artist, and how do we reconcile that fact with printing and upright slant and the materialism of heavy pressure of the scientist—analogous, by the way, to the writing of our own great scientist Thomas Edison? Well, we must confess that the world of Leonardo was primarily material rather than spiritual—one of the reasons perhaps that regard for him has never been higher than today—and as for his painting, remember that he used oil color or egg tempera in which the work is more painstaking and methodical than the fresco common in his time and took years trying to capture the Mona Lisa's smile. But with all these contradictions, we see in the terrific speed of his writing and that beautiful shorthand an enormous vitality and indeed a sleight of hand which could have put Houdini to shame.

One of my biggest surprises recently was noting the number of broken letters in the writing of Howard Hughes. One thinks of him as the super-businessman as well as the engineer and inventor, but of course the well-known urge shown in his broken

*Writing of Leonardo da Vinci *

* From *Handbook of Facsimiles of Famous Personages*, Karl Geigy (ed.). (Rudolf Geigy Pub., Basle, Switzerland)

Boston Feby 3ᵈ 69

Received of Samuel W Ropes Jr
The sum of Thirty 30 dollars -
being full amount received from
him ———

Thomas, A. Edison

Writing of Thomas A. Edison *

but unusual writing, as in Franklin Roosevelt's, to ride off in all
directions, is most unbusinesslike. Oh, well, my opinion doesn't
matter to Howard, as he once wrote a specimen of his writing
for me in which he claimed to have no faith whatever in graphology!

---

* From *Collecting Autographs and Manuscripts* by Charles Hamilton.
Copyright 1961 by the University of Oklahoma Press. Reprinted by permission of the publisher.

Speed, Saudek

How important is the speed at which handwriting is produced? According to Robert Saudek, speed is a critical factor in understanding personality through handwriting. He gives us numerous clues "for a reasonably reliable estimate of the speed of production," as Sonnemann puts it, and the latter adds that the writing trail cannot be copied, while every other quality of the writing but the speed of it can. To Harry Brooks, Saudek's faithful disciple, "it seems almost incredible that by merely determining the indications of speed and slowness in a given script, one can obtain a vivid glimpse into the mind of another person." To Saudek himself great speed is automatically a concomitant of intellectual ability or even genius, but most subsequent graphologists, in-

Little point on the small "s" and "r"

cluding Dan Anthony, have disagreed with this premise. In attempting to define good rhythm, I have said that two essential factors might be speed and beauty of lettering. Even an office manager, wrote Saudek before the general use of typewriters, was in duty bound to know whether beauty and legibility were produced at the expense of rapidity, or whether an applicant was able to produce a beautiful and legible script rapidly. (One test of this ability, by the way, is the retention or omission of the little point on the usual small "s" and small "r," which is rather difficult to make even when writing slowly.) Perhaps the best explanation of my definition of rhythm is that the speed which begins to show itself in adolescence acts as a dramatic challenge to the school-copy and has one of three effects upon it. Either it builds up a resistance in the copy, which instead of changing becomes, one might say, more reactionary and only exaggerates the curlicues and unnecessary strokes of immaturity; or the copy tends to disintegrate under pressure, and one finds a predominance of misshapen letters and the kind of strokes we

Exaggerated curlicues

Napoleon—deterioration of rhythm under the pressure of speed *

* From *Universal Manuscript.*

Animals talk to each other, of course. There can be no question about that; but I suppose there are very few people who can understand them. I never knew but one man who could. I knew he could, however, because he told me so himself. He was a middle-aged, simple-hearted miner who had lived in a lonely ~~corner~~ corner of California, among the woods & moun-

The beauty with speed of Mark Twain's writing *

call threads; or finally, the challenge is taken up by the copy, and the writing is given a simplification on the one hand and a flair on the other which produces a real style. Speed, in other words, magnifies the photo of the personality, which is why graphologists ask for a fast, natural specimen of writing when reading character.

*Reprinted by permission of Thomas Chamberlain for the Trustees u/w Clara Clemens Samossoud.

The beauty which one sees in the rapid writing of many great men, such as Scott, Dickens, Mark Twain, and President Kennedy, has always led me to believe that rapidity rarely exists in great handwriting at the expense of such beauty. In his summary of Shaw's writing, Saudek comments that in this very rapid writing restrained by self-control, one is struck by the fact that simplification resulting from speed is never achieved at the expense of distinctness. I like to point out the rapid but extremely confused writing of Karl Marx and Napoleon—the indecipherable orders of the latter being given as one of the reasons for his failure at Waterloo—as indicative of their neurotic personalities. On the other hand, there is a rumor even in graphological circles that illegibility is somehow a sign of brains, and of course the writing of doctors and others is offered as an example. Of one subject Dorothy Sara comments that "he is such a speedy thinker and worker that he hasn't the time to devote to writing legibly."

Writing of George Bernard Shaw *

Writing of Karl Marx

* From *The Psychology of Handwriting* by Robert Saudek. Reprinted by permission of Dr. A. Saudek.

Writing of Jean-Jacques Rousseau *

And I must confess that when I compare the extraordinary precision of the writing of Michelangelo and Rubens, of Voltaire and Rousseau, of George Washington with the somewhat incomprehensible scribble of many other great men, particularly the greatest composers such as Beethoven, Schubert, and Tchaikovsky, I am confused. Perhaps the irregularity of excessive haste, as Jacoby puts it, suggests a person who is moved far more by strong feelings and impulses than by self-control, as one might expect to find in the case of musicians; but then how does one explain the handwriting of such intellectual geniuses as Pascal, Goethe, and Talleyrand with their own varieties of scribble? I believe the answer lies in the extent to which the scribble upon careful study comes to life—the extent to which it falls into that distinguished category which Louise Rice calls legible-cryptic, understandable only when your eyes become accustomed to the shorthand in which it is written.

Saudek spends a good part of his book *Experiments with Handwriting* in discussing the differences between fast and slow writing. A key factor is the beginning stroke of words. To Saudek

* From *Autographic Mirror* Volume 2.

Ludwig van Beethoven *

the degree to which this stroke learned in childhood is retained
or eliminated during adolescence and after is a fundamental
indicator of speed and in turn of the maturity of the writer. A
classic example of what I have named a primary beginning stroke
is that found in the writing of Clare Luce. (Missing unfortunately
in the charming letter of the illustration, which I could not re-

---

* From *Handwriting Tells,* copyright © 1936, 1959, 1969 by Nadya
Olyanova, reprinted by permission of the publishers, The Bobbs-Merrill Company, Inc. and Peter Owen Ltd.

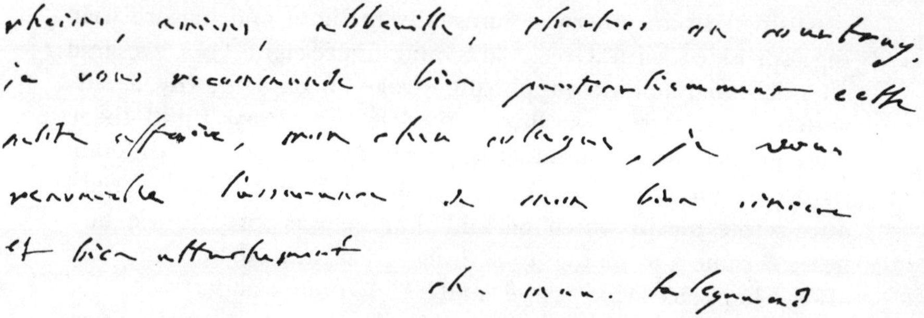
je vous recommande bien particulièrement cette petite affaire, mon cher collègue, je vous renouvelle l'assurance de mon bien sincère et bien attachement

Ch. Maur. Talleyrand

Talleyrand *

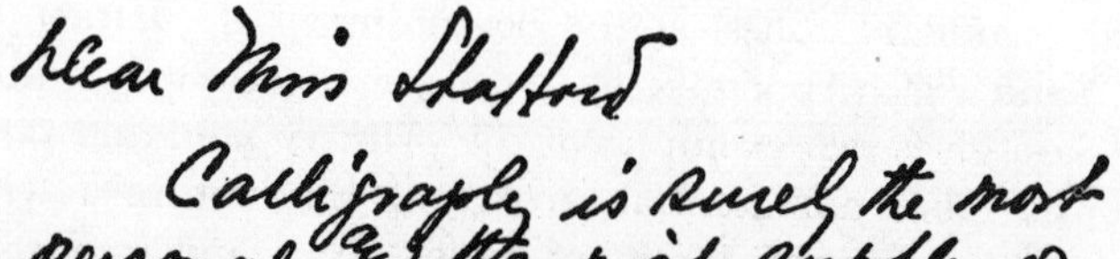
Dear Miss Stafford

Calligraphy is surely the most personal and the most subtle of the arts. The Chinese, who place it among the greatest of their arts, realize as you do, that with one stroke of his pen, a man reveals his heart, his mind, the depth of his culture, and the uniqueness of his own personality.

What joy you must have of your work!!

Cordially,

Clare Boothe Luce

Clare Luce †

* From *Autographic Mirror.*

† From *You and Your Handwriting* by Muriel Stafford. Reprinted by permission of the author.

sist using.) In an otherwise unusually brilliant and mature writing, sprinkled with Greek "d"s and figure-eight "g"s, we find
an occasional telltale supporting stroke to explain why a lady
with talents in so many directions does not always fulfill them.
Though my own graphological shortcomings are of a different
nature, I am reminded of a letter which Frank Lloyd Wright
once wrote me in which he said that he was sorry to see how
near I came "to doing something great and then something
always happens—what is the matter?" I often wonder!

In three studies made at my Handwriting Institute in New
York several years ago, Harriet B. Linton, Lawrence Epstein,
and I differentiated between "primary" beginning strokes—at the
beginning of words commencing with "a," "c," "d," "g," and
"q"—and "secondary" ones—at the beginning of the letters "u,"
"v," "w," and "y." (Appendix C is comprised of these studies.)
Dorothy Sara gives two examples of the primary kind and points
out that the more nonessential strokes of this nature a writer
eliminates as he matures, the more he is "direct and resourceful
in his approach to new ideas." Louise Rice—teacher of Miss Sara
and myself and innumerable others—comments that the elimination of the beginning stroke is the first step that the writer takes
in showing developing mental processes (as he emerges from the
copybook stage). She is speaking essentially of what I call "primary" strokes, as she does not differentiate between the two
kinds. She goes on to say that educated writing in which the

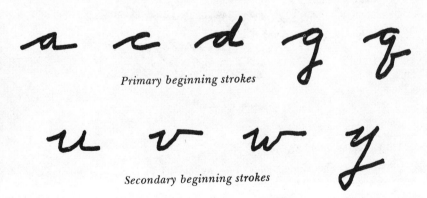

Primary beginning strokes

Secondary beginning strokes

Extreme *speed*

beginning strokes are long shows that the mentality has still far to go before reaching maturity, regardless of age. In discussing the small "c," Miss Rice remarks that when the superfluous first stroke is used by a person of mature years, we can be sure that the convictions and ideals of the writer are those learned in youth or adolescence.

To what extent can we assume that speed causes the primary beginning stroke to disappear? During adolescence, of course, speed generally increases as primary strokes diminish, but there is little proof that those with faster writing do not sometimes retain the strokes while slow writers drop them. Certainly it is true that there are many adults who retain unnecessary beginning strokes when writing slowly and carefully, as in the case of addresses, but drop them in their more informal script. This fact is constantly observed by the graphologist when he makes three or four requests for a fast, natural specimen of writing and frequently finds that there are fewer beginning strokes—both primary and secondary—after each request (just as he is sometimes amazed to find an isolated figure-eight "g" appear in a later script where he would never have expected it in the earlier ones). On the other hand, it is equally true that there are many cases where all the speed in the world will not cause the writer to drop one single beginning stroke or make one figure-eight "g" in his whole life.

To Irene Marcuse the primary beginning stroke points to the past and symbolizes a crutch on which to lean. Others have seen in it a clinging to convention, a hesitancy to rush into any new and unfamiliar plans, which has occasionally developed into contrariness or opposition. Sonnemann as usual puts it beautifully. "Prolonged initial upstrokes," says he, "thus indicate that the person, before going into action, has to traverse a certain margin of accumulated inner resistance, which accentuates his activities as experiences of personal effort rather than of service to the goal, while inner absorption by the objective headed for, correspondingly, would tend to disemphasize [sic] the initial upstroke in the direction of its total omission. . . . The person letting himself be guided by past experience and generally by his memories can be expected to emphasize the initial upstroke, while absence of it can be said to indicate a freer, more unbiased attitude toward the future and the task ahead." All this "inner resistance," of course, consumes time, and Saudek divides the sheep from the goats in regard to the speed with which one gets past that initial stroke to the task at hand. First of all, he tells us, motion pictures have been taken showing the momentary pause at the beginning of *all* words—for planning, adjusting the pen, and so forth. The primary beginning stroke, since it moves clockwise in the form of an arcade, is a difficult, unnatural one to make, a bar to spontaneity, and such strokes "require more effort and entail a greater loss of time." To Saudek, "the complexity of the initial adjustment [including variations on the beginning stroke] informs us of the degree of deliberation of awkwardness or ceremoniousness, or the degree of graphic immaturity, but in any case the degree in which the automatic fluency of the act of writing was restrained or impeded."

There was once a famous phrase in baseball—by which we date ourselves in remembering, but about which my old school acquaintance Barclay Cooke could tell us every detail—"Tinker to Evers to Chance." Robert Saudek gets most of the credit for expounding on the subject of speed in handwriting, but a great deal of what he wrote was derived from Pulver, and the complexity of his own work, in turn, was supposedly reduced to simple terms in a popular textbook—*Your Character from Your Handwriting*—written by his admirer Harry Brooks. Pulver to Saudek to Brooks—and to a few others such as Alfred O. Mendel and Klara Roman. In a foreword to Brooks's work Saudek praises it highly, and obviously it has virtue, but I spent a day or two trying to relate it to Saudek in order to bypass the master with dubious success. Anyway, before starting with Brooks let me comment once again that many graphologists do not agree with Saudek on the importance of speed. To Saudek "rapid handwritings . . . are completely mature handwritings," but in my opinion speed is no more essential to dynamic writing than it is to reading; it not only brings out the good points of a "positive" personality but on the other hand the faults—both of omission and commission—of a "negative" one. It can mean hysteria as well as energy and brains.

Brooks opens his chapter, "The Movements of Handwriting," by demonstrating the close connection between the spontaneity of a handwriting and the speed at which it was written. To illustrate the value of this spontaneity to collectors of manuscripts, he observes that Goethe had two handwritings, the natural and

*Signatures of J. W. von Goethe *

the calligraphic, and collectors pay four or five times as much for the former as for the latter. As another example he points out the differences between a specimen of writing dictated at speed and one dictated or copied slowly. The latter frequently shows signs of immaturity which may disappear in the high wind of speed. Brooks then gets down to business and proceeds to consider what he calls the chief laws governing the movements of handwriting. "Our list," he says, "is a shortened and simplified version of that given by Dr. Saudek."

Here is the list:

1. When writing quickly no one can bring his pen to a dead stop. This is clearly exhibited, he says, by the simplest graphic form, the dot: in quick writing the dots invariably take the form of commas or accents.

* From *Collecting Autographs and Manuscripts* by Charles Hamilton. Copyright 1961 by the University of Oklahoma Press. Reprinted by permission of the publisher.

[handwritten facsimile]

Misplaced "i" dot and "t" bar

2. When writing quickly no one can direct the movement of his hand with perfect accuracy. In this case the "i" dot and the "t" bar will rarely be exactly where they are supposed to be.

3. When the hand changes its direction without arresting its movement, a curved stroke always results, generally a garland; but in forming an angle, the movement is always arrested for a fraction of a second. (Long strokes, incidentally, are written faster than short ones because, I imagine, of the momentum which they attain.)

4. Wavering or broken strokes are inconsistent with quick writing.

[handwritten facsimile]

*Writing of Charles Dickens on the day before his death ***

* From *Universal Manuscript.*

5. There is a contraction and release in normal writing which produces a rhythmic sequence of thick and thin strokes. When the muscles are not working properly we get a so-called pasty or smeary writing. (He cites the writing of Dickens on the day before his death as an example of this.)

6. In quick, Western writing (moving from left to right) the rightward movements are performed with greater vigor and emphasis. This affects the letters: strokes which are normally leftward are eliminated or turned rightward; it affects the left-hand margin, which grows wide as the writer proceeds down the page; and it affects the width of the script, illustrated by the small letters "m," "n," and "u."

7. When the pace is retarded and spontaneity is checked, a tendency to the left appears. Here we have a narrowing left-hand margin and an exaggeration of leftward movements in forming letters; a tendency to the left is proof, according to Brooks, of inhibitions and the curbing of natural impulses.

8. The "initial adjustment" of which I have already spoken at length—the beginning strokes.

Brooks's second chapter on speed starts off with another table "related to the laws of movement dealt with in the preceding chapter." Here we have a number of quick signs offsetting an approximately equal number of slow ones. We have lines rising toward the right opposed to lines sinking to the right. We have

Leftward handwriting with narrowing left margin

frequent signs of tendency to the right and frequent signs of tendency to the left. We have fluent, unbroken strokes and excellent rhythm contrasted with wavering, bent and broken strokes, and pasty writing. We have inaccurate aim in placing "i" dots and "t" bars contrasted with accurate. We have letters clipped and incomplete, becoming almost illegible toward the ends of words contrasted with careful formation of letters. Finally we have much continuity and linking up of signs, letters, words, etc., contrasted with pauses, angles, dots, changes of pressure, and grasp of pen; and we have the presence or absence of the beginning stroke. In conclusion, Brooks adds that many factors may contribute to retard the speed of a script, and here he includes the physical and emotional condition of the writer and the quality of the writing materials.

So much for those signs which Saudek calls the primary signs of the speed of execution and which Brooks seeks to interpret. There now remain a few "equivocal" signs with obviously more than one meaning which often appear contrary to the dominant tempo of the writing. Saudek goes into this subject in great detail, but to do so here might confuse the reader, as it did me. One example given by Brooks is of tremulous and broken strokes in a primarily fast writing which are caused by faults of the writing instruments or physical disorder. Another is of sinking lines caused by depression rather than by the usual reasons for a slow script. A third is increased continuity which is caused by

Tremulous and broken strokes

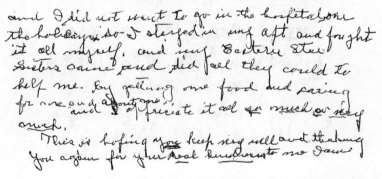

"laziness," as Brooks puts it, or by adherence to routine which results in inability to adapt to new conditions. A fourth is the omission of "i" dots and even "t" bars which can be caused either by negligence or, as in the case of Scott, by an increased speed and continuity which is too rushed to go back and make these isolated signs.

If my readers, generally tolerant because graphology is new to many of them and ready to accept much with an open mind, find inconsistencies and duplication in these lists which are hard to overlook, I can only say that after studying Saudek and Brooks with care I would prefer to give them self-contradictory Saudek and Brooks from the source than by way of Hartford!

Can we, however, make any concluding generalizations on the subject of speed? Roman has one or two. Physiological studies, she tells us, have shown that the tempo of thinking and writing are intimately correlated, and subsequent experiments, she adds, have substantiated that it is the sweep of ideas which carries the writing along and ultimately determines speed. In my opinion

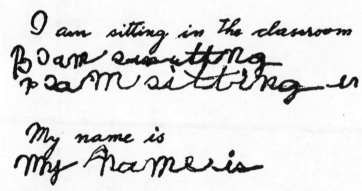

Feeble-minded
The first sentences were written by the teacher; underneath are the feeble-minded thirteen-year-old boy's attempts to copy them. *

* From *Handwriting—Revelation of Self* by Herry O. Teltscher. Reprinted by permission of the author.

this judgment should be modified, as I have said, by taking into account the extent to which form and style are retained, improved, or lost, under pressure. Roman next tells us that individual speed is variable and changes according to the writing situation—the where, the how, and the what of writing. I agree. Finally, she notes that speed increases with practice and particularly during the very early years. Roman says in her *Encyclopedia* that at the age of fourteen the average boy has reached 85 percent of and the average girl has equaled the habitual writing tempo they will display at the age of eighteen. There are cases, of course, such as those of the feeble-minded, in which speed rarely changes throughout life, even with fluctuating moods and conditions.

Pressure

Pressure, or the depth component, as Lewinson and Zubin call it, is a difficult subject to write about. I have spent several days fussing with my notes and am far from being able to claim, as Elbert Hubbard could regarding his little masterpiece, *A Message to Garcia*, that "this literary trifle . . . was written one evening after supper, in a single hour." When you compare the vertical and horizontal dimensions of handwriting with the minute variations in the third dimension, the depth, it is apparent that not only is this third dimension extremely restricted but buried in the paper in such a way that we can do little more than make calculated guesses about it. While I am thus floating far from the safe shores of scientific certainty I am going to wrap my security blanket around me and quote from Roman's definition in her *Encyclopedia of the Written Word*, which defines "Pressure in Writing" as:

> The graphological term for the summation of forces exerted
> by the writing fingers to press the point of the moving pen
> downward on the writing surface.

95

Writing pressure manifests itself in line quality, i.e., thickness, darkness, sharpness, and shading of the stroke.

The pen guided over the paper with slight pressure produces a fine stroke; heavy pressure, a broader, darker stroke. Differences in application of pen to paper—i.e., firm or gentle, rapid or slow, an easy, rhythmic motion or a tremulous, shaky one—leave corresponding impressions.

The fingers usually apply more pressure when making the downstroke than they do with the upstroke. The rhythm of emphasis thus produced parallels the interplay of muscular contraction and release that underlies the "healthy" writing movement. It results in variations of line thickness; relatively thick downstrokes alternate with thinner upstrokes, while curves show gradations of thickening and thinning. This effect is known as *shading*—one of the best indices of writing pressure.

However, pressure may also be exerted sideways instead of downward; this lateral emphasis is termed *displaced writing*

More pressure on the downstroke *

---

* From *The Psychology of the Movements of Handwriting* by J. Crépieux-Jamin (translated and arranged by L. K. Given-Wilson). (George Routledge & Sons, Ltd., London)

pressure. [Anthony calls this horizontal displacement a manifestation of psychological disturbance and claims that it means
that the writer is overcompensating for feelings of inadequacy
or expressing in numerous ways his lack of ego-fulfillment.]

The tendency to exert heavy writing pressure is not attributed to sheer muscular force or "will power." Pulver conceives
of writing pressure as a primordial phenomenon, a discharge
of libido, understood not merely as psychosexual energy but
as the total psychic energy vested in all life activities of the
individual. In this sense, it is an index of alertness and intensity of needs, of drives and cravings seeking either physical
or psychic expression.

Writing may be produced with instruments of different construction—pen, pencil, stylus, ball-point pen, or goose quill—
yet, except for certain differences that identify the tool rather
than the user, the script is a form of expression that bears
the unique stamp of the individual writer.

Though the various types of writing instruments have to
be considered to the extent that they modify the stroke, it
must be borne in mind that the tool functions as an extension of the hand; in fact, in this context the pen may be
thought of as a part of the body, hand and pen moving as a
single member. The fingers and thumb transmit to the pen
the directive impulses and the variations in muscular tension
that occur during the act of writing, according to the nature
of the writer's nervous organization. Each writer has his own
way of manipulating the pen and exerting pressure, and his
own rate of speed in moving the pen. The same pen in different hands will produce different strokes.

The study of handwriting for the disclosure of subtle variations in psychomotor activity has gained considerable recogni-
tion in the field of clinical psychology. A number of researchers have investigated the operational characteristics of writing
pressure and have constructed special devices such as . . .
Roman's graphodyne . . . [and] Tripp's electrographodyne
[which he invented while a member of my Handwriting Institute several years ago] . . . to make visible and measurable,

in recorded wave-form tracings, the variables of writing
pressure and speed.

The pattern of these tracings, illustrates that the pressure
phenomenon involves two components: (1) the activated energy
expended in writing, represented by the action pattern;
(2) the store of retained energy (tension), represented by the
blank area upon which the action pattern is superimposed.

Though it is recognized that there are wide individual
differences in the particular patterns of energy mobilization,
activated energy and muscular tension are in due balance,
i.e., when the area of the action pattern exceeds the blank
area (retained tension).

Graphologists, following Saudek, distinguish two kinds of
writing pressure apart from tension: point pressure, the pressure brought to bear by the point of the pen upon the writing
surface; and grip pressure, the pressure exerted by the fingers
in gripping and holding the pen. The distinction is mislead-
ing, inasmuch as grip pressure is a function of tension
significant only as one of its visible indicators.

In another of her books Roman says that "the tendency to
exert heavy pressure in writing is not attributable to possession
of sheer muscular power. H. Jacoby studied this possible relationship by examining the handwriting of several hundred shoe-
factory hands whose work involved the use of pliers in a routine
manipulation requiring great strength primarily. Yet Jacoby
found that those workers who turned out more than the average
number of pieces per hour, i.e., who had the greatest muscular
strength, invariably wrote with no more than average pressure."

Not only Roman, but many others have debated about light
and heavy, even and uneven pressure. Most graphologists agree
that light pressure points in the direction of sensitivity, sensibility, delicacy of feeling. Surely a person who writes with light
pressure is easily hurt and in my opinion gets over the wound
less quickly than those who write with heavy pressure and, as
one writer puts it, soak up emotional experiences like a blotter.
Louise Rice finds perverts, as she calls them, primarily among

[handwritten lines]

Light pressure—a letter from Marjorie to me. As Courbet says, "One does not need to take the trouble to conform to rules of spelling when writing to such a shady character."

light-pressure writers, but of course the world is full of homosexuals with heavy pressure. On the other hand Miss Rice remarks that heavy-pressure writers are rarely of as fine calibre as light-pressure, and she writes that "very even pressure, which is light and delicate and yet conveys the feeling of virility, is the finest indication of character development." To both Pulver and Mrs. Lewinson, the greatest energy and creativity lie in heavy pressure, and certainly I would have to testify on their behalf, taking as evidence the writing of composers, and particularly of Mozart, whose handwriting is not only heavy but uneven and almost muddy. Let us not write off light pressure, however, as an index of vitality. In many respects my former wife Marjorie has a highly aggressive handwriting, but she also has the lightest pressure I have ever seen, so light that when she used to leave a note for her roommate in Laurel Canyon in Hollywood before we were married, the roommate, thinking the paper was blank, would write another note across it. Certainly there was no lack of energy in an actress who was picked by Elia Kazan, as was Marjorie, for the forty-minute monologue of Maggie in *Cat on a Hot Tin Roof* for a full year on Broadway and across the country. But it may also be that when light-pressure people exert their energies to the fullest there is a toll taken which is unknown to the exuberance of the heavy-pressure people. In a study made at New York University, Dr. Leo Goldberger has some interesting comments about pressure and other aspects of handwriting. He finds medium-light pressure to go along with intelligence, but also with features of overcontrol, whether of the conscious kind issuing in secretiveness or the unconscious manifestations of neurosis. He finds light pressure correlated with "social withdrawal" and shyness, indicating, he believes, the degree to which the person "avoids having to cope with his controls." I must admit that I will never forget the way Marjorie used to tell everyone in the living room that she would "be down in just a second" and then disappear for the rest of the evening.

Heavy pressure belongs to those who have a strong development of the senses of music, odor, color, flavor; whose imagination is highly visual, with an affinity for the occult and the supernatural; to those with extrasensory perception; to public speakers and actors and dancers and athletes and cooks; to inventors and engineers, who often admit, like Howard Hughes, that their interest is greater in things than in people; and to alcoholics. When the heavy pressure is even and rhythmic, it can be a sign of perseverance, diligence, and resolution; of warmth, wide experience, capacity for enjoyment, and sense of humor; of discipline and self-control.

Louise Rice had much to say on the subject of heavy pressure and her so-called "material type" of people who generally use it. Heavy pressure, she told us, denotes the temperamental ardor which gives nervous vitality to any action of the body. She rated every writer of heavy pressure as belonging in either the sensuous or sensual category. She declared that there is no exception to the rule that heavy pressure shows materialism but that there

Heavy pressure *

* From *Encyclopedia of the Written Word* by Klara G. Roman. Reprinted by permission of the Frederick Ungar Publishing Co., Inc., New York.

Dear Hunt

Thank you for your invitation to sign me up into the world of Beauty. Fortunately Beauty has as many meanings as man has moods.

Hunt,

Heavy pressure

are quite a number of exceptions to the rule that light pressure shows idealism. In her opinion, heavy-pressure important people are more aggressive success-getters than light-pressure important people, but their ultimate place in the memory of man is often less. Elaborating on her definition of "material" people, she held that their love of money and of physical ease and comfort is strong and their ardor is apt to turn into coldness or sensuality. She believed that physical courage is characteristic of this type, but high moral courage rare; that their affections are possessive; that their tempers are often violent and strong; and that men of the "material" type, instinctively possessive, and with their feelings of altruism deeply rooted within the family, are often ardent fathers. Finally, Miss Rice believed that it is from this type that we have a disproportionate number of sudden deaths from heart disease.

The highest and lowest of humanity have written with heavy pressure. They have run the gamut from the Marquis de Sade,

Sacher-Masoch (to whose name we owe the word "masochism"), and Casanova, to such prodigies as Elizabeth I, Nelson, Newton, Darwin, and Dickens. The uneven and muddy pressure of the former group illustrates Werner Wolff's concept of the paper as the medium or "object" upon which the writer releases his "libidinous impulses." The desire for bodily contact, or the impulse to caress or to hurt or be hurt, Roman comments, is thus vicariously realized on the paper. The *positive* counterpart of such physical desires and impulses is excellently described by Jacoby: "The man who shakes hands forcefully, treads forcefully, or when writing presses the pen forcefully, follows an unconscious desire for or expectation of resistance—an attitude characteristic of the energetic, active type of person whose strength and vigor seem to thrive on opposition." I. Pascal obtained results on the correlation between writing pressure on the one hand and "energy, dominance, and determination" on the other.

GEORGE L. HARTFORD &
JOHN A. HARTFORD, Trustees

By _____
George L. Hartford

and

By _____
John A. Hartford

Note the artistic Greek "d" at the end of John's writing (and the long stubborn stake into the ground at the end of George's!).

In my opinion the polemics between the partisans of light and heavy pressure are barren, for certainly there have been many great men in both categories. I believe that handwriting can be highly creative at any level of pressure, that the business-man can be fully as creative as the artist, the astronaut as the philosopher, the emphasis on the one hand being on transforming his environment and on the other on understanding it. My late Uncle John, almost totally responsible for the growth of the A & P in this century, had the writing of a great artist, but with heavy pressure. It was perhaps the characteristics manifested in the heaviness of Albert Schweitzer's writing that made him capable of performing his immortal work isolated in the jungle; a less physically masterful person would not have lasted. Finally, I believe that pressure is one of the basic characteristics of writing which is strongly affected by environment and occupation, and it is quite possible for someone to have light pressure at one period of his life and heavy at another. Miss Rice calls this change the most drastic that a writer can effect and claims that it usually takes place over a long period of time, as was the case with my mother, who, starting her adult life with light pressure, ended it using a stub pen.

We come around at last to a mention of uneven and wavering pressure. Here we find the tremulousness of ill health, both

Addict under influence of heroin *

---

* From *Handwriting Tells,* copyright © 1936, 1959, 1969 by Nadya Olyanova, reprinted by permission of the publishers, The Bobbs-Merrill Company, Inc. and Peter Owen Ltd.

mental and physical, and of old age—to be discussed in later chapters. In any case such uneven pressure, whether heavy or light, is rarely a "good" sign. It is analogous to the wavering slant of which I have spoken in another chapter, and when accompanied by it indicates people who can never make up their minds and have a way of looking at a horse, as Conrad said in *Heart of Darkness*, which is far more immoral than the thief who goes out and steals it (as Conrad put it, if I remember correctly, perhaps he can ride!). Wavering and erratic pressure can be the sign of an indecisive nature, of emotional instability, of an inferiority complex, of hysteria, of drug addiction, of petty crime (the nature is generally not consistent enough for big crimes). Sudden pressure on an occasional stroke, according to Rice and others, indicates temper and ill-regulated passions; heavier pressure on perpendicular strokes than on horizontal, passions and appetites which are probably without expression save as they ravage the inner nature. One wonders about the inner nature of the great Franklin Delano Roosevelt, whose writing so clearly illustrates this observation.

If we are to speak of uneven pressure, we cannot leave the subject without a word about writing which alternates between the pasty and the muddy. According to Roman's *Encyclopedia*, pastose or doughy writing indicates "sensitivity to tactile stimuli and need for bodily contact." The pastose stroke is described as uniform in width (without any rhythmic contrast) and dense

Writing of Franklin Delano Roosevelt *

* From *Handwriting—Revelation of Self* by Herry O. Teltscher. Reprinted by permission of the author.

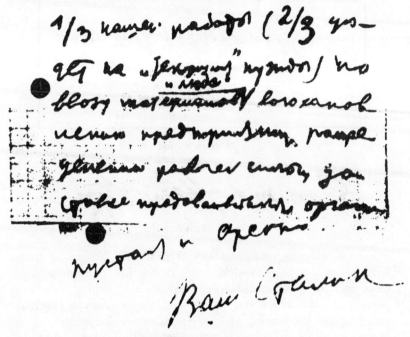

Writing of Josef Stalin *

with ink. The stroke is less written than daubed upon the writing surface, as if with a paintbrush, with little effort or strain. Muddy writing of course is not necessarily heavy and can be written with a sharper stroke involving an ebb and flow of the pen, occasionally interrupted by pauses and sudden changes of pressure causing smears and blots. Sometimes there is writing which is both pasty and muddy, as was probably the case with that of Josef Stalin, whose script might have given concern to the world if people had taken graphology seriously enough during the Twenties and Thirties or at Yalta. It is extremely violent and, like that of Napoleon and the Marquis de Sade, expresses

* From *Handwriting Tells,* copyright © 1936, 1959, 1969 by Nadya Olyanova, reprinted by permission of the publishers, The Bobbs-Merrill Company, Inc. and Peter Owen Ltd.

Marquis de Sade *

Lady Hamilton †

crudeness, excesses, and brutality. The sensual nature of pasty writing, according to Saudek, has been verified in thousands of cases, and his favorite examples of it are the writings of Casanova, Lady Hamilton, and Byron. He has an amusing vendetta going against the writing of Lady Hamilton, which in the course of two pages he describes as ugly, demoralized, mendacious, ignoble, hysterical, cruel, unintellectual, sensual, grotesque, savagely grasping, repulsive, and criminal. Poor Nelson, who had to live with her! As for Byron, I believe Saudek included him in his attack rather to fill out his trio of sex symbols than because his handwriting is pasty, which it isn't; it is sharp and clean with the ebb and flow of great rhythm and an occasional blot. Byron may have been sensual, but it is hard to deny him the title of the greatest romantic of his age.

Since this chapter is essentially a discussion of doctrines that Roman originated, I will conclude it by describing, partially in

* From *Diagrams of the Unconscious* by Werner Wolff, Ph.D. Reprinted by permission of Grune & Stratton, Inc., New York and Mrs. Kate A. Wolff.

† From *Collecting Autographs and Manuscripts* by Charles Hamilton. Copyright 1961 by the University of Oklahoma Press. Reprinted by permission of the publisher.

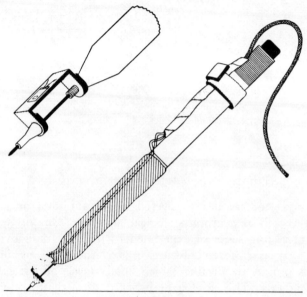

The graphodyne *

her own words, one of her most important projects, the graphodyne. She invented this instrument for the measurement of
writing speed and pressure in 1931, going far beyond the
"balance" developed for this purpose by the great psychiatrist
Kraepelin in the Nineties. The graphodyne permitted the trans-
mission, at first mechanical and later electrical (as devised by
C. A. Tripp at the Handwriting Institute which I set up in
New York), of writing pressure from a movable stylus to a
recording device. The variations in writing pressure affect a metal
drum attached to a lever and are transmitted to an ink writer
and recorded. Tracings thus obtained show the ebb and flow,
the tension and release of healthy writing of which we have
spoken earlier, as well as other dynamic components such as
accented beats and interruptions of flow. Work with the grapho-

* From *Encyclopedia of the Written Word* by Klara G. Roman. Reprinted
by permission of Frederick Ungar Publishing Co., Inc., New York.

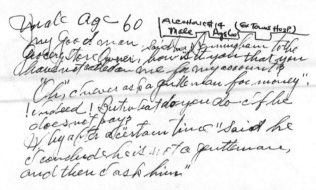

Writing while under the influence of alcohol *

dyne, says Roman, has uncovered significant data on psychological as well as neurophysiological problems. One of Roman's most interesting series of experiments with the graphodyne disclosed that as children advance in age, their writing pressure shows a progressive decline, which finally levels off with the onset of puberty. This level is maintained through the adolescent years except for a short crisis period, in which pressure drops to an unprecedented low; within less than a year, however, it jumps back to the writer's former level. For this unique phenomenon, occurring around the seventeenth year and more pronounced in boys, Roman has no explanation.

Other experiments at the Handwriting Institute using a graphodyne stylus to examine the behavior of people writing while under the influence of alcohol, clearly indicated that a raggedness of stroke and a definite disturbance in rhythm (due to impairment of muscular and neural control) result as the brain becomes sluggish with alcohol. Further, I firmly believe that the graphodyne and the microscope as used by Kanfer in his work on cancer will one day unveil great vistas to psychiatric and medical research by correctly diagnosing the role of pressure in handwriting as an indicator of subtle variations in psychomotor activity.

* From the files of The Handwriting Institute, Inc., New York.

Spacing, Width, Size

When they examine writing for signs of judgment, sensitivity, good taste, and similar estimable qualities, students of the subject are likely to think first of either the figure-eight "g" or the arrangement of words, lines, and paragraphs on the page. Alfred Kanfer, of whom I will write at length in Chapter 14 on the effects of cancer, tells us that certain areas of handwriting show stability through all conditions of health and illness. One such area is spacing. A close relative of Mr. Kanfer's was dying of tuberculosis, and when he became unable to talk he jotted down a few notes. Comparison between these last notes and his previous writing indicated that the spacing was practically unchanged even though the writing itself was already utterly disintegrating.

Is there an intrinsic difference between spacing and the nature of the strokes themselves? There is; for while the strokes derive primarily from the organism of the writer, spacing relates to the

Great South Street
Tuesday Morn

My sweet Fanny,

On awakening from my three days dream ("I cry to dream again") I find one and another astonish'd at my idleness and thoughtlessness. I was miserable last night. the morning is always restorative. I must be busy, or try to be so. I have several things to speak to you of tomorrow morning. Mrs Dilke I should think will tell you that I purpose living at Hampstead. I must impose chains upon myself. I shall be able to do nothing. I should like to cast the die for Love or death. I have no Patience with any thing else. if you ever intend to be cruel to me as you say in jest now but perhaps may sometimes be in earnest be so now. and I will. my mind is in a tremble, I cannot tell what I am writing.

Ever my love yours
John Keats

Later writing of Keats, who died of "consumption." *

Certainly no one could have done more to make a mother proud and happy than you did.

Pat and I want you to know our prayers are with you in these sad hours —

Dick

Handwriting of President Nixon *

outside world with which the writer is communicating. Spacing and margins are thus acquired characteristics and up to a certain age susceptible to arbitrary changes by the writer; but with advancing years they become fixed and automatic, spacing more so than margins. As Kanfer has pointed out, spacing within sentences has a dual function: through narrow spaces to indicate that certain letters belong together, forming the unit of a word, and by wider spaces separating one word from the other. The objective is communication, clarity to the reader, enabling him to recognize at a glance which letters belong to one word and at the same time keeping each word clearly distinct.

Is the writer concerned with clarity and order? Is he capable of recognizing the necessity for proper control and organization and is he capable of carrying it through consistently? A harmonious distribution of words and free spaces—and of paragraphs—

* From *Handwriting Tells,* copyright © 1936, 1959, 1969 by Nadya Olyanova, reprinted by permission of the publishers, The Bobbs-Merrill Company, Inc. and Peter Owen Ltd.

would show that he is, says Kanfer, and we have the handwriting of President Nixon as a prime example. Such distribution argues the ability to separate thoughts and impressions logically and to present them with clarity and logic to the outsider. The way the writer can control the alternating process between actual writing and moving the pen through the air to the proper place for the next word, is also the way he controls other activities in his life—methodically or carelessly, aware or unconcerned, impulsively or acting almost automatically.

The average writer is concerned with clarity only to a necessary degree. Emphasis on clarity is diluted by the need to economize space, which often gives a crowded appearance to his writing and reminds one of bookkeeping. On the other hand, there is frequently a classic beauty in the spacing of the writing of people with strong personalities which seems to belie the tumultuous natures which are expressing themselves. It is only where the intensity of the creative temperament veers toward the worldly and domineering, where social involvement and ambition become driving forces, that this classic beauty is distorted, not so much by crowding as by occasional outbreaks from the concentrated middle zone which spill forth vertically as long upper and lower loops and elaborate capitals and horizontally as long and dramatic "t" bars and word endings.

The analogy between the symmetry (or lack of it) of a painting or drawing and a page of writing has been observed by Werner Wolff and Sonnemann. Yet Wolff associates symmetry with sameness and a pedantic search for security, and this view coincides with Sonnemann's derivation of the calligraphy of earlier centuries from the "greater security which the more stable values of past ages were able to afford. . . ."—terminating in the twentieth century, of course, with a general breakdown of style not only in writing but in other areas of culture. To Wolff, symmetry is a static concept which he identifies in extreme cases with "the artistic manifestations of mentally diseased people" and in handwriting in which Schmidl-Wachner found "the rigid . . . rhythm [of] . . . demented and feebleminded children." Wolff places symmetry on the side of "necessity, unchangeableness, fate, and fatality" as opposed to the self-concept of modern man who, with his striving for independence, has become "very sensitive to the problem of freedom. . . ." It is the dynamism of rhythm—in handwriting and elsewhere—which Wolff identifies with change and progress rather than the perfect and Platonic world of symmetry.

Ideal spacing of a page *

* Reprinted by permission of Yale University Library.

Mondrian, Composition in Red, Yellow and Blue (Collection Haags Gemeentemuseum, The Hague)

Be that as it may, if we can associate the ideal symmetry of a page of writing—with emphasis on margins and the indentation of paragraphs as well as the clear separation of words and lines —with the symmetry of a great painting, then we can hardly regard it as critically as does Werner Wolff. It is true that symmetry, when reduced perhaps to a combination of lines and shapes as one might find in a Mondrian painting, has a limited and static quality. But symmetry, in a page of writing as in a painting, ought not to be an end in itself but, as Kanfer observes of spacing, a means by which the overriding purpose of communication may be accomplished. Symmetry dramatizes; it places the subject of the painting at the ideal focal point for the viewer; in the painter's supreme effort to communicate his feelings, he puts the object or objects in the most significant light. In setting down his thoughts on paper, the intelligent and creative person arranges his words and frames his thoughts in the manner by which they will be most easily and quickly assimilated. The lines and paragraphs, like Mondrian's forms, are indeed symmetrical, but in a symmetry created to present the sensitive or tumultuous emotions within in the most effective way.

I have referred to margins only in passing, and it is time to say a few words about them. Someone has likened margins to the frame surrounding a picture. Louise Rice says that the way margins and paragraphs are used has a great deal to tell the graphologist about the artistic taste of the writer but that it is the appreciators of art and the connoisseurs who are more likely to arrange the page with meticulous care than the artist himself. Great talent, in other words, often lies somewhere between the desire to produce a perfect page and the vitality which overflows its medium. We see this antithesis in the careful address of an envelope on the one hand and the more spontaneous variation and elaboration inside the letter. The contrast is dramatically illustrated by the frequently even left margin, which reminds Mendel of a bed before one gets in at night and the analogy of the right margin (where the writer plunges into the environment and the future) to the same bed disarranged in the morning.

It is the conventional practice of Western writing to have

The two pages designed by William Morris (Reprinted by permission of Kelmscott Press, London, 1895)

margins at the left; Roman speaks of their relationship to the outside world. The painter and graphic genius William Morris, she tells us, declared that the unit of printing was two open pages. These he designed, following the model of medieval books, with inner margins narrowest and the top, outer and bottom successively wider; and such a design is now still in use and highly regarded. Apart from these conventions handed down from one age to another, what are the psychological factors which today affect the width of margins and the angles at which they descend from the top to the bottom of the page? Little has been said about the top or upper margin except that it tends to denote respect and, where it is particularly wide, submissiveness; the absence of this margin, on the other hand, "has clearly a clumsy, 'obtrusive,' disfiguring influence," says Sonnemann, "upon the whole appearance of a text."

It is the left and right margins about which almost all graphologists have expressed themselves and with a good deal of agree-

But AMANDA *has suddenly stopped dead, covered in confusion. For the* PRINCE *has pushed aside the* BUTLER, *who since his entrance has stood as though petrified, and stands there in the doorway, pale with anger.* HECTOR *stops humming, and the* DUCHESS *and the* HEAD WAITER *turn round, dumbfounded.*

PRINCE. Aunt Melisande!

DUCHESS. Albert!

PRINCE. What is the meaning of this masquerade?

DUCHESS. Theophilus, what have you done?

BUTLER (*looking ten years older, as he bows his head*). I came to warn Your Grace, but I was so dumbfounded by what I saw that I fear I——

DUCHESS (*terrible, with an imperious gesture*). Theophilus, you are dismissed!

The BUTLER *creeps out, a hundred years older.*

PRINCE (*dry, to the others*). Perhaps the rest of you would be kind enough to leave us also. I must speak to this young lady alone.

HECTOR *and the* HEAD WAITER *beat a hasty retreat. The* DUCHESS *also prepares to go. The* PRINCE *looks at* AMANDA *for the first time, to her great embarrassment. Suddenly he sees the Venetian negro. He leaps to it.*

Who has dared to lay hands on this statue?

DUCHESS (*at the door*). I did, Albert. I wished to clear a space for——

PRINCE (*in a fury, as he puts the statue back in its original place*). I gave orders that nobody, under any pretext whatsoever, was to touch anything that she had touched!

The DUCHESS, *who is really not very intimidated by this display of temper, is making complicated signs to*

42

AMANDA *behind the* PRINCE'S *back. He studies* AMANDA *silently. The* DUCHESS *goes.*

PRINCE. I am afraid that my aunt has placed you in an embarrassing position, mademoiselle.

AMANDA (*simple*). I'm afraid she has, sir.

PRINCE (*unkind*). I don't doubt that you were desperate to find employment of some sort——

AMANDA. No, sir. That is to say, yes, sir. You see, your aunt had taken the trouble to get me dismissed from the milliner's where I worked before she summoned me here.

PRINCE (*amused*). She's an amazing woman.

AMANDA (*a little bitter*). Amazing is right. (*Pause.*) But since yesterday I've got to the point where nothing amazes me any more.

PRINCE. You have been here since yesterday?

AMANDA. Yes. You even spoke to me last night, in the park, by that obelisk with the stone bench round it——

PRINCE. Was that you? I must beg your pardon for not recognizing you. It was very dark. Why did you ask me the way to the sea?

AMANDA (*soft*). Apparently that was the particular phrase of which you had to be . . . reminded. . . .

The PRINCE *stops as though thunderstruck, and murmurs:*

PRINCE. Excuse me, can you tell me the way to the sea?

He sits down in an arm-chair, saying nothing, as if in a trance. Endless pause. AMANDA *clears her throat. No effect. She starts to tiptoe out. He suddenly cries:*

PRINCE. Don't go! Come back, where I can see you! You are plain. You walk badly. You are not in the least like her. You never could be like her. You're just a common little milliner, with no mystery, no aura——

T.R.—4   43

The margins of an open book—no change from the Middle Ages *

ment. Unusually wide margins, it has been said, are generally the sign of an emotionally withdrawn or extravagant ego, while very narrow or completely absent margins have on the other hand been called a sign of domination or greed or at best—this is Kanfer's judgment—of a neurotic personality who fears that if he cannot express himself fully he will be misunderstood and misjudged. The total absence of a right-hand margin is also an indication of speed, as is the constant increasing of the left-hand margin by the writer who is carried away by his momentum to the right. Conversely, a progressive decrease of the left-hand margin indicates slowness and reduced spontaneity.

As Sainte Colombe tells us, "the enterprising Western civiliza-

* From *Time Remembered* by Jean Anouilh (English version by Patricia Moyes). Reprinted by permission of Dr. Jan Van Loewen Ltd., London.

tion writes from left to right, moving always forward toward action, accomplishment, goals." (Writers in Hebrew and Arabic, of course, go from right to left and the Chinese from top to bottom.) Pulver referred to movements in the lateral dimension —from left to right—as moving metaphorically toward the environment. As our first step in that direction, at the left side of the page, we are self-conscious and wish to make a good impression. As Mendel puts it, the left margin remains the "face" that writers insist on "showing": it is the "show window." Wide left margins, according to Mendel, may therefore be interpreted as an indication of the writer's respect or reservation toward others and are found in the letters of "shy or proud" people. By the time the writer reaches the right side of the page, on the other hand, he has come to terms with his subject and his audience and is far less concerned about a margin, especially since he does not have the same control over the end of a line as he does of the beginning. Of a wide margin at the right, therefore, graphologists are not as tolerant as they are of one at the left, and what they sometimes praise when found at one side of the page they often condemn at the other as neurotically fearful of the future.

As usual, it remains for Sonnemann to have the final word on the subject. He is speaking about the angle of the left-hand margin. "The person allowing his left-hand margin to broaden," says he, "appears so much absorbed by his activity that he experiences the necessity of returning to the left-hand side as more and more unwelcome disturbance." The respect of the wide but even left margin thus declines into neglect. Conversely, Sonnemann sees a shrinking of the left-hand margin as a compulsion to "put things behind one," both economically and psychologically, and to behave in the reactionary manner which leftward writing suggests. Such a writer, like the bird that flies backward, is less interested in seeing where he is going than where he has been.

As I have discussed the evenness or unevenness of margins and their tendency to spread to the right or left, I will discuss the evenness and unevenness of lines and their tendency to veer up would have written sooner but had no idea where you are. The only way that I can keep up with you is by reading exalted personages of Journal-American Cholly K. and such—

Have been fairly busy rehearsing to un E.L.T. (Equity Library Theatre Production) Hotel Paradiso by Fedeau + Desvallieres une petite part. I am one of tour daughter

Broadening of margin

Through a series of bad fortunes, my funds have run dangerously low, I have no financial aid from anywhere no passage anywhere (which doesn't matter so much as I want and need to stay) and o remunerative possibilities here.

Shrinking of margin—and spirits

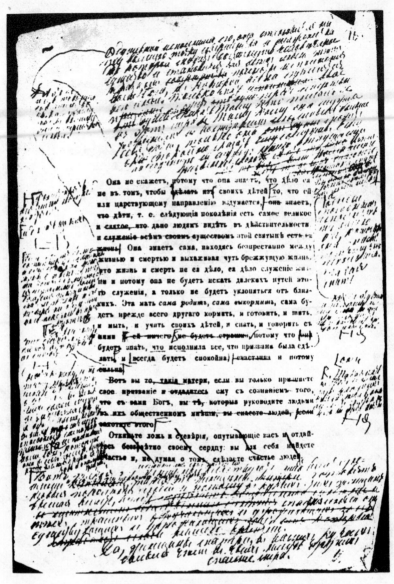

Она не скажетъ, потому что она знаетъ, что дѣло са
не въ томъ, чтобы сдѣлать изъ своихъ дѣтей то, что ей
или царствующему направленію вздумается, она знаетъ,
что дѣти, т. е. слѣдующія поколѣнія есть самое великое
и святое, что дано людямъ видѣть въ дѣйствительности
и служеніе всѣмъ своимъ существомъ этой святынѣ есть са
жизнью Она знаетъ сама, находясь безпрестанно между
жизнью и смертью и выхаживая чуть брежжущую жизнь.
что жизнь и смерть не ея дѣло, ея дѣло служеніе жиз
ни и потому она не будетъ искать далекихъ путей это
го служенія, а только не будетъ уклоняться отъ бли-
кихъ. Эта мать сама родитъ, сама выкормитъ, сама будетъ прежде всего другаго кормить, и готовить, и мыть,
и мыть, и учить своихъ дѣтей, и спать, и говорить съ
ними ей ничего не будетъ страшно, потому что она
будетъ знать, что исполнила все, что призвана была сдѣлать и всегда будетъ спокойна, счастлива и потому
сильна.

Вотъ вы то, такія матери, если вы только примаете
свое призваніе и отдаетесь ему съ сознаніемъ того,
что съ вами Богъ, вы тѣ, которыя руководите людьми
въ ихъ общественномъ мнѣніи, вы спасете людей, если
захотите этого.

Откиньте ложь и суевѣрія, опутывающіе васъ и отдай-
тесь безраздѣльно своему сердцу: вы для себя найдете
счастье и, не думая о томъ, сдѣлаете счастье людей.

Proof sheet of Tolstoy in later years *

* From *Married to Tolstoy* by Lady Cynthia Asquith. Reprinted by permission of Hutchinson Publishing Group Ltd., London and Houghton
Mifflin Co., Boston.

or down. To begin with, there can be "crowding" vertically as well as horizontally. One cause is speed or slowness; in the case of fast writing, the lines tend to rise, sometimes approaching the lines above; and the man who writes fast frequently takes little time to separate a new line from the one before. Wherever there is crowding there is confusion, both on the paper and in the mind; and as Sonnemann warns, "the lack of verbal and conceptual articulateness generally disclosed by 'crowding' will of course be found accentuated where lines get entangled. . . ." Overlapping lines are a sign of mental disorder and an early and obvious one; Tolstoy, writing in his last days, when he was under very great stress, showed such an overlapping of lines that it was almost impossible to read them.

Speed may cause upward writing, but what are the psychological factors involved? According to Crépieux-Jamin, while ascending handwriting signifies ardor, it may also mean "ambition, activity, good humor, excitement, fever, hope, and sudden joy!" Other graphologists have seen in the rising line perennial optimism and enthusiasm. But some of the conclusions drawn

Rising lines *

* Reprinted by permission of Grune & Stratton, Inc., New York and Dr. Ulrich Sonnemann.

which forked up 200 gallons of gas. We've been having a hysterical forty-eight hours. Spent last night in Pittsburgh — driving like maniacs. We've only been stopped once and that was outside of Princeton

Downward slant

from this rising line are not so favorable. Mr. Micawber, always waiting for something to turn up, is hardly the person to approach for business advice. And the joy of those with their eyes constantly fixed on the rainbow in the sky can turn to terrible frustration when the pot of gold is not forthcoming. The lines of suicide notes rise as well as fall. And the euphoria of those who feel that nothing is wrong, from playing God to committing murder (the graphologist Nadya Olyanova points to the rising script of Lee Harvey Oswald), may create more havoc on society than the deepest depression. As a final word on the subject of uphill writing let us refer to the illiterate, who, writing with his arm instead of his hand, can move only in an upward arc!

Next, what about a downward slant of the line? As certainly as we know that when we are sad or depressed or ashamed we hang our heads, so does the graphologist know that such a downward slant often means depression—or worse. For many long years I had a Swedish cook named Ellen—who made the best chocolate cake on earth—and Ellen always seemed reasonably happy with her adopted home in the United States (in spite of the fact that the English language never ceased to baffle her). But whenever I noticed her handwriting, it was running downhill; and it was only when she finally retired and I received cards from Sweden with every line horizontal that I realized the sad truth. Again, I had a girl friend, many years ago, who wrote me dozens of letters with lines running down across the page at a 45-degree angle, and it was not until seeing some recent letters that I became aware that she had apparently been very unhappy. Swift, who hated the artifices and concealments of fashionable women, mockingly observed that his Lilliputians' "manner of writing is very peculiar, being neither from the left to the right, like the Europeans; nor from the right to the left, like the Arabians; nor from up to down, like the Chinese; nor from down to up, like the Cascagians; but aslant from one corner of the paper to the other, like ladies in England."

Downhill writing, then, implies depression—mental or physical. Mental depression culminates in suicide notes which frequently travel evenly across the page and drop off abruptly at the end; and the signature of Hitler in his last days is dramatic evidence of a combination of mental disorder and physical deterioration probably due to poisoning. On the physical side, Crépieux-Jamin claimed that "descending handwriting is a pathological indication of no small importance to an observant physician." Louise Rice was firmly convinced that the persistent droop of the basic line is never totally dissociated from serious physical ailments, and Roman felt that the slope of the line is less affected by a state of mind than by physical conditions, some of them temporary, like fatigue, and others more serious.

We come now to our last pair of opposing types of lines: the even line versus the fluctuating and wavering. I have not personally made much study of this subject, but after reading the comments of other graphologists I have reached one general conclusion. Where the basic line is even, we find vitality and

The political atmosphere is much brighter than it was, and we are now looking forward to a year of peace, good will, and, I hope, plenty of work.
Though we are almost in Winter the weather is exceptionally mild for this season of the year; the Sun is still quite warm.
I hope that you are keeping well, and that I shall have the pleasure of seeing you again in 1955.
Will you kindly remember me to Mr. Finch.
With kindest regards and renewed good wishes,
—believe me
Sincerely Yours

Even basic line

pleased to have;
Thanking you;
reply as possib

Wavy line *

supremacy of the mind and will; when it is uneven, the writer has become the victim not so much of deep emotions as of neurotic whims and moods. The wavy line, the rising and falling line, are signs of emotional instability; and they are frequently accompanied by changes in slant and by light and variable pressure. In more extreme cases, says Mendel, wavy lines may

* From *Graphology A Handbook* by Henry A. Rand. Reprinted by permission of Sci-Art Publishers, Cambridge, Massachusetts.

be indicative of a grievous loss, "or in a more lasting state of confusion, an ambivalence of reality and hallucination." And Louise Rice believes that eccentric basic lines point the finger of danger—of a nervous or mental breakdown.

The steadily horizontal but relaxed and rhythmic line is not significantly influenced by passing moods and uncontrolled emotions. But when the steadiness is under pressure, there are signs of tension. As one graphologist puts it, "self goes, travels, imagines, 'escapes,' but always returns 'home'"—to an even basic line. Sometimes, to contest the pressure, the line becomes as straight as a ruler; and to reinforce the evenness, the letters themselves become more angular. Occasionally, as in the case of Thomas Mann, we find the "stepped lines" in which the lines as a whole

"Spacing is too close"

are straight but each word slants either up or down. Here you have self-criticism, self-control, and a stubborn energy which, in spite of emotional strain, rarely fails to "hold the line."

Alfred Kanfer adds as a footnote to the subject of spacing that there is great importance in judging the spacing of lines and words at the two extremes of tightness and width. Narrow distances between words indicate a predominance of action, of emotions which are stronger than the critical and separating force of intelligence and of will power—in other words, an outgoing and integrated personality. But where spacing is too close, where there is no clear separation, the writer lacks either the ability or the concern to muster the control and attention to develop logical order in his thoughts and actions. To such a person, says Kanfer, facts may become confused by wishful thinking, fears, and hopes. The writer becomes too closely involved with his environment and lives in constant friction and turmoil; his is a driven, difficult, frequently talkative, and neurotic temperament, unable to see the forest for the trees. At the opposite pole of wide space between words and lines, "thereby distintegrating the context of the writing," you have the script of the independent writer who wants to be free of the crowd, who takes time to think and decide for himself, taking a broad and bold outlook on his problems. (The writing of Howard Hughes.) In cases of extreme width you have the person with a fear of being involved, of coming to grips with problems and people; a person in danger of developing deep-seated complexes and neuroses.

While we are on the subject of tightness and width, let us note briefly what other graphologists have to say in regard to the widths of words and letters. To Lewinson and Zubin the space between letters means "reciprocity between the individual and the environment." Whereas contraction might indicate the writer's inhibitions and repression of impulses toward his environment, they explain, its release might indicate too much dependence on the environment and a consequent scattering of oneself. When I asked Kanfer about the difference between this inner relationship to the environment and that of words to free space, he held that while the condition *within* words is a deep-seated psychological one, the spacing outside is generally more susceptible to outside influence. Sonnemann sees an obvious relationship between the crowding and dispersing of letters and words and the activities of saving and spending. And Louise Rice draws a comparison between the narrowness of letters and that of words. Words formed of letters which are "squeezed," she writes, which have very short connecting strokes, and are placed close together, show a cautious spirit which is too greatly engrossed with things as opposed to people and ideas and emotions. However, she continues, scripts in which the letters of the words are widely spaced but the words themselves and the lines are only narrowly separated show generosity checked and deflected from expression by circumstances, training, and environment.

Narrow letters, in writing of what earlier graphologists used to call a "high standard," are probably more characteristic than their opposite of talent and ability, for with such writing we find dependability, a realistic and practical approach to life, and a patient and sensitive willingness to analyze complexities rather than simply "to cut the Gordian knot." But extremely narrow writing has been held by various graphologists to indicate anxiety, inhibition, calculation, distrust, deception, repression, selfishness, avarice, and hostility! Very wide writing, on the other hand, is accused of displaying the opposite failings: inconstancy, lavishness and extravagance, prodigality and conceit, and in extreme cases, feeble-mindedness or a hint of paranoia. Excessive spacing of words and letters is indicative of the spendthrift, says Mendel; and he writes that Pulver calls such writers prodigals, egotists, "semi-gods," little concerned with the rights of others. On the bright side of the coin, as Daniel Anthony points out, we see the moderately narrow writer as, at his best, expressing restraint and self-control and the moderately wide writer as a generous outgoing personality of self-confidence and courage.

I have referred in the chapter heading to spacing, width, and finally to size. Why is handwriting large or small? According to Sonnemann, size is graphologically taken as a measure of the person's spontaneous self-estimate of his feeling of self-importance, and he notes how we relate "big" to important, "small" to negligible, and how we speak of magnanimity and a "grand gesture" as opposed, for example, to a "narrow" mind. When the graphologist speaks of size he generally means the size of small letters (as Saudek did), especially because the small letters are contiguous and the effect of the emotions on them is cumulative. The relationship between small letters and loops, however, cannot be ignored. As Sonnemann maintains, with the shrinking of the middle zone, the upper and lower lengths, rather than being reduced, are often expanded. As the rope of words of the tightrope walker of whom Sonnemann speaks becomes thinner, the sticks or loops by which he balances himself become longer due to the need for emotional security. (Hysterics are sometimes to be recognized by the reductions of the middle zone without the compensating loops.) While vertical reduction and undue emphasis on the width of writing goes with a yearning for the future, with a consequent endeavor to escape from the present, vertical development of the middle zone, on the other hand, places the inner focus on self-confidence and enjoyment of present activity. Where the vertical thrust is thus translated from the loops and the upper zone to the middle one, and especially where the latter is narrow, we have a person whose striving for power is reduced to a more self-contained or domestic level. To Kanfer this is a person "with strong needs for attention and for

Shrinking of the middle zone *

* Reprinted by permission of Grune & Stratton, Inc., New York and Dr. Ulrich Sonnemann.

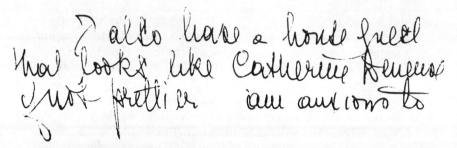

Vertical thrust translated from the loops and upper zone to the middle zone

domination without giving much in return, with concerns centered essentially around his own family and his own interests": satisfied, perhaps, to be a big fish in a little pond.

Into what categories does large handwriting fall? That of expansiveness and the ego, of childhood, of illiteracy, of illness and old age, and occasionally of mental disorder. But the picture is not quite as bad as it sounds, and let us take these up one by one. Large writing "of high standard" is generally synonymous with strong personality on a brilliant and dramatic though sometimes superficial level. We find it frequently among entertainers

High standard writing—Constance Collier re Marjorie

and performers in the musical world, though it rarely belongs to great creative artists. On the good side, it can indicate pride and generosity, enthusiasm and passionate concern, and the imagination and temperament of a born leader. It can also mean, of course, exhibitionism and impatience with detail and responsibility, which can point the way to delusions of grandeur. Saudek comments that "considerable amplifications in writing of high-standard always testify to an inclination to broad, epic, highly colored linguistic expression, to confiding intimacy, and to that geniality which finds expression in a superabundance of words." What a beautiful epitaph to my old friend Osty, now dead many years!—I wonder if anyone reading this book remembers him.

Let us run quickly over the other categories of large size. Children write large because they are just learning to make the letters and the element of design is of more concern to them than the thought which they are expressing. Lack of motor control causes the increase in size associated with illiteracy and certain illnesses, a striving to communicate causes it in the case of failing eye-sight, and sometimes an attempt to *mask* lack of motor control in old age. Finally, Roman points out that the combination of a large middle zone and rigid letters of stereotyped regularity is one of the hallmarks of what may be called the schizoid pattern, and largeness is often a characteristic of feeble-mindedness.

Osty

Sat Nov 28 - Sleep Pill
Sat Nov 28
Tuesday Dec 2
Wensday Dec
Thursday the 4
Friday Dec 5

*Lack of motor control ***

I received the proof. It seemed pretty rough to me, so I corrected it as written, adding a few more italics where the original seemed obscure or seemed reaching. Your reason for the change, i.e., that with italics only 2 different

Writing of William Faulkner †

The writing of the average literate adult tends more toward small size than large. Small writing, of course, can be a mark of brilliance, of the psychologist or writer who can see life with detachment, yet at the same time forges ahead into the environment. It is characteristic of many of the greatest people in history, from philosophers to statesmen. But where handwriting is excessively small, or where it is small and contracted, or especially if it diminishes in size, there are sometimes red flags flying. Ex-

* From the files of The Handwriting Institute, Inc., New York.

† Reprinted by permission of William Faulkner's sister: Mrs. Paul P. Summers.

cessively small writing can signify an interest in science or minute detail, like the writing of Proust and Faulkner, but it can also mean mental illness. And Werner Wolff points out that while increase in size can mean fatigue and exhaustion of emotion, a sudden decrease can indicate inhibition and frustration, possibly leading to breakdown; in this connection he cites a study made of the small handwriting of depressed children.

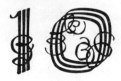

Slant

If I were asked what were the most important characteristics of a specimen of handwriting, I might very well answer rhythm and spacing, the small "t," the small "g," and the slant. Rhythm and spacing I have discussed. The small "t" relates to will power and drive, the small "g" to the part of awareness which we might identify with sensitivity, and the slant, to the emotions, the degree of forward slant giving a bearing on the degree of emotion. To Louise Rice the angle of inclination, as she calls it, is of the utmost importance, not only because she considers it "the love register" because of its link with the affections, but because it registers a host of other characteristics, from repression on the left through degrees of creativity to warnings of possible mental disease on the extreme right.

Slant or the angle of writing can be divided into four categories: forward, backward, generally upright, and mixed—the latter subject to much variation. One factor in the more con-

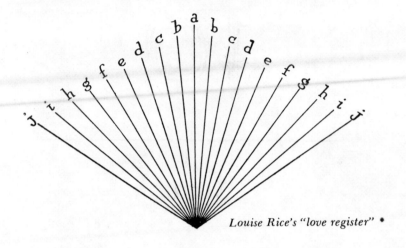

Louise Rice's "love register" *

Equally formal from the White House

sistent shifts of slant, affecting whole sentences and groups of
letters, is the gradual break with the school pattern, from the
Palmer method or some version of it, or, in the case of a few
young ladies, with the vertical, rounded script which they learn
in American boarding schools. Another factor is the varying
angles of the paper to the writer, and though Klages finds a

* From *Character Reading From Handwriting* by Louise Rice. Copyright,
1927, by Frederick A. Stokes Company. Reprinted by courtesy of J. B. Lippincott Company.

psychological reason here, the causes seem to me to be primarily mechanical. Then we have to take the addressee into account. When one addresses oneself in brief jotted notes, the slant is generally vertical. When one is writing the White House or addressing the envelope of a letter, the slant tends to be at an extremely correct 70 degrees, reminiscent of the Palmer script. When one dashes off a letter to a close friend, the slant tends to be forward leaning, increasingly so as one warms to the subject. One other reason for more consistent changes of slant is a deliberate attempt to alter one's writing: consciously for purposes of disguise (with emphasis on the slant) or subconsciously because one wishes to be all things to all men, as Miss Rice and the Apostle Paul put it—or simply because a young person admires someone's writing and wishes to copy it. The young lady who tells you proudly that you can't read her writing because

Whimsical variations—and incidentally misplaced capitals discussed later

she writes in several different ways is generally referring un-
knowingly to those variations in slant which betray her youth.

Whimsical variations within sentences and within words are
generally considered to reflect the inner conflicts, irresolution,
and transient moods of immaturity, particularly that of adolescents whose writing and personality have not completely found
themselves. Such writing sometimes resembles a line of soldiers
standing at ease after a long march. Miss Rice has hard things to
say about such variations, should they persist into later years;
she concludes her chapter on what she terms "moral diseases" by
stating that "the writing which cannot find an angle of inclination at which to stick, which cannot find a solid basic line, which
persists in uneven pressure, which has a wavering t-bar, is the
usual writing found in the criminal records of the police departments."

We now turn to the three remaining categories of slant. The
upright is the handwriting of the businessman, of the person
who places the certain present before the uncertain future, but
at the same time refuses to hide in the shadows of the past. It
is to be found in the handwriting of Admiral King, who sat at
his desk in Washington as Chief of Naval Operations and plotted
the day-to-day activity of the fleet during the Second World War,
not in the outgoing writing of General MacArthur, who risked his

Writing of Admiral Ernest J. King (Department of the Navy)

Writing of General Douglas MacArthur (From Instrument of Surrender. Signed at Tokyo Bay, September 2, 1945.)

life on the battle front in the Pacific. It is in the writing of Bernard Shaw, whose plays are more famous for their brilliant dialogue and wit than for their movement and warmth, who proudly proclaimed his atheism because there was no philosopher or mathematician clever (or spiritual) enough to prove otherwise to him, who lived into his nineties on vegetables and not, like Churchill, on hard liquor. It is the writing of those who are more interested in things than people, and as such, when at its best, is sometimes mistaken for the writing of a great scientist. And for once I must disagree with Miss Rice. It is not, as she says, the writing of the British as much as of the French, whose interest in detail and the fashion of the moment is supreme. It is the handwriting of neutrality, which some graphologists interpret as artificial, unhealthy, escapist. (If two thousand letters which the German physiologist Preyer received from his father have any meaning, it might more frequently be the writing of age than youth.) At the same time it is the writing of the person who, standing up straight, resists the urge to be absorbed into the environment and perhaps become its victim. It is the writing in which one most often finds loops, both upper and lower (in my opinion a sign of worldly ambition), perhaps because the horizontal direction is thus replaced by the vertical. The upright writing at its best represents, as Sonnemann suggests, an intensity

"Extraordinary slant" in the writing
of Immanuel Kant *

of emotional experience, if not in contemplation of the panorama of the future, at least in the physical love of present activity.

Now a word about the real key to the emotions, the forward-leaning slant. Considering the extent to which proponents of the Gestalt theory permit us to give independent meaning to any one sign, the rightward slant represents a sure expression not only of the emotions but indeed of the mind itself. "The more extreme the high level of the mind," says Louise Rice, "the more ardent, flaming and intense are apt to be the reactions of the feelings" (represented by the forward slant). The greatest of German philosophers, Immanuel Kant, with his "extraordinary slant," as Saudek calls it, was a perfect illustration of this theory; but Saudek, surprisingly, cites him as a contradictory case, apparently visualizing the purest mind as untainted by emotion and forgetting the writing of most of the great thinkers of the modern world from Voltaire to Einstein. "I do not blame Mr. Saudek for this mistake," comments Miss Rice in her book. "It is constantly iterated and reiterated, not only by generally educated people, but by educators and those whose jobs are intimately connected with the expert appraisal of human nature." The less sensitive, the more worldly people are glorified at the expense of the truly great. The Alfred Austins become the poet laureates instead of the Kiplings; the Picassos rule supreme. Intelligence tests, notoriously better at rewarding mediocrity than at detecting genius, are too often based on agility of mind and memory by rote instead of feeling and creativity. Such distortion of priorities is amply demonstrated by Professors Jacob W. Getzels and Philip W. Jackson in their book *Creativity and Intelligence*.

* From *Autographic Mirror* Volume 1.

Since writing, like walking, says Roman, is an act of progression, it follows that the easy-running "cursive script" will lean from left to right in the direction of the action—the forward movement. CBS ran several ads on television quoting Justice Holmes to the effect that a man must share the passion and action of his time at peril of being judged not to have lived. "Get involved," CBS put it in contemporary language. It is the people whose writing slants forward who get involved. They do so through love, but the object of their love, of course, is not necessarily a worthy one. Hitler's insane passion for a pure German race destroyed millions of innocent people. It is common for graphologists to identify vertical and backward writing with the writer's self, forward-leaning with others. The warmth and humanity of such great writers with forward-leaning script as Dickens and Scott and Goethe and Voltaire is immortal proof that the forward slant, when controlled, lives up to its best interpretation. But books on graphology are also full of warnings about how the temperament of those with forward-leaning script can signify anything but harmony and beauty. Laura Doremus, writing in the Twenties, starts the chorus softly by commenting that forward-leaning writers demand a great deal of life, that they are not satisfied with plain comfort but want luxury, personal ease, and exotic pleasures. Louise Rice joins in, noting the ability of the forward-writers to "beat down the opposition . . . to dominate by sheer weight of the personality." Jacoby says that the forward-leaning writer tends to be too easily influenced, that he is not sufficiently anchored in his own self, and too dependent on

Pulver's own example—a very right-handed slant *

* From *Symbolik Der Handschrift* by Dr. Max Pulver. Reprinted by permission of Orell Füssli Verlag, Zurich and Leipzig.

the outside world (what Sonnemann calls "self-exposure"). To Frederick Stehman, extreme slant indicates a person "who can't stand to be alone. He may even submerge his own personality by trying to show others what he thinks they want to see. This conduct- on his part usually results in what he feels most, rejection." Finally Pulver states that "a very right-slanted script lacks the ruler of reason . . . it throws itself stormily against the You: hurls itself into the environment and is dissipated in it." And Roman, speaking of those who "wear their hearts on their sleeves," claims that "excessive rightward slant goes with uncontrolled irresponsible behavior and lack of resistance to internal and external stresses." Here, of course, she speaks of the "excessive"; a moderate rightward slant she deems natural and the most frequently occurring one: the forward-pitched body of the jockey, she calls it, as he gallops his horse down the home stretch. The rightward slant, in any case, is the slant of creative men and women, with all their eccentricities, their vices and virtues; it is the slant of Hitler, but it is also the slant of George Washington. Often, as Saudek appears to admit rather reluctantly, it is the slant of the English, for with all their tradition about writing in a stiff and upright manner, they refuse to conform, and their forward slant, according to Saudek, "may all the

Rightward slant in the writing of George Washington *

* From *Universal Manuscript*.

more reliably be taken to indicate lack of discipline, excessive zeal, exaggerated optimism, hastiness, great excitability, extreme sensibility . . ."—many of the traits for which, may I add, we loved Churchill. This does not mean, of course, that everyone with forward-leaning slant is creative. Since the days when the Abbé Michon placed a fixed meaning on each sign regardless of context, graphologists have warned us against such dogmatic and unscientific assumptions. But we *can* say, despite the inflexible approach of the Gestalt doctrinaires, that the forward slant is frequently a straw in the "wind of love."

Finally, there is the most difficult and unhappy type of slant, the backward- or leftward-leaning. When the person who writes this way is left-handed, it is more natural for him to write backward than forward, though not so natural as to an Arab writing from right to left. (Some left-handers slant their writing forward anyway, and it is not easy to evaluate this characteristic.) In any case when the right-handed person goes to the trouble—consciously or unconsciously—of turning his body and arm around in such an awkward manner as to make it natural for him to write backhand, it is apparent that there must be some psychological basis for his doing so. Roman sees in it a political analogy with the dissidents, the nonconformists, the iconoclasts, the radical "left" as opposed to the conservative "right." Grapholo-

Backward leaning slant with arcades *

* From *Encyclopedia of the Written Word* by Klara G. Roman. Reprinted by permission of Frederick Ungar Publishing Co., Inc., New York.

Darling —

I am so _thrilled_
with my "Easter bonnet"
that I couldn't wait until
you returned to thank you.
When it was delivered I
thought there must be a
mistake so called John
Fredrics and they said it
was from you!

Forward leaning—joy

It breaks my heart that all the beauty
that has gone between us should come to
an unhappy end. but you have given
me no other choice— Believe me if

Backhand—the same writer in a different mood

gists have few favorable comments to make about backhand writing. Some claim that the writer is hiding from life and retreating toward his mother's womb. June Downey says that back-slant is indicative of diffidence, reserve, a masking of the self, which may be carried so far that it shows disguise of the self, or even deceitfulness. She claims that it was taught in no school and that to use such an uncomfortable method of writing shows an impulse toward concealment or repression. The arcade which frequently accompanies this method appears to draw a kind of curtain or tent over the body of the writing. Dan Anthony finds in it—on the negative side—self-centeredness, resentment, cruelty. Louise Rice claims that it is among those who write with the more extreme leftward angles that we get nearly all of the greatly involved and sometimes morbid temperaments, and finds perversion, as she calls it, more commonly associated with the slant of repression. Alfred Mendel expands the latter comment thus: "The boy who adopts the left slant, even though he acts in a revolutionary manner . . . relinquishes his usual role in life," of following his father as the head of the family and may gravitate toward the feminine. Mendel finds the converse in a girl who adopts backhand writing.

With all its negative connotation, the backward slant has one element which can be looked upon as positive, especially when the writing is otherwise of a generally high quality, and that is its strength. The signatures of Joseph Conrad and of Charles Dickens, with their high, narrow letters, build a wall against the intrusion of strangers into the warm, forward-leaning writing of the body of the text. The "curls," loops, and hooks of which Lewinson and Zubin speak, interpreted as signs of persistence and stubbornness, have a general backward trend. And when Lewinson and Zubin, basing their research on the work of Klages, seek their ideal rhythm midway between the control of leftward forces and the release of rightward, one visualizes rather a partnership between complementary factors than a struggle between good emotion and bad repression. Sonnemann puts it thus: "Psychologically, emphasis on contraction relates to ego emphasis with its possible implications of relative increases in volitional, emotional, and concept control: emphasis on release relates to object emphasis with its possible implications of relative increases in spontaneity, impulsivity, and fantasy life." In speaking about general dynamic qualities, as he calls them, Sonnemann divides them into three categories—width, rightward and leftward slant, and the relation of rightward and leftwardness. It is the interaction of the forces manifested in these qualities that, he feels, is primarily responsible for the composition of the personality.

Capitals and Signatures

Two of the commonest questions asked of graphologists deal with the capital "I" and the signature. How important are they —what do they mean? In answer to these questions I usually reply: Just as Pulver divides handwriting into three zones, upper, middle, and lower (with an analogy, he tells us, to heaven, earth, and hell and to the Freudian divisions of the psyche), so one may relate the signature to the exterior or façade of the personality, the body of the writing to the personality, and the capital "I" not to what the writer wishes us to believe about him, as in the signature, but to what he secretly thinks of himself. It is because of this relationship that I have linked the signature with the capital "I" in this chapter and both with the other capitals.

The capital "I" very probably originated in primitive times as the conventionalized drawing of a man. In sign language one

Origins of the capital "I" *

Backhand and broken capital "I"s—signs of an inferiority complex

finger held up means "one," and if it is pointed at oneself it means
I or me; it is natural for one to think of the capital "I" as a
symbol of oneself. An inflated capital "I" can mean pride and a
large ego, a small one—sometimes broken at the top or even
written in the form of a small "i"—the opposite, a deflated ego
or inferiority complex. Where there is no capital "I" present in
the writing, the graphologist studies the upper loops and the
signature for other indications of ego. In Latin script the capital
"I" finally became a simple straight stroke, but not of course
meaning the self. This single stroke was carried into modern
English as the ego symbol, where it contrasted with the two- and
three-letter words of other countries—the French *moi*, the German *ich*, and the Slavonic *ja*. For decades on the Continent, observes Saudek, "decency, custom, and school training" demanded
that the "I" of the first person should be kept in the background,
and accordingly the foreign ego words all begin with small letters. (Pascal said, *"Le moi est haïssable."*) The Anglo-Saxons, on
the other hand, more famous for their individualism than their

* From *Character Reading From Handwriting* by Louise Rice. Copyright,
1927, by Frederick A. Stokes Company. Reprinted by courtesy of J. B. Lippincott Company.

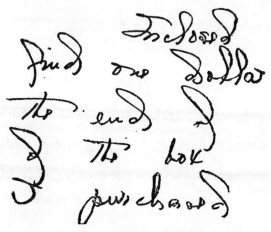

Spreading sails in a stormy sea *

modesty, take pleasure in exhibiting the capital "I" in their correspondence as frequently as possible. Father A. J. Becker has likened it to a sailboat attempting to navigate rough seas. When sails are too small or remain furled, a boat floats idly about; when there is a strong breeze and too many sails are filled with wind, the boat is in danger of capsizing.

Crépieux-Jamin, in the dawning days of scientific graphology, claimed that after considering all the possible ways of forming the capital "I," he calculated the total number of possible variations (at a conservative estimate) at 857,560,950,025,227,457,643, 187,000. From the zeros at the end, I assume this was only a round figure! In any case let us run quickly over a few billion of them, or at least eight or ten, and start with the opinions of Louise Rice. It is impossible to find a really vain person, she states, who uses the small and unobtrusive capital "I." The vanity of those with an inflated "I," on the other hand, unlike that of people who inflate upper loops in general, can disappear under

---

* From *Character Reading From Handwriting* by Louise Rice. Copyright, 1927, by Frederick A. Stokes Company. Reprinted by courtesy of J. B. Lippincott Company.

Jackie

PS I hope, perhaps in vain, that you will overlook the spelling and the handwriting

The "simple upright stroke" of my son

2

The squatty capital "I"

the pressure of hard work or suffering. She finds the printed "I" to be a sign of good taste and modesty in ordinary handwriting, less so where all the capitals are printed; and she finds the simple upright stroke to be that of the person who is simple and perhaps uncommunicative through choice rather than ignorance. Lastly, she identifies the capital "I" which has become squatty and looks somewhat like a capital "Q" or the figure 2 as belonging to someone with old-fashioned and reactionary tendencies.

Other graphologists variously describe the capital "I" which leans backward as indicating guilt feelings and a lack of self-confidence. It is interesting when we are speaking of guilt to observe the capital "I" of Richard Speck, the mass murderer whose crime was at least partially the result of brain damage. Although his "t" bars are fairly weak, he has crossed his tiny capital "I"s with a strong tie similar to that of a "t" bar, thus transferring his persistence from the normal channels of the body of the writ-

*I understand Dr. Ziporyn is writing a
book about me. I am glad he is doing this,
because he is the only person who knows
anying thing about me. I want the world
to know what I am really like, and I
fell he is the one who can tell about me.*

Richard F Speck

Note capital "I" in writing of Richard Speck *

ing down into the inner recesses. At the same time where there would usually be an upper loop in the "I," we find instead a diminutive sharp point showing how the ego has been crushed.

Let us turn to the other capitals. Again it is Louise Rice to whom we look for guidance. The "protective A," she tells us, softly rounded with a curved line for a bar, shows a tendency to protect the weak and poor, and those who use this letter (witness Abraham Lincoln) are likely to possess a deep humanity. The printed capital "A," by the way, originated as a symbol of the ox's head and in many languages where it has a name as against a sound means "the ox." The "B" at one time represented two Bedouin tents, as one can visualize when the letter is laid on its side; with curlicues in the upper area it can mean pride in externals. The capital "C" is chiefly of interest as a test for the angularity of the writing; being identical with its small letter,

Protective "A"

---

* From *Handwriting Tells,* copyright © 1936, 1959, 1969 by Nadya Olyanova, reprinted by permission of the publishers, The Bobbs-Merrill Company, Inc. and Peter Owen Ltd.

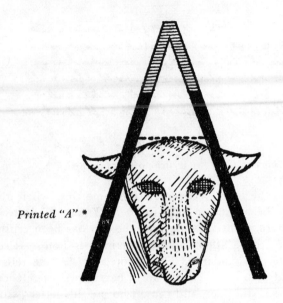

Printed "A" *

"B"—curlicues in upper area

it is also the capital most often substituted by the illiterate, the immature, and the criminal (my own observation) in place of the small letter—ungrammatically—for the purpose of emphasis. The chief distinguishing characteristic of the capital "D" is the final stroke at the top, indicating conservatism and timidity when it is brought to the left and tightly closed, generosity and open-heartedness when it is open. The capital "E" with a centrifugal

* From *Character Reading From Handwriting* by Louise Rice. Copyright, 1927, by Frederick A. Stokes Company. Reprinted by courtesy of J. B. Lippincott Company.

The open capital "D"

Capital "E" with centrifugal curve

curve at the top appears, according to Miss Rice's description of it, as a good test for the vanity of upper loops; it also probably reflects some of that concern for convention and the window-dressing of culture which Miss Rice attributes to its small counterpart. The printed capital "F" is a touchstone of good taste, and conversely a vulgarly ornamented "F" is the opposite. The normal "F" is severely plain, and when any other capitals are printed, the "F" is likely to be also. The "G," susceptible to a long beginning stroke, shows mental development—as does the "E"—when the stroke is eliminated; and the capital "G" made like an enlarged figure eight is the same criterion of true cultivation as its small version. The *simple* "H," like the "F," is a sign of good taste—and vice versa.

The "I" we have already discussed. The "J" is a test for loops —upper and lower. Regarding the capital "K," when the upper stroke on the right-hand side is elongated we have the inborn rebel, says Miss Rice. One is reminded of the high and intolerant third "point" of the "M" of which I speak in a moment. When the capital "K" is made by one upright stroke and one stroke which "ties in" to the upright one, there is the indication of a bright and active but superficial mind. The printed "K" is another touchstone of good taste.

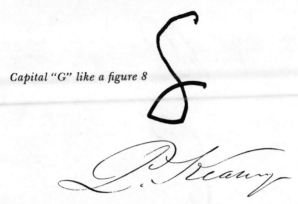

Capital "G" like a figure 8

*"The inborn rebel" —signature of Philip Kearny, Civil War general and soldier of fortune ***

The "L" has a curious history. Its origin is in the recumbent figure of the lion, and the name of the lion in most languages has begun with the sound which we mark as "L." The capital "L," says Miss Rice, when flowing, rightwardly inclined and made with strong pressure is indicative of a word which I could not find in my 1946 Webster, "charisma," but today is on everyone's lips. The "M" and "N," which can be read together, have a good deal of space devoted to them both in Miss Rice's book and by Saudek, who notes that the capital "M" has assumed such importance in France due to so many possessive words beginning with it—*monsieur, madame, mon cher,* etc. The "M" made of three uprights and one horizontal is to Miss Rice indicative of cool efficiency and the modern age. The "old-fashioned M," with the beginning stroke on the basic line, is similar in meaning to the "protective A"—interest in the welfare of others, often with a paternal or maternal instinct. When the beginning stroke of the "M" is turned in on itself, a characteristic known as the incurve, possessiveness and clannishness are shown. These writers

* From *Collecting Autographs and Manuscripts* by Charles Hamilton. Copyright 1961 by the University of Oklahoma Press. Reprinted by permission of the publisher.

Three uprights on capital "M"

Incurve on capital "M"

Third point higher on capital "M"

are "never humanitarians," according to Miss Rice, but rather ardent partisans. Finally we have the capital "M" in which the third point is higher than those preceding it; the users of this formation, analogous as I have said to the upper right-hand stroke of the "K," possess "a tenacity and aggressiveness unsurpassed," we are told, "by any type." (If we analyze Miss Rice's own writing, we find an emotional intensity which appears to express itself best in extremes, a condition usually looked upon less kindly by the scientific community than by the literary world of which Miss Rice, a journalist for many years, was a part.) In any case the users of this formation are pretty stubborn, as I have verified many times by my own observations!

Next we come to the capital "O," with which we are concerned only as to whether the letter is made clockwise or counterclockwise. The latter is the common version, analogous to the garland. The "right to left" version, essentially backward in movement and difficult like the arcade, is rarely seen and indicates a more complex personality. "P," our next letter, is governed by the rules which apply to "R," and "Q"—the capital, of course—is subject to the same analysis of direction as "O."

*Capital "R" in one
continuous formation*

Printed "R"

Miss Rice has almost two pages of comment about the capital letter "R." The "R" made with a large, full half circle is indicative of the showman, the actor, the politician; it is the paradigm of the upper loops. The printed capital "R" ideally expresses, we are told, "development of mental assurance and self-understanding." The capital "R" which is made in one continuous formation is the indication of extreme rapidity of thought. Miss Rice compares these latter two forms of "R." While the printed-R writer is accurate about concrete things and material facts, she says, the continuous-R writer is accurate about "ideas, thoughts, and philosophies."

Now, the capital "S." The printed "S," derived from early times, is the ordinary one used both in the capital letter and the small one, and it has only one unusual meaning: when a line is drawn through it from top to bottom, the writer may have dollar signs on his mind! When the capital letter is preceded by a long beginning stroke which starts at the base line to the left and connects at the upper right, Miss Rice claims that we have an ideal example of the superfluous and conventional, though certainly there is a grace and a continuity of flow in this formation lacking in the more elementary one. When the capital "T" is printed in a hand with few printed letters, it is a sign of "some instinct for constructive thought." When it is made with one action of the pen, consisting of an upper rightward stroke, a

I'd give anything in the world to see you Sweetheart — and my coming for Saturday looks dubious — father and

Printed "S" like a dollar sign

Capital "S" preceded by a long beginning stroke

long stroke downward and a curve back to the left at the bottom, we have, according to Miss Rice, the epitome of the commonplace. This she calls "the great common denominator of humanity," found to be used "by all sorts and conditions of men." Lastly, we have capitals "U," "V," "W," "X," "Y," "Z"—and if Miss Rice was not simply bored and tired when she lumped them all together we can accept her statement that they are to be read for "legibility, pressure, width, rounded and angular formations, and so on, through all the general graphological indications." (The rules governing loops also apply to "Y" and "Z.")

The capitals of our Western languages, we recall, are derived from the simple block letters of the Romans. These frequently evolved with the rich embellishments which we find in the manuscripts of the Middle Ages, before the invention of the printing press, when capitals often formed a grand ornamental device at the head of a page. As I have observed, we still use many of the printed letters of Roman days. But when we find the embellished capitals or vestiges of them carried into the twentieth century, we come to various conclusions. In the writing of genius, as in the case of the signature of Dickens, they reflect the lively imagination of a brilliant personality. In the writing of lesser people we often detect the superfluous strokes of immaturity, as Louise Rice finds, for example, in the capital "B," "F," "G," and "S"; or to quote Jacoby, "a craving of pathological proportions to attract attention at all costs." Jacoby refers here in particular to the address on an envelope, where both the capitals and the writing in general tend, as they do in the signature, to be concerned with ornamenting a façade.

Finally, we come to the signature. According to Miss Rice, it represents "personality" as opposed to the mind and character represented by the body of the writing; but when this outer "personality" is at odds with the writing in general, in my own opinion, we must always turn to the latter for a true evaluation of the writer. The signature, in fact, can be an actual barrier between the real personality and casual acquaintance, as in the case of Charles Dickens, with a flamboyant but high and narrow wall of letters standing between himself and the outside world, and the even more obvious case of Joseph Conrad, whose handwriting in general slants forward but whose signature slants upright. When the signature is wholly at one with the body of the writing, of course, as Miss Rice says, the personality is a close replica of the character. Even in this case, however, it is not possible to analyze a specimen of writing from the signature alone, as much more variety is needed. Although the signature is of less value to analyze than the body of the script, it is none the

Signature of Charles Dickens ✱

✱ From *Collecting Autographs and Manuscripts* by Charles Hamilton. Copyright 1961 by the University of Oklahoma Press. Reprinted by permission of the publisher.

grew austere with disappointment at our silence and immobility in the gathering dusk of the low room. "What? Nor Archie Powell?

Joseph Conrad—contrast in slant between body of writing and signature *

Joseph Conrad.

Signature of Joseph Conrad †

less, according to Roman, "the most distinctive part of the hand-writing."

The foundation of the ultimate pattern of the signature is laid in the formative period of life, and one of the first expressions of a child's emerging ego is the writing of his name. Because it develops so early, because it is generally separated from the body of the writing, and because of its close identification with the ego, the signature is capable of more "imaginative projections," as Roman puts it, than any other graphological unit. As we see in the famous signatures of Napoleon and Franklin Roosevelt, it can go through a series of drastic changes during a lifetime. Like the capital "I," the signature is particularly significant in regard to the ego. It is certainly true that an interesting and even eccentric signature, as in the case of the heads of some of our large American companies, often reflects a strong and dom-

---

* Henry W. and Albert A. Berg Collection; The New York Public Library; Astor, Lenox, and Tilden Foundations. Also permission to reprint granted by J. M. Dent & Sons Ltd., London.

† From *The Psychology of Handwriting* by William Leslie French (copyright 1922 by William Leslie French). Reprinted by permission of G. P. Putnam's Sons, New York.

Signature enclosed by a sweeping stroke *

inant personality. (It is also true that the signatures of some of the greatest men in history, from Ben Franklin to Robert Browning, have differed little from the body of their script.) There are negative aspects to flamboyant signatures, also, which might be suspect even in the handwriting of greatness. Illegibility, for example, has been interpreted as an indication of a desire to hide, to evade commitments, somewhat like the defects Sonnemann finds in diminishing letters of words which seem to be trying to "slip through." When the signature is enclosed by a sweeping stroke, said a graphologist in 1920, self-interest and excessive secretiveness are indicated. And when the signature is unexpectedly small and unpretentious in an otherwise large and aggressive hand, we wonder if the writer is not attempting to hide his aggressiveness.

Perhaps the surest sign of ego in a signature, for better or worse, is the underscoring, and Louise Rice spends five pages of her book on this subject. The underscore, she tells us, "is always an indication that the writer has gained some assertiveness and that the personality is one which has more or less force and distinction," and it is seldom that the actor or orator or statesman fails to use it. She goes on to give us examples. "The short, straight underscore with medium pressure," she says, "is assertive of rights and of possession; such people are eager 'to have and to hold'" and are often without much tact. "The long, straight, and rather heavy to very heavy underscore is the ex-

* From *L'Écriture et le Caractère* by J. Crépieux-Jamin (Translated and edited by John Holt Schooling). (Kegan Paul, Trench, Trubner & Co., Inc., London)

Curved underscoring in the signature of Charles Dickens *

pression of a nature" which is both clannish and aggressive. The long straight underscore with delicate pressure transfers these characteristics to a higher, less materialistic plane. Curved underscores accentuate indications of the personal charm of the writer; the smoother and more gracious the curves, the more magnetic the charm. Angular underscores, on the other hand, show "temper, force, ambition, and an overbearing personality," often unattractive, perhaps, but rarely dull. Next Miss Rice tells us that "the underscore which takes on a very eccentric form is the indication of a personality which is eccentric—there is no deviation from this rule." How much surer we were of ourselves in the Twenties than we are today—but I love Miss Rice for her prejudices! Finally we have the signature which is underscored with a straight or curved line crossed by two perpendicular strokes. This is indicative of business ability and reminds us of the capital "S" bisected by a vertical line—like a dollar sign.

The importance which Louise Rice gives to the underscore is emphasized by her dictum that if it is absent, and we are yet to attribute any unusual elements of personality to the writer, the letter forms must be exceptional. Conversely, she finds in the underscore a kind of magic key to the personality, and it appears to be her experience that in those rare cases where the underscore is not used in early life and begins to blossom forth after thirty (as in the situation of a talented woman released from a confining and unhappy marriage) we are likely to discover an exceptional person with a bright future.

* From *Collecting Autographs and Manuscripts* by Charles Hamilton. Copyright 1961 by the University of Oklahoma Press. Reprinted by permission of the publisher.

The Small Letters

If you were to ask a graphologist what was the most significant small letter in the alphabet he would probably reply "the letter 't,'" the index of will power and procrastination and a lot of other things. But there is another letter which to me is fully as important as the "t" and perhaps more so: the letter "g." To many students of graphology the "g" is primarily of interest as a potential indicator of cultivation and good taste; but I believe it goes far beyond that. Let us examine it. To begin with, the copybook "g" with the conventional lower loop, if used without variation, gives a strong hint of a conventional personality. When the return stroke is eliminated and the "g" resembles a figure 9, here we have a step upward on the intellectual scale; the users of this form, as Nadya Olyanova argues, may have mathematical ability; and it appears in the hand of people who are good at facts and figures and who often tend to be highly critical and see everything in black and white. But now we

Copybook "g"

Figure-9 "g"

come to the sign which to me is the most interesting of all in Western graphology, the "g" made like a figure 8 or some segment of it. To Louise Rice, the users of this "g" "never fail" to have a certain amount of intuition and instinct; they have gentleness "in the blood" and show innate understanding of humanity. To Olyanova, they also show an ability to adapt themselves to varied circumstances and "see the way clear ahead"; with their temperamental flexibility they are "at home in a tent or a palace," and to them difficulties become a challenge by which the personality grows.

Olyanova, of course, speaks of the good taste and education suggested by this sign, the literary flair, and Louise Rice indeed calls it "the cultured g" and claims that the people who use it are good judges of art and literature. With such perfunctory praise, most graphologists generally leave the "figure-8 g's" and go on to other subjects. But it is my opinion that this sign is of far greater significance than even Rice and Olyanova attribute to it. If there were any one sign by which we might intellectually separate the sheep from the goats in Western handwriting it would have to be the figure-8 "g." (Incidentally, writing, like art, should be judged by its best samples, and this "g" need not be used uniformly throughout the writing.) If it is necessary at this

Writing of President Kennedy.
Note figure-8 "g"'s and high and bowed "t"'s.

late date, by the way, to argue about the equality of blacks and whites, one can point to the innumerable figure 8s in the writing of the former. What gives this sign such significance? My explanation is as follows: every small "g" except the figure 8 makes a right angle or the semblance of it after circling around counterclockwise before descending to the lower zone. It is only the person with that sixth sense, with the instinct for the unspoken word, who realizes that he will still communicate the meaning of the letter "g" if he eliminates the right angle entirely before moving quickly to the next letter. It is amusing to note which of our recent Presidents have made the figure-8 "g" and which have not. Franklin Roosevelt, Eisenhower, Kennedy, and Johnson, yes; Truman and Nixon, so far as I know, not. In defense of the latter, however, I must add that I have rarely seen so aggressive a handwriting as that of the humble gentleman who claimed that he felt as if "the moon, the stars, and all the planets had

February 10, 1953.

*Your good letter congratulating
me on the past national administration's work for all the people,
and wishing Mrs. Truman, Margaret
and myself happiness and prosperity
for the future is highly appreciated.
Thank you very much.
Sincerely,
Harry Truman*

Letter of President Truman *

fallen on him" on Roosevelt's death, nor as perfectly balanced
writing as Nixon's. And one wonders if the thin-skinned nature
of the maker of figure 8s will be able to cope with the Presidency
of the future. (Yes, Washington and Jefferson and Lincoln made
them, too.)

Also, I would be less than honest if I did not admit that there
have been a number of great people who apparently *did not*

* From *Collecting Autographs and Manuscripts* by Charles Hamilton.
Copyright 1961 by the University of Oklahoma Press. Reprinted by permission of the publisher.'

*Writing of Ernest Hemingway. Note the neurotic and violent pressure of the downstrokes.**

make figure-8 "g"s. (After all, there are exceptions to every good rule!) I have not seen them, for example, in the writing of Marcel Proust, Hemingway, and Dali—if anyone has observed otherwise, I hope he or she will let me know. What is the explanation? The writing of all three, as I remember, has many broken letters, a sign of intuition, and of two of them at least, Proust and Dali, the brilliant Greek "d," which I come to in a moment. Now, the figure-8 "g" is the sign of the general versus the particular; that is why it indicates philosophy and a sense of humor. The brilliant people who do *not* make it may conceivably be geniuses of detail—as was certainly the case of Proust—at the expense of deep understanding. There may well be a certain insensitivity in genius without figure 8s which drives it to extremes in search of a philosophy which always remains out of reach—Proust to the microcosm, Hemingway to violence and suicide, and Dali to an exhibitionism often unworthy of him and, incidentally, to his recent desire to be immortalized by being frozen at his death.

Since graphologists generally associate figure-8 "g"s with culture and the arts, they often lump them with the Greek "e" and the Greek "d"—which remains suspended in the air instead of returning to the base line. The Greek "d" is a unique sign. It is found rather rarely in the United States, a lot more frequently in the writing of the English (where of course it harks back to

* Henry W. and Albert A. Berg Collection; The New York Public Library; Astor, Lenox, and Tilden Foundations.

The Greek "d" in the word "aiding"

the days of early manuscripts). To Louise Rice it is the sign
which indicates that "the higher levels of existence and of mental
companionship are of supreme importance" to its users. She finds
it to be a beacon of the intellectual possibilities of a writer, but
at the same time not always used by creative people, to whom its
leftward tendency can be a check on spontaneity. To me its unfinished counterclockwise curve is a signal of the perfectionist,
of the person who is always seeking and never satisfied with the
world as it appears on the surface. In spite of Miss Rice's reserva-
tions about its use, most geniuses have made it, and it is generally
accompanied by the figure-8 "g." Where it is not, there is a
conflict. The maker of the Greek "d" without the figure 8, as
I have said, can be a very unhappy person, for in spite of the
fact that he is always searching he often fails to come to grips
with his problems. People with Greek "d"s but an otherwise
mediocre writing may take to drugs, for example, or prostitution,
for frequently when the person cannot find what he seeks on
the mental level he resorts to the physical.*

* Appendix D, page 329, describes a handwriting research project in which
the small "d," "g," and "f" are analysed.

eated, at this time, in Poems, essays or plays like make novels about the South or any

The Greek "e" in the writing of Margaret Mitchell

The Greek "e" is made like a small form of a copybook version of the capital "E." Louise Rice pretty well wraps up the description of it when she says that it indicates "the aspiration rather than the realization" of culture. It is found, she says, in the writing of people who desire to be "refined" and whose ideals of life are "nice." I believe that, like the Greek "d," it indicates a talent for detail but on a more pedestrian and domestic level. Its greatest exponent who comes to mind is Margaret Mitchell (who *occasionally* made figure 8s) and it is possible that without her sometimes partisan interest in Southern tradition and trivia her book, *Gone With the Wind*, might not be the masterpiece it is. The pedantic nature of the small Greek "e" is lessened on very rare occasions by a long and outgoing middle stroke, found usually in the writing of those who tend to print.

I have spoken of the importance of the small "t," and let us now examine it. Since the characteristics of the "t" bar are similar to those of the "i" dot and the "j" dot, we will discuss those at the same time. Lastly, it occurred to me only a short time ago that the ending strokes of words are also similar in many respects to "t" bars—a fact rarely brought out by graphologists—

Copybook letter "t"

Writing of President Eisenhower

"t" bar ahead of the "t"

and should be included here. Certainly the "t" bar has the greatest variety of meaning of all the small letters; it is also capable of much variation throughout life. Where the figure-8 "g" is essentially a product of heredity—or heredity combined with early environment—the "t" is highly subject to change, including day-to-day moods. What are its meanings? When the "t" bar is small and placed fairly low in the center of the "t," it is the copybook letter with all that implies. When it is to the left of the "t" we have one of the surest signs in graphology—that of procrastination and emotional dependence; the bar does not keep pace with the writing. (Eisenhower continually made this sign, but the weakness was offset by the fact that the bar usually slanted downward, indicating strength and aggressiveness.) When the "t" bar flies ahead of the "t" to the right, we have a quick mind which tends to give way to impatience and impulsive decisions. When the bar points upward, like an arrow shot into the air, it indicates ambition, like all upward signs, and possibly a certain withdrawal and snobbishness, as if the "archer" were not quite ready and willing to follow straight through. (We will come to long "t" bars in a moment.) When the "t" bar flies high above the stem, we have a sign of imagination and leadership in superior writing but of prejudice in lesser scripts. When it is high and bowed—that is, when the end of the bar is turned down —one has the sign, according to Louise Rice, of a nature in which strong appetites and passions have been conquered. Jack Kennedy and Lincoln both made this type of "t," but with very different writing. A bar with a wave in it, finally, is an interesting sign. I saw it in the writing of a young lady, a great unknown poetess whom I knew years ago, and it reminds one of the "threads" which we sometimes see at the end of words (to be found in the writing of Henry Kissinger) in which a fast and intuitive mind seems to reduce script to a kind of shorthand or graphological electrocardiogram, similar to what Miss Rice describes as legible-cryptic.

"t" bar upward

[handwritten text] thought they, do not remember the particular day. I therefore, on account of his tender age, have concluded also to pardon him, and to leave it to yourself whether to discharge him, or continue him on the

N. Lincoln

*The bowed "t"s of Lincoln **

[handwritten text] can't help thinking you were either terribly depressed because of the school and Miami or rather bored with wrt

"t" bar with a wave

We now come to the more aggressive type of "t" bars. When the "t" bar is long and strong, says Miss Rice, no other indication of the character in the writing can dilute this "outstanding evidence." It is evidence of will power, strength, aggressiveness, enthusiasm, the precise quality depending on the nature of and pressure on the bar, heavier pressure of course indicating a more overtly domineering person. (My former wife Marjorie's became heavy only on rare occasions, but that was enough.) When the bar is heavier at the end than the beginning—club-shaped, as they call it—you have a sign of brutality; the reverse, in which the bar starts heavily but is pointed at the end, is said to indicate sarcasm, the rationale, I suppose, being that the initial brutality is refined. The bar which points downward rather than upward, as in the case of Eisenhower's writing, is a sign of determination and an argumentative nature, as all such downstrokes are. The hook at the end of the bar means persistence, as do all such hooks, but the most definite sign of persistence in writing is the

* Manuscript Division; The New York Public Library; Astor, Lenox, and Tilden Foundations.

"*t*" *bar long and strong*

"*t*" *bar club-shaped*

"*t*" *bar pointed at the end*

Hook at the end of "*t*" *bar*

"t" which is made by one continuous stroke which after producing the stem turns back and then ties a knot or lassoes the stem with a forward movement. Such people rarely give up. When the loop of the lasso is wide and full and sometimes encompasses two "t"s in a word, this is a sure sign of exhibitionism and often occurs in the writing of entertainers. These "persistent" ties or knots are seen infrequently in the writing of the most creative people, as the continuity of the stroke emphasizes logic and materialism over intuition, but their concentration is unquestioned and many scientists have used them, including Einstein. They are sometimes characteristic of obsessive mental cases in which concentration is carried beyond the point of no return. A variation of the "persistent" lasso is the stroke which flies leftward through the "t" and stops there, perhaps indicating a reactionary nature which moves more aggressively backward than forward.

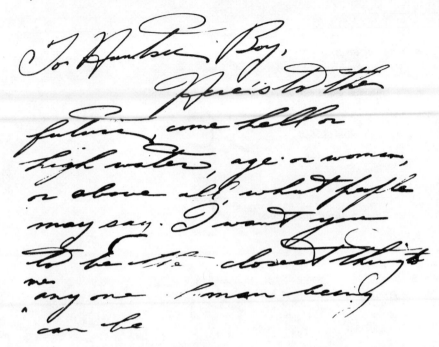

Knot or lassoes in writing from a close friend of mine

Last of all, we have the absence of a "t" bar. Some graphologists call this a sign of absent-mindedness, and perhaps they are
right; but in very fast writing, such as that of Walter Scott, the
"t" bar is obviously omitted because the writer had no time to
go back and cross it and he assumed, as do the writers of figure-8
"g"s, that his readers would still recognize the letter in its abbreviated form. The same holds true, of course, for the omission
of the "i" dot, which relates so closely to the "t" bar.

In speaking of the small "t," I promised to go into the subject
of the small "i," the "j," and the ending strokes. The fact is, of
course, that after discussing most of the variations of the "t"
bar there is not much new to be said about affiliated letters, and
to quote one of our famous American sayings, "When you've
seen one, you've seen them all." An "i" dot before the letter

Writing of Walter Scott—few "t" bars! *

Club-shaped "i" dot

Tent-shaped dot

means procrastination, for example, and beyond it, impatience; a club-shaped "i" dot, temper, brutality. There are three or four meanings peculiar to the "i" dot, however, about which most graphologists agree. For some reason they often link the dot precisely placed above the "i" with a good memory and a wavy dot with a sense of humor. (I am not 100 percent convinced!) They ascribe a critical faculty to those who make a "tent-shaped" dot and a greater power of concentration to those who, in superior scripts like those of Einstein, Lessing, and Pasteur, connect the dot with either the preceding or the following letter. Finally, there is the "i" dotted with a complete little circle. Before the days of Walt Disney, with the circular dot over the "i" in his famous signature, Louise Rice informed us—I believe most correctly, in spite of some dissenting opinions in more recent books —that the users of this sign are "the adapters of art." It is true that they may be mildly eccentric and prefer an unconventional life, as other graphologists have pointed out, but according to Miss Rice such eccentricity remains well within bounds so long

* From *Autographic Mirror* Volume 2.

Signature of Walt Disney.
Note "i" dot with complete circle. *

as they are doing work which is congenial to them: interior decorating, fashion designing, certain types of sculpture, needlework, and so forth. There is generally a physical or commercial element in their works of art, as there was in Walt Disney's. I assume that they are more interested in making a design out of an "i" dot than reducing it to a mere symbol, as most of us do. (The circle was also a talisman against evil spirits, as the Egyptians encircled the hieroglyphic name of their king. Apart from the "i" dot, the circle in handwriting today sometimes retains a connotation of protection and fear.)

The letter "j" is to be read, with regard to its dot, by the rules which apply to "i."

Now, what about ending strokes? Dorothy Sara has a good short chapter on the subject in her book *Handwriting Analysis for the Millions.* Ending strokes, as I have said, have many of the characteristics of "t" bars: slanted sharply downward, they indicate determination, stubbornness; curved upward, they show aspiration and ambition, and, if the curve is unusually long, some immaturity; hooked backward, either above or below, they show the persistence which we associate with hooks in general. Long, outgoing, final strokes indicate enthusiasm and ardor and a potential for leadership; somehow the emphasis here seems to be less on domination, as it is in the "t" bar, than on warmth

---

* From *Handwriting—A Key to Personality* by Klara G. Roman. Reprinted by permission of Pantheon Books, Inc., New York.

Downward ending strokes

Note long outgoing final strokes in the writing of Ingrid Bergman.

and unselfishness, possibly both because it is at the end of the word (where psychologically it may relate more to the other person) and in the middle rather than the upper and domineering zone. The coldness suggested by high and narrow letters is often ameliorated by long ending strokes. The total elimination of ending strokes, conversely, indicates—at least in writing with unusual letter forms—the concentration of the mental worker, of the writer or lawyer or scientist.

In order to confuse the reader as little as possible, I have been discussing the small letters in the natural groups into which they fall rather than taking them up alphabetically as I have done with capitals. The last major group is constituted of letters with loops—that is, of "b," "f," "g," "h," "j," "k," "l," "q," "y," and "z." Many graphologists consider loops so important

My dear Mrs. Carnegie,

You have made me very happy by your generous decision to restore the income of the scholarship fund established by Mr. Carnegie for my laboratory, and I am deeply indebted to you for the most efficient support thus given to my work.

Writing of Marie Curie—elimination of ending strokes *

Graphology	UPPER ZONE MIDDLE ZONE LOWER ZONE

Pulver's theory of zones †

that they devote a separate chapter to them in their books, under the influence perhaps of Pulver and his theory of zones. According to Pulver, the upper zone—the upper loops and strokes, including those of capitals—corresponds to heaven and the intellect, the middle, the earth and "reality," and the lower the nether regions of the physical and the material; he also found an analogy to the components of Freud's concepts of personality structure, the id, the ego, and the super-ego. To Pulver the upper zone is the area of intellect and the spirit, of idealism. Roman speaks of it in terms of creativity and preoccupation with dreams and illusions and associates it with a disposition to "the holy curiosity of inquiry," as Einstein phrased it; and Anthony equates it with the conscience. Where the upper zone is high in relation to the middle, Pulver gives us the analogy of trees growing toward heaven without sufficient rooting in the earth. Mendel claimed that the theory of zones had never been successfully challenged, but there are now at least two dissenting opinions in the liter-

---

* Manuscript Division; The New York Public Library; Astor, Lenox, and Tilden Foundations.

† From *Encyclopedia of the Written Word* by Klara G. Roman. Reprinted by permission of Frederick Ungar Publishing Co., Inc., New York.

The ambitious capitals of Roosevelt and Nixon *

ature of graphology—the first by Preyer, who finds in his collection
of specimens numerous examples of short upstrokes among
writers following intellectual pursuits, and the second by myself. Rarely seeing high upper loops in the handwriting of great
thinkers and artists throughout history, and frequently seeing
them in the writing of politicians and businessmen and actors—
witness the capital "R" in the signature of Franklin Roosevelt
and the capital "D" in Dick Nixon's—it has gradually become
clear to me that the aspiration and ego ascribed by Werner Wolff
to the upper area of writing issue forth far more in a craving
for power than for knowledge. Louise Rice, who attached some
significance to the fact that she found high upper loops prominent in the writing of young aviators, claimed that upper loops
mean "reaching up"—but *what* they reach for depends on the
remainder of the script. In any case I believe that the knowledge
for which people with high upper loops reach is generally of a
kind that will help them on their path to practical business or
public success, or possibly even to a fixed body of information
which they seek for scientific reasons. Theirs is rarely the instinctual and compulsive search of the purely creative person.

* The Roosevelt sample is from *Collecting Autographs and Manuscripts*
by Charles Hamilton. Copyright 1961 by the University of Oklahoma Press.
Reprinted by permission of the publisher. The Nixon sample is from
Handwriting—Revelation of Self by Herry O. Teltscher. Reprinted by permission of the author.

[handwritten sample:]

arising out of the money I brought
back on Saturday Aug 9th. after I
made an ass of myself by getting
stupid thru drinking with my
friends at Lexington; I felt that
perhaps my signing a transfer
slip for the money over to Jack,

Long and large lower loops *

What about the rest of Pulver's theory? So far as the middle
zone goes, in my opinion, it is true that here we find a middle
ground which we can, if we choose, term "reality"; it is also
true that if idealism is to be found in a particular zone, it is
certainly the middle rather than the upper, as Pulver suggests.
About the lower zone there is that kind of universal agreement
among graphologists whose rareness continues to hold back our
scientific progress; it is the zone of materialism and the physical.
We see long and large lower loops in the writing of dancers and
fighters, of salesmen, of politicians and entertainers who must be
in continuous contact with their public. The urge toward power
is directed downward—and to some extent secretly—instead of
upward as in the case of upper loops. The fact that a long
lower loop is generally a simultaneous indication of physical
vitality, of libido, and of a hypocrisy inherent in the inward and
downward direction of its thrust has always intrigued me. However, I agree with Miss Rice when she says that there is a "certain
good-heartedness" indicated by long lower loops which may be
absent in upper loops. The ambition of the upper-loop people
is out in the open, often without diplomatic frills.

* From the files of The Handwriting Institute, Inc., New York.

What else can we say about lower loops? Well, when they extend backward you have a sign of introversion, and when the downstroke is pulled forward in the direction in which the writing is heading you have one more sign of forward movement, as with the "t" bar and the "i" dot. When they tend to be curtailed one finds mental powers on the threshold of more than ordinary development. When they have ties and lassoes in them the same persistence noted in the "t" bars is removed to the lower zone. When the return stroke of the loop turns toward the right rather than the left, as in the case of the "f" and the "q," there is what Miss Rice calls the "altruistic" loop, the rationale being, I suppose, that the writer gives up a small and rather fussy bow in favor of a swing forward to the right. Finally, there are inflated loops, indicating pride or a gay and happy disposition, depending upon their nature, and narrow and restricted ones, indicating repression and narrow-mindedness. (The "heart ticks" of loops and other characteristics affecting health I have taken up in the chapter on that subject.)

Since the small letters remaining to be discussed are relatively few, let us introduce them alphabetically. First the "a" and the "o," with which it is associated. When they are open at the top, we have a sure sign of generosity and openmindedness, as in the case of the capital "D"; when tightly closed, of caution and reticence and of generosity which responds only to the appeal of logic. When slightly open at the bottom, "with a curious break in the continuity of the stroke," we have, according to Miss Rice, the love of large sums of money which Miss Rice spends two pages in analyzing and which, as I point out in my chapter on crime, has been observed by many graphologists, though I have never seen it.

"altruistic" loop in the small "f"

[handwritten letter]

I shall stop being subtle and
bid you good night — and maybe tonight I
can rustle up a dream about you.

Love,
Catherine

P.S.

Today I got mad and made myself very
unpopular!

Inflated loops—even the doodle is inflated!

"a" and "o" open at the top

"a" and "o" tightly closed

"a" and "o" open at the bottom

"b"—pendulous lip

Next the "b," in which Miss Rice informs us there sometimes appears a "pendulous lip," which, like its physical analogy in the slack human mouth, suggests weak credulity, the people who can "be sold the Brooklyn Bridge," as they used to say. The small "c," once again according to my favorite oracle, Miss Rice (whose book *Character Reading from Handwriting* is long out of print but worth looking for), is a test for the angularity or curvature of writing. In my opinion it is also the letter most easily changed from a small letter into a capital and is thus frequently seen among those "misplaced capitals" of which I speak in the chapter on crime; prisoners constantly write home about getting out of that Cell, which is thus capitalized as a God for its power over them and a devil for its inhumanity.

The "f" is of interest because it possesses two loops that are supposed to be of exactly the same size and shape, and when this is actually the case, particularly in a creative hand which ignores convention, we have a strong indication of poise and emotional balance. The small "m" and "n" are to be read in the same manner: when the initial stroke tends to be large and flourishing, we have the sign of executive ability and diplomacy; when the final stroke is higher than the other, particularly if it is pointed, the sign of stubbornness and eccentricity.

The letter "p," according to Miss Rice, has a special conformation, a very long lower stroke, which she calls the "physical p." This shows not only physical vitality, common to all lower loops, but a special delight in sports and in the development of the body—with perhaps some remote relationship to the love of nature. Like the "d" and "t" above the line, the stroke of the "p" below the line has a cleanness and sharpness absent in

The balanced "f"   𝑓

m

Small "m"—final stroke higher than the other

p

"physical p"

ordinary loops which perhaps give it a less material and more sensitive quality. Finally, we have the small "r" and "s." Since both of these letters are tricky to make, whatever the individual variation may be, in my opinion the ability to make them correctly at high speed—especially when the little point is retained at the top of each letter—is a primary sign of agility and alertness of mind and of persistence.

HEALTH, CRIME,
BUSINESS

Health, Illness

There have been many studies of mental health as observed in handwriting—though not nearly enough—but very few of physical health. One exception, of course, has been the work of Alfred Kanfer on cancer detection, carried out for many years in New York hospitals, of which I write in the next chapter. During the Twenties, Adelle Land of the University of Buffalo observed that undoubtedly there were correlations between physical health and motor performance but that they had not really been proved. Her description of the instruments needed to carry out her program of correlation must have been discouraging to future graphologists! "Some few of them," she said, "we can name here. First is a good chronoscope. . . . Then we need at least two Roemer keys and a Marey tambour, as well as the necessary electrical and mechanical connections and supports. We will also need a sphygmomanometer and a sphygmometroscope, two or more kymographs, tapping boards, erographs, and tachistoscopes." She concluded with the statement that her tests were "merely preliminary . . . and . . . only roughly indicative of what could be

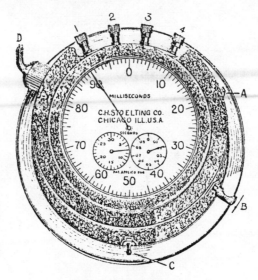

The chronoscope *

done were all [her] apparatus . . . used." Heaven forbid! Around the same time June Downey commented that the few researchers in graphology not only failed to discriminate between graphic and contentual disturbances—between the physical and the mental—but in general failed to realize the necessity of obtaining the normal writing of a patient to compare with a pathological specimen. For adequate comparison, she said, one should have a series of samples showing the progressive effect of the disease (as Kanfer of course has done in the case of cancer). It is nearly half a century since this comment was made, but, unfortunately, research on the motor aspect of graphology is still grossly inadequate. This side door to the study of handwriting may one day turn out to be the one through which the all-important medical profession is drawn into a thorough examination of the building.

* From *Medical Physics* by Otto Glasser. Copyright © 1944, Year Book Medical Publishers. Used by permission. Courtesy of C. H. Stoelting, Co., Chicago.

There are physical handicaps, it is true, that have little effect on handwriting; for example, as Saudek comments, the really mature writing of a blind man and the mature writing of the same writer before he lost his sight are more nearly related than are two mature manuscripts of the same "sighted" person, one written with good and the other with extremely bad writing materials. But it is safe to assume that when disease, like the iceberg, shows mildly above the surface, it is often a warning of serious danger. Kanfer tells us to "keep in mind the following basic points: 1. Individual differences of movement are caused by individually different constitutional structures and individual peculiarities of organic function. 2. These differences in movement are manifested in the basic structure of the handwriting. 3. The truth of these statements may be demonstrated by the observation that certain elements of movement, such as speed, are changed in a particular way by specific physiological changes. 4. Handwriting shows characteristic physiological changes which can be related to organic disturbance." When Preyer said that "handwriting is brainwriting," declares Kanfer, he referred to more than the intellectual function of the brain, for the brain is the director of our physical as well as of our mental activity. Just as our writing (or our walking, for that matter) is a mirror of our personality, so it is of certain aberrations or deteriorations in our physiology.

What are the diseases whose signs graphology has made any serious effort to detect in writing? Cancer, heart disease, arteriosclerosis, nervous and glandular disturbances, tuberculosis, and, if you wish to call it a disease, alcoholism. (Kanfer also comments that a high fever and accelerated pulse increase movement in handwriting while diminishing its strength, whereas a small, slow script is generally found to coincide with a low pulse frequency and low basal temperature.) As for alcoholism, Robert Holder in a recently published book finds the following similarities in the writing of certain alcoholics: easy legibility, fast writing, overinflated loops, increase in pressure or hooks at the ends of words, and a rhythmic sweep to the forward-slanting script. These are indications, he says, of personalities easily car-

The writing of an alcoholic *

ried away by excesses; and from my own observations I would
tend to agree, generally finding in the writing of alcoholics a
certain basic immaturity combined with definite extraversion
and—when the subject is drinking—a marked increase in pressure.
(Sonnemann finds a combination of "an 'indented' type of tremulousness with smeariness" of the pen or pencil track in such
writing.) Holder cites experiments at my Handwriting Institute
in New York City (see the Appendix G, p. 352) which used a
graphodyne stylus equipped with a strain gauge to measure and
record script variation in persons under the influence of alcohol.
These experiments clearly indicated that a raggedness of stroke
and a definite disturbance in rhythm (due to impairment of
muscular and neural control) were further results of the brain
becoming fogged with alcohol. Such results are hardly surprising in the light of the statement of Dr. Melvin Knisely of the
Medical College of South Carolina in 1968 that the bodies of
"skid row" drunks revealed such extensive destruction of cells

* From *You Can Analyze Handwriting* by Robert Holder. Reprinted by
permission of the author.

"heart tick" *

that their brains were worthless for use in neurological teaching.

Cancer I omit from this discussion as it is taken up in the next chapter. What about heart disease? Crépieux-Jamin in the late nineteenth century wrote of two signs which he felt were indicative of it. Both have been frequently mentioned by later graphologists, some after independent research and others, I presume, by simply repeating the words of their famous predecessor (a practice less highly regarded in the literary world than in the scientific). The first sign Crépieux-Jamin called a break: a slight interruption in the up- and downstrokes, especially in the loops of the letters. His faithful disciple in America, Louise Rice, called this a "heart tick" and found it particularly in the small "h" and to a lesser degree in the "l" and "b." Another early writer finds an analogy here with bonds of affection and broken hearts, and it is an interesting sidelight that Miss Rice claims that one of her basic "types" of humanity, the "mental," is particularly susceptible to heart disease and at the same time "depends largely upon the state of the mind for health." With my Greek "d"s, figure-8 "g"s, simple capitals, and small writing, I appear to fall into this category.

The other sign of which Crépieux-Jamin speaks is abnormal "dotting" in the course of the writing "trail" (as Sonnemann calls it). In the act of writing, he says, a man with heart trouble—

* From *Character Reading From Handwriting* by Louise Rice. Copyright, 1927, by Frederick A. Stokes Company. Reprinted by courtesy of J. B. Lippincott Company.

as the decision grew a
they finally decided
the issue till a later

Abnormal dotting *

and often with resulting shortness of breath—instinctively rests himself by resting his pen on the paper, as he would do with a stick when walking. On this subject Sonnemann himself agrees that dotting shows a need for rest, adding that the specific frailities and incomplete ataxias marked by partial dotting of the course of strokes indicative of cardiac disease have been found sometimes at very early and clinically still entirely undetected stages. Finally, Kanfer has a word to say on the subject of arteriosclerosis. In general, he claims, all sclerotic persons exhibit increased width and heaviness in their writing; the strained form of movement reflects the additional work which the heart muscles are required to undertake in pumping blood through the constricted arteries.

In some of the earlier studies at two New York insurance companies, undertaken to test Kanfer's method for early detection of the presence of cancer (discussed in the next chapter), Kanfer stumbled upon further information regarding heart disease. While he was able to clearly separate the healthy handwritings from the ones with cancer or heart disease, he erred by diagnosing a considerable number of the heart cases as positive for cancer. In later studies, with sharpening of the cancer criteria, this cause of error was practically eliminated. But the errors made at that time pointed out a potentially very important factor: a difference between the handwriting of persons who

* Reprinted by permission of Grune & Stratton, Inc., New York and Dr. Ulrich Sonnemann.

The U.S. Navy war and after signed of it again the Belgian rely the war end

Arteriosclerosis *

subsequently suffered heart attacks and of those persons who remained free of them. These chance observations might in the future form the basis for developing a predictive test for early detection of a trend to heart attacks, particularly in the younger generation.

The following microphotograph is from the handwriting of a man, age 39, who died at age 43 from a heart attack. He had medically a clean bill of health. The handwriting shows the

* Reprinted by permission of Grune & Stratton, Inc., New York and Dr. Ulrich Sonnemann.

absence of a regular, normal upstroke-downstroke pressure pattern and many segmented strokes. What makes it different from handwritings of cancer patients is, however, his ability to perform narrow, unbroken turns.

A final word about the heart: The heart issues a primary electrical impulse principally summarized by the electrocardiogram which, if properly interpreted, contains patterns that can be classified or somehow reduced to significant information about the proper functioning of the cardiovascular system. A new method for interpreting this electrical signature has been formulated by Dr. J. R. Levitt of New York City and is called the Omnicardiogram. Here the primary electrical impulse is transformed and examined against a crescent space bounded by two tangent circles. If the Omnicardiogram pattern breaches either of these circles the patient is abnormal—even if he has no apparent symptoms. Werner Wolff's *Diagrams of the Unconscious* brings to light the fact that writing is a signal, and according to the cardiogram, so is the electrical activity of the heart. Both must be properly evaluated.

Regarding the effects of tuberculosis on handwriting, little is known. Many years ago Crépieux-Jamin reported that out of forty-eight handwritings of sufferers from tuberculosis, forty-one were "descendant"—adding that "we do not see our way clear to report any other fact." Louise Rice, who felt strongly that the persistent drooping of the basic line could be an indication of

Upswing of basic line with sudden drooping *

* From *Character Reading From Handwriting* by Louise Rice. Copyright, 1927, by Frederick A. Stokes Company. Reprinted by courtesy of J. B. Lippincott Company.

ill health, found a sudden upswing of the basic line coupled with a sudden drooping at the end to be a probable sign of a well-developed tubercular condition. The upward swing, she felt, corresponded to the "curious optimism" characteristic of the disease, analogous perhaps to the marked increase in speed and extension of movement in the writing of hyperthyroid patients. Dr. Wladimir Eliasberg, in an article entitled "Graphology and Medicine" in the *Journal of Nervous and Mental Disease,* observes: "A very interesting sign in the handwriting of tuberculosis patients is one that has a certain resemblance to that of paresis patients. Letters are omitted, confused, syllables are doubled, and even whole parts of sentences and paragraphs are repeated. This sign is about equal in frequency in men and women. Jenoe Kollarite, himself tubercular and a very talented Hungarian neurologist and psychiatrist, described it two years before the graphological authors. This sign points to an intoxication of the cerebral cortex and it would be important if it could be elicited in other cases of toxic fatigue, e.g., in hyperthyroidism, etc."

We are left finally with disorders of the nervous system, and especially with Parkinson's disease. One of Klara Roman's early studies at the University of Berlin showed what a contribution the graphodyne could make to the treatment of stuttering. She proved it to be a general disorder in which almost any stress could induce immediate hypertension in the stutterer and could

Writing of a stutterer *

* From *Encyclopedia of the Written Word* by Klara G. Roman. Reprinted by permission of Frederick Ungar Publishing Co., Inc., New York.

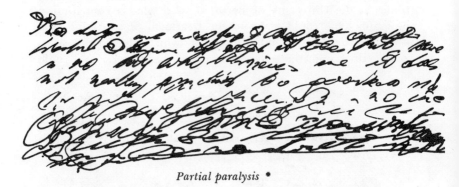

Brain-organic graphic symptoms *

often gravely impede his writing. In some cases of brain injury, she later found that where a subject had written "garlands" prior to the damage to his dominant brain hemisphere, he wrote "arcades" after he regained ability to write, but with the other hand. As a result of Roman's research with the graphodyne, handwriting analysis came to be widely employed in various countries of Europe to diagnose and treat speech disorders. Of the most prominent types of brain-organic graphic symptoms, Sonnemann has the following to say: "Both cerebral thromboses and tumors tend to show a 'shivering' of the ductus far coarser than that found in psychogenic conditions dominated by anxiety. Blotting is frequent, particularly in tumor cases . . . ataxia is prominent and may be found in conjunction with doubling of strokes and marked disturbances in spatial orientation; . . .

Partial paralysis *

* Reprinted by permission of Grune & Stratton, Inc., New York and Dr. Ulrich Sonnemann.

[handwritten text]

Epilepsy *

[handwritten text]

Epilepsy *

Aphasias . . . [impairment of the mental functions of speaking and understanding speech] tend to show peculiarly abrupt changes of letter directions and occasionally of pressure. . . ." In the case of partial paralysis, tremors of writing are particularly irregular, blotting frequent, and in contrast with that of patients with tumors, the writing tends to be "fast and flighty." The pre-eminent feature of focal epilepsy, says Sonnemann, like that of all convulsive disorders, is the tendency toward abrupt changes, particularly of the pressure. "All conditions marked by an increase in cerebral pressure . . ." he concludes, "are characterized by an extreme slowness and resulting lack of graphic 'slenderness.' . . ."

In 1959 Dr. Eliasberg published a paper on the relationship of handwriting to Parkinson's disease, a disorder of the central nervous system, in which he states that a routine check of the

* Reprinted by permission of Grune & Stratton, Inc., New York and Dr. Ulrich Sonnemann.

Parkinson's disease *

handwriting of elderly patients—the samples to be kept in the
case record—is a simple and valuable diagnostic tool. Handwriting samples, he says, taken before the patient has been spoken to
in a friendly and comforting manner, enable the physician to
distinguish between tremor and rigidity as psychological reactions and aid in the selection of patients with Parkinsonism who
are likely to benefit from surgery. Psychological factors he found
to have a strong influence on the moving muscles and practically
none on the fixating muscles. It is easy to understand, he explains, that the fixating muscles guaranteeing the necessary rigidity should not be easily amenable to the succession of emotions;
it is also understandable that the typical symptom of the working muscles—the tremor—should be extremely subject to their
influence. Forgery, for example, would tend to increase the
tremor (with an analogy to reactions which the lie detector en-
deavors to pick up), while on the other hand Dr. Eliasberg claims
that after three minutes of "befriending" he has seen tremor
diminish or even disappear in the writing of a patient who has
had Parkinson's disease for twenty years. In patients whose
tremor may diminish, however, the postural or fixating muscles

* From *Handwriting and the Emotions* by Malford W. Thewlis, M.D. and
Isabelle Clark Swezy. Reprinted by permission of the American Graphological Society, Inc., New York.

are strongly amenable to fatigue, and after a period of "befriending" we have the apparent paradox of less tremor but increased rigidity. The patient with tremor, Eliasberg considers, is dependent, weak, and passive as compared to the rigid patient who gives the impression of a "retracting, unbending, supercilious, independent personality." Dr. Eliasberg's findings (reached with the help of H.O. Teltscher and E. C. Trautman) make it easy to distinguish between these two personality types.

One last word on Parkinson's disease. In 1967 Dr. Robert S. Schwab of Massachusetts General Hospital and Dr. James E. McLennan of the University of Minnesota Hospital published in the *Medical Tribune* the results of a study of the handwriting of 800 patients with the disease. One hundred who displayed signs of micrographia were sent questionnaires and requests for serial samples of their handwriting. Of the 63 who responded, "17 showed well-defined changes in their handwriting before or contemporaneous with the onset of their disease." Drs. Schwab and McLennan include a striking and sadly memorable example of the progressive diminution of the writing of a patient developing micrographia—the shrinking signature of the lamented Margaret Bourke-White.

Let me conclude this chapter on health and illness with one more quotation from Dr. Eliasberg. Medicine may use graphology, he tells us

> (a) for the diagnosis of disease entities and differential diagnosis; (b) for the prognosis of the development of the disease and for the prognosis based on the character of the patient; (c) for better knowledge of the subjective factors, among them the adjustments of the patient to his disease; (d) for records showing the course of the disease and the effect of treatment; (e) for better use of the psychological factors in treatment; (f) for special applications: (1) for the psychological evaluation in accordance with the above-listed aspects in the prognosis of life insurance prospects, (2) evaluation of the subjective and the physiological age of the writer as compared with his chronological age.

Cancer: The Kanfer Test

Alfred Kanfer's "Neuromuscular Test for Determination of High-Risk Groups for Cancer" is performed through microscopic examination of the handwriting and logically belongs in any book on graphology. It became a prominent and integral part of the Handwriting Institute in New York which I organized. The Institute closed, but I continued both to finance and to seriously study Mr. Kanfer's work. He has specially authorized me to present this report, which derives not only from many years' acquaintance with his work but also from a complete dossier of his research results and correspondence in my files.

The origin of Kanfer's test lies in the graphological interpretation of children's handwritings (more about this later on). It deviates from normal graphology technique in that neither the shapes of letters nor any overall arrangement of a person's handwriting are examined, but only the finest variations of the stroke itself, too fine to be seen with the naked eye or even with a strong magnifying glass.

As an outsider in the field of medicine and with a method for identifying cancer-prone individuals, so highly unorthodox, Kanfer has had a stiff uphill fight in proving his method and finding acceptance for it. This was to be expected. What is surprising, however, is the cooperation Kanfer found throughout his more than thirty-five years of work from many prominent doctors and hospitals, from that of the great City Hospital of Vienna at the beginning to that of the Hospital for Joint Diseases in New York, and finally to an association with the Preventive Medicine Institute-Strang Clinic in New York. Between these main stages there were other institutions which provided financial and material support to Kanfer's work: the Equitable Life Assurance Society, the Metropolitan Life Insurance Company, and the American Cancer Society, which helped to bring Kanfer's method to its present form.

Kanfer was born in Vienna in 1901. After completing school he spent all his time in handwriting work, first as an amateur, later on as an expert for the Ministry of Justice and as a consultant for major banks and industries. His early interest was, however, the study of the handwritings of children—normal, healthy children at the elementary schools, problem children at special institutes, and sick children in the wards of children's hospitals. There was a reason for this special interest. Kanfer was the worst writer, not only in his class but in his entire school, and no training or punishment helped to make his writing any better. The hardship this inflicted on the young student can be understood only when you consider the importance of good handwriting in the days of old Austria and Germany. A child with bad handwriting was considered inferior or lazy or both, and no good marks in other subjects could make up for that. As a result of this Kanfer developed a fixation about problems of handwriting, and specifically about why some children have good handwriting without having to make any effort and others do not. He never forgot the shadow this disability threw on his school years, and when he returned to the question later on in life he speculated that it might have been the fine tremor of his hand together with a state of physical weakness in his early years which caused his writing problem. In any case, it was this factor which led to his investigation of children's handwritings from the point of neuromuscular coordination and its influence on the mental and emotional development of the child. From his own experience he was able to assume that handwriting must be an extremely fine recorder of neuromuscular conditions and developments and, therefore, that handwriting could be made into a tool for studying and measuring the state and development of neuromuscular conditions. His observations were still comparatively crude and unsophisticated at that time, but even by gross observation certain stages of development in the children's writing could be discerned.

In the initial stages of the learning process, the child cannot control the writing pressure to the degree which is necessary for fluent and integrated movement. The writing pressure is either too heavy, thereby slowing and interrupting the flow of movement, rendering the strokes stiff, clumsy, inflexible or uncontrollable in size, or too light, rendering the direction of the stroke unstable and wavering. In a child's writing only a single form of movement is applied, contraction, which does not allow for uninterrupted changes between downward and upward strokes and specifically does not allow for carrying out narrow turns in an uninterrupted flow of movement. Therefore, children's early writings are stiff, rigid, angular or else too wide and horizontal.

Subsequently the child learns to control the degree of pressure, and by achieving continuity of movement within the stroke and greater flexibility learns to apply differentiated movement (contraction for the downstroke and extension movement for the upstroke, involving different muscle groups) and later on to make narrow turns and switch gradually without interruption from contraction to extension. With this, the child has reached neuromuscular maturity and also maturity in writing performance. These stages develop gradually and with individually different degrees of speed and completeness. The individual differences thereby provide the yardstick for measuring the child's neuromuscular advances.

Later on the question arose as to how one could be sure that the developments in writing processes do actually represent and manifest neuromuscular conditions; and it was speculated that if neuromuscular conditions are at the roots of writing performance, then these performances must change with any changes of the neuromuscular conditions in the person, not only of the child but also of the adult. These speculations led to the studies in the wards of the City Hospital of Vienna. The findings on cancer thus came accidentally out of these studies.

Studies of the handwriting of cancer patients at the City Hospital were from the first startling. They all gave the appearance of a high degree of neuromuscular immaturity, regardless of the shape of a writing or of the social-economic state or age of the writer and regardless of the type of cancer that was involved. The surprise grew later on when it could be seen from follow-up studies that, with the development of cancer, handwriting gradually retrogressed from normal and mature neuromuscular functioning into a stage of immaturity, a process which started long before there was any clinical manifestation of cancer. With these observations, the study of the correlation of handwriting with cancer began in the early 1930s. Whether the observed changes in handwriting were actually related to cancer and whether they occurred also with other conditions or with changes of age could only be determined in a large series of blind tests on different types of population. These tests were made in and outside hospitals, employing different investigators in order to determine the objectivity of the criteria and the reproducibility of the findings of one investigator by another. Such studies have now been carried out for over thirty-five years, first in Vienna and then in New York and elsewhere. The path of these studies was not an unbroken upward line. Great successes were sometimes followed by severe setbacks. Techniques changed. At the first, many criteria had been taken into consideration; it was a long time before they could be condensed into the handful of which the test now consists. The criteria were first developed out of empirical study; then each one had to be evaluated for its statistical significance measured by the presence or absence of cancer while controlling for physical conditions and the age of the subjects. Starting out with a simple magnifying glass, it advanced step by step to the use of the projection microscope; the types of lens, eyepiece, and light source had to be most accurately determined in order to provide the optimum field of observation under different magnifications. All this was a process of trial and error, and some changes which seemed to promise progress resulted in abysmal failure when used in blind tests.

Description of Technique

MICROSCOPIC APPEARANCE OF THE NORMAL HANDWRITING
(FIGURE 1).

1. *Marked difference between down and upstroke pressure in regular sequence throughout a given writing sample.*

Characteristics: downstrokes (a flexion movement) are broader and show greater ink density than upstrokes (1 and 2 in figure 1). All downstrokes in a given writing have about the same width, and so do all upstrokes.

2. *Elasticity of strokes.*

The width of downstrokes gradually increases toward the end at the base line toward the joining with the upstrokes, and at the same time the upstrokes thin slightly out along their course.

3. *Uninterrupted flow of movement.*

    a. through downstrokes

    b. through upstrokes

Characteristics: uniform, even density of ink throughout the length of down and of upstrokes (1a and 2a). Continuous, uninterrupted and unwavering delineations of down and of upstrokes (1b and 2b).

4. *Uninterrupted flow of movement through area of transition (3 in figure 1).*

Characteristics: as above.

Specific importance: Uninterrupted joining between down and upstroke, that is, between flexion and extension movement,

VARIATIONS OF NORMAL HANDWRITINGS

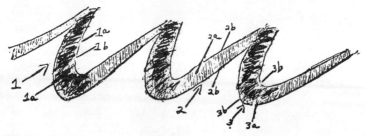

Figure 1

Figure 2   *Figure 3*

NORMAL CHANGES WITH OLD AGE

requires a maximum degree of neuromuscular coordination, and therefore is of the highest order of significance.

5. *Shape of transition (angle between down and upstroke).*
   a. narrow oval turn (figure #1)
   b. hyperbolic turn
   c. narrow angular turn

Essential characteristic: the writer's ability to proceed from down- to upward movement via the shortest, in time and effort, most economical way which is the curvature and narrow turn. It is, as in criterion #4, achieved by a maximum of neuromuscular coordination, and therefore also of the highest order of significance.

6. *Overall regularity of the length of downstrokes and of upstrokes.*

NORMAL CHARACTERISTICS OF HANDWRITINGS IN OLD AGE
(FIGURES 2 AND 3).

1. *Changes taking place:*
   a. increase of absolute pressure in down- and upstrokes
      (characterized by wide spread of pen nibs and with it
      greater width of strokes)
   b. greater irregularities of ink deposits within stroke, and
      greater irregularity and waverings of delineations of
      strokes
   c. loss of elasticity, stiffer shapes of strokes
2. *Characteristics which remain unchanged:*
   a. continuity of movement through area of transition
   b. narrow and/or curved turns

MICROSCOPIC APPEARANCE OF ABNORMAL HANDWRITING

Disturbed pressure ratio between down and upstroke

marked irregularity of stroke
pressure (irregularity of width
and ink shading)

sudden change between down-
and upstroke pressure at base
line

partial rigidity
(absence of pressure difference
around area of transition)

full rigidity
(absence of pressure difference
throughout major parts of
writing

strokes are disintegrating
(each stroke consists of many
parts of different width)

Figure 4

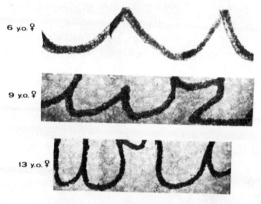

6 y.o. ♀

9 y.o. ♀

13 y.o. ♀

Handwriting Specimen 1-3 *

HANDWRITING SPECIMEN NOS. 1–3.

These specimens should demonstrate the maturation process taking place in the handwriting of a normal child between the ages of six and nine.

At age six the strokes are stiff, inflexible, and equally heavy pressure is applied to downstrokes and to most of the upstrokes. The uneven distribution of ink within the strokes manifests the slow, halting advance of writing movements. Characteristic of the state of neuromuscular immaturity is the absence of a regular pressure pattern of heavier downstroke and lighter upstroke, the flat, horizontal change from one downstroke to the other in the first part of the writing, and the complete interruption of movement in the upstroke leading to the third downstroke.

At age nine something like a pressure pattern is developing, the downstrokes are already slightly heavier (wider and darker) than the upstrokes, in a fairly regular sequence, the movements within the strokes show greater continuity, and in most parts of the writing specimen the turns from downstrokes to upstrokes are carried out via narrow though still angular turns at the base line.

* Reprinted by permission of Alfred Kanfer.

At age thirteen greater flexibility has developed, to be seen in the curvatures at the base line over which one downstroke is connected with the next one. Also a certain pressure pattern has evolved, which can be seen in the slight thinning out from downstrokes to upstrokes. The increased flexibility and control of writing movement can also be seen in narrowing distances between the downstrokes if one compares this writing with the two preceding ones.

With this writing a stage of neuromuscular maturity has been reached. The importance of this development in the normal writing will be seen by looking at the handwriting of incipient cancer, with its step-by-step retrogression and neuromuscular maturity to full immaturity.

(The following sample, no. 4, is from a healthy woman, aged eighty-two. It is important to note that with age, in the absence of cancer, the ability to carry out narrow turns in a continuous movement is not affected; nor is the pressure differentiation between heavier downstroke and lighter upstroke. At this age one

*Specimen No. 4 **

* Reprinted by permission of Alfred Kanfer.

can assume the presence of certain degenerative conditions and must also conclude that they do not affect the writing movements in the way cancer does.)

With the following three handwriting specimens (nos. 5, 6, and 7), the logical conclusion of the evidence of a child's writing emerges and the nature and technique of the Kanfer test can adequately be demonstrated. These samples are microphotographs of the same person's handwriting, a woman's, the first one written at the age of twenty-eight, the second one at the age of thirty-three, and the third one at the age of forty. The samples were taken from the death-claim files of an insurance company.

The first sample shows the typical criteria of normality—that is, of a mature neuromuscular condition with a normal, adequate state of coordination. The criteria for normality are manifested in the smooth, continuous flow of movement—both in the descending and ascending strokes (uniform flow of ink throughout the strokes, sharp, continuous lineations to both sides of each stroke). The strokes have an oval shape, the turns from descend-

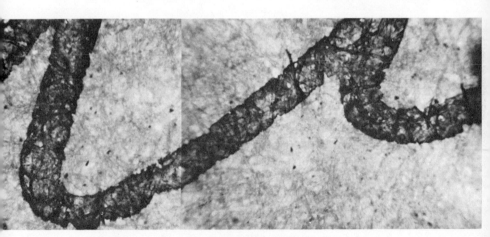

Specimen No. 5 *

* Reprinted by permission of Alfred Kanfer.

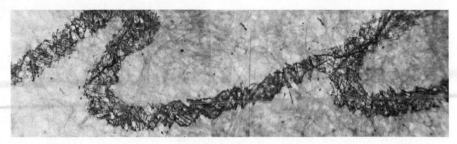

*Specimen No. 6 **

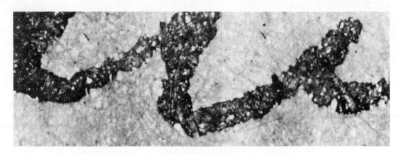

*Specimen No. 7 **

ing to ascending strokes are narrow, curved, and show continuity of movement throughout the turns. Throughout the writing a regular pattern of heavier (wider and darker) descending strokes and lighter ascending strokes prevail.

The second writing specimen already shows a marked change. Although the overall pattern of heavier descending strokes and lighter ascending strokes is still preserved, the narrow turns have disappeared, the writing spreads out widely, the strokes are much weaker and highly unstable, and in most of the ascending strokes clear segmentations can be seen (continuity of movement is interrupted and the direction of the stroke is seen on a microscopic examination to be wavering). Clear interruptions between descending and ascending strokes are also visible.

* Reprinted by permission of Alfred Kanfer.

The third samples show breakdown of every phase of the writing process. The strokes are stiff or formless. The pressure is uneven, sometimes too heavy, in other strokes too light. There are clear interruptions between descending and ascending strokes. And specifically descending as well as ascending strokes show marked, low-amplitude, high-frequency segmentations.

According to the rating system of this technique the first sample was rated as negative (nos. 1 and 2), the second sample as suspicious (nos. 3 and 4) and the third sample as positive (no. 6).

This is the history of this person. By medical standards she was found to be healthy throughout the span from the date of the first to the date of the third writing. One year after the date of the third writing, at the age of forty-one, an advanced cancer of the breast was found, and she died at the age of forty-two.

Discussion of the Case History

These three handwriting specimens and the history of the writer present not only the technique in a nutshell but also the meaning of, and the problems involved in, the work; they also show why it cannot be called a "cancer test," but only a test for "high-risk groups for cancer." The definitions and requirements for a "cancer test" are strict and narrow. If a test proves positive, it is to be expected that cancer will very soon appear to clinical examination. The samples here show that the Kanfer criteria precede by many years the clinical manifestation of cancer, producing thereby what is called a "false positive rating" (i.e., the test rating is positive in contradiction to clinical findings taken at the same time). In fact, these "false positives" are the most important aspects of the Kanfer test. They provide a warning of a trend to cancer in the person and, if heeded, can put the physician or the clinic on guard to provide for more frequent examinations. Cancer can then be detected at the earliest stage.

Test Results

From the inception of this test, Kanfer and his co-workers had to struggle with a never-ending stream of questions. Answers could be found only in blind tests carried out for more than thirty-five years under varied conditions and controls. No single study at any institution could produce a total answer, and therefore his work can only be judged by considering all the test results. Nevertheless, a final judgment should be based on the most recent findings over the past five or six years made at the Preventive Medicine Institute-Strang Clinic in New York. These were the essential questions:

1. Do all forms of cancer affect the handwriting in the same way?

2. At what stage of the development of cancer do the alterations in handwriting become manifest? Do such changes proceed at the same rate with all types of cancer?

3. How does age *per se* affect a person's handwriting, in health, and then as severe degenerative conditions develop?

4. How is handwriting affected by other neuromuscular diseases? What is the influence of different moods and mental conditions?

5. Do benign tumors, cysts, or other lesions affect a person's handwriting, and, if so, how do such changes compare with those caused by cancer? And what effect have other, more transient, physical conditions?

6. Does the social and economic status of the person have any effect on the neuromuscular status of the handwriting?

Some of the studies made over the years were specifically designed to answer one or other of these questions. Other studies were more general, addressed to several of the stated problems at once.

The first blind studies were undertaken at the City Hospital of Vienna in 1934–1936. The first study was made on 500 cases and the second on 600; the findings were reported in the *Wiener Medizinische Wochenschrift* for November 1935 by Alfred Kanfer and in the *Oesterreichische Review* for October 1936 by Dr. Arnold Baumgarten. The combined results were 82 percent correct for cancer, and 80 percent of the noncancer cases were correctly diagnosed as negative. The controls (noncancer cases) in this study came from patients with all types of disease, taken from all departments of the hospital and from the Old Age Home of Vienna which adjoined the City Hospital. The patients in this group were suffering from severe chronic degenerative conditions and a number of them also from neuromuscular diseases. The test findings therefore indicate that a differentiation between the handwriting of cancer patients and the handwriting of patients with other severe disabilities was obtained at a highly significant statistical level.

In 1940 Kanfer came to the States as a refugee from Dachau. In 1945 he resumed his researches, at the Hospital for Joint Diseases of New York, under the wing of the Director of Laboratories, Dr. Henry L. Jaffe, and with the support of the hospital administration and a number of staff members. He was also aided by various grants. These researches fell into several separate categories. The examiner of the first group was Alfred Kanfer. The source of his material was all patients admitted during the time of the study—with all the great range of diseases to be found among the patients entering a general hospital, from all age groups and walks of life. The overall number of cases examined was 3,460, 221 being cases of cancer. Results ranged from 63 percent (in the first study) to 90 percent correct for cancer and from 76 percent to 84 percent for noncancer cases. All findings indicated significant differences between cancer and noncancer cases. The next group of studies at the hospital was undertaken by a staff of six members under the chairmanship of Dr. Daniel Casten. Their assignment was threefold: to determine the validity of the test itself; to determine the objectivity of the criteria; and to investigate the usefulness of the test as a diagnostic tool. First the six doctors examined 1,361 handwriting samples of the hospital's patients, 489 of them of patients with cancer. Each doctor worked independently of the others. The results are in the form of a statistical average taken from the findings of the six doctors. They were 90 percent correct for cancer cases and 73 percent correct for the negatives. The findings were again within the level of statistical significance and demonstrated the validity of the neuromuscular test for separation between cancer and noncancer cases—that is, patients with all possible diseases except cancer.

Of greater importance were the predictive studies, carried out at the Hospital for Joint Diseases, the Equitable Life Assurance, and Metropolitan Life Insurance companies—studies which will be discussed later on. All these studies worked from old handwriting samples of patients admitted more than once to the hospital who at the time of writing were clinically free of cancer. They returned subsequently, within one to five years, some again with a nonmalignant condition and others with what proved to be cancer. The six physicians had to predict from the first samples which patients were likely to develop cancer and which were likely to remain free of it.

The studies at the Equitable Life Assurance Society and the Metropolitan Life Insurance Company examined signatures on insurance forms taken from the death-claim files. To medical examination the people concerned were healthy at the time they signed the insurance forms; but they had died within one to ten years, some from cancer. But to the six doctors at the Hospital for Joint Diseases and the two Metropolitan Life actuaries who conducted this investigation, the study was truly prospective, since in the hospital study no one among the analysts knew the subsequent disease or, in the insurance study, the cause and time of death.

Since the studies of the hospital and the Equitable cases were made by the same six physicians, the findings can be combined. There were 279 samples altogether, 129 from people who subsequently developed cancer. The examiners were 92 percent correct in predicting both the presence and absence of cancer. *With these findings it was for the first time shown with statistical significance that the manifestations of cancer in handwriting precede the manifestations of cancer by clinical signs. And it was again shown that the criteria were objective enough to produce identical findings from different investigators.* *

* Published in the *Bulletin of the Hospital for Joint Diseases* by Kanfer and Dr. Daniel Casten, April 1, 1958.

Subsequent studies made by Kanfer and others essentially confirmed these findings. These consisted first of three made under the auspices of the American Cancer Society. For the first study Kanfer was given by the Cancer Society 935 handwriting specimens gathered from five different hospitals in the New York area, 88 of them from patients with cancer. Kanfer detected 84 percent of the cancer cases and 79 percent of the non-cancer cases. It is especially significant that Kanfer was correct in 22 of 23 cancer cases designated as being at stage one, the earliest stage of cancer. Furthermore it was important because the variety of hospitals, and patient populations with diverse socio-economic backgrounds, had no influence on the findings.

The second study was the only one that failed. It was carried out on samples gathered at a Detroit Cancer Detection Center. The reason for this failure, as later established, was faulty technical arrangements. The patients were made to write with a hard glass plate as writing support and had to use a rigid fine pen point—a combination which made the finer segmentations in the stroke, on which the test is based, practically invisible, even to the microscopic equipment then available. When this error was recognized some changes were made in the microscopic technique and some of the samples were reexamined by an actuary of the Metropolitan Life, Mr. Gordon Shellard. His results were then considered "very good" by the Cancer Society. But this failure set Kanfer's work back many years and showed the importance of the technical considerations.

The third study was the predictive study mentioned above, carried out at the Metropolitan Life Insurance Company, first by an actuary, Mr. Gordon Shellard. Of 252 cases of cancer appearing within three years after the date of signature, 98.4 percent appeared in his "positive" list and 0.8 percent appeared as "doubtful." In 44 cases of death from cancer from 4 to 10 years after the samples were written he predicted 16 percent with certainty and 77 percent as possible. He was correct in excluding cancer in 90 percent of the deaths from nonmalignant causes within three years, and he was 100 percent correct in excluding it when death occurred more than 10 years later from nonmalignant causes. The total number of cases examined was 1,082. These findings were confirmed by the studies of another of the Metropolitan Life actuaries, Mr. Tap Taves, who examined two separate batches of handwriting samples.

With these findings it was determined on a larger scale that positive handwriting criteria preceded clinical manifestations of cancer by up to ten years, and it was further confirmed that different examiners arrived at identical results, so that the technique could be considered objective.

An additional study of the Memorial–Strang Clinic samples was carried out at the Handwriting Institute by Kanfer. The study was arranged and supervised by Dr. Emerson Day, director of the Strang Clinic at that time. Essentially, it tested the power of the test to differentiate between malignant and benign tumors. Kanfer was correct about 72 percent of the cancer cases, 60 percent of the benign tumors and 87 percent of the non-tumorous cases. Although the correct predictions were fewer than previously, the degree of statistical significance remained great. This study was later repeated by three independent investigators at the Strang Clinic, Mrs. Naomi P. Roman, Miss Joyce Farro, and Mr. John Donahue, members of the Strang Clinic staff assigned to this study. Their combined result was 94 percent accurate on cancer cases and 89 percent accurate on the non-malignant cases with a range of from 100 percent to 85 percent accuracy among the three examiners. Especially notable in this study was the fact that one of the examiners, Mrs. Naomi P. Roman, who achieved the highest results, applied a simplified method, using only the three most important criteria (pressure ratio, continuity of movement at the points of transition, and shape of angle between downstrokes and upstrokes). This technique was later applied in the following study at the Preventive Medicine Institute–Strang Clinic by two other independent examiners and brought about considerable progress.

Preventive Medicine Institute—Strang Clinic Studies

Of all the studies made over the past thirty-five years, the Strang Clinic studies can be considered the most important. The reason for this lies not only in the great number of subjects studied—35,000 as compared to a total of 10,000 examined in all Kanfer's previous experiments—but in the type of population involved. The "patients" or, rather, visitors coming to Strang Clinic are essentially healthy persons of all age-groups and from all activities of life as well as socio-economic groups. They do not come for treatment but for yearly routine checkups. Often they are young couples starting their yearly examinations right after marriage. Others just come as a precautionary measure, and there are also groups brought in as a benefit by large industrial companies. Thus a study of these cases comes closest to a study in general of the seemingly healthy population at large. This is the purpose of the test and what it has aimed for and for which it is best qualified: to screen the seemingly healthy population before there are any complaints and before any suspicion of cancer may arise. There was an additional advantage in the yearly return of the same persons which made a long-range follow-up possible.

The Strang Clinic studies divide into three separate parts—the last two being the most important.

The first Strang Clinic study. Undertaken from 1964 to mid–1968. In this study only the signatures of patients making their initial visits to the clinic were examined. Throughout the years of experiments the patients wrote on the same kind of plain white bond paper with the same kind of flexible steel nib pen.

The total number of cases was 20,216.

The Test rating was negative for 78 percent and positive for 22 percent.

In this group were 70 clinically proven cancer cases, of which 84 percent were rated positive or suspicious and 16 percent negative.

The chance factor was less than one in a million.

The ratio of cancer present in the group rated positive compared with the groups rated negative was 19:1.

Subsequently 33 patients with no signs of cancer at the time of the first examination were diagnosed as having cancer on re-examination from one to four years later. Of these 33 cases, 32 were rated suspicious or positive by the neuromuscular test at the time of their first clinical examination.

The second Strang Clinic study. From October 1968 to December 1969 another study was undertaken; this time, however, the handwriting samples of all visitors to the Strang Clinic both for initial and for annual examinations were rated. In this study, a standard sentence was used, instead of the patient's signatures. Pens and paper were standardized as before.

In this study, 15,402 samples were examined: 68 percent being rated negative, 17 percent suspicious, and 15 percent positive.

Of the 15,000 subjects, 90 were found on clinical examination to have cancer. Of these 90, 6.7 percent had been rated negative by the Kanfer test, 26.7 percent had been rated suspicious, and 66.6 percent had been rated positive.

The possibility of this being due to chance alone was less than one in a million.

The ratio of cases of cancer in the group rated positive to those in the group rated negative was 42.1. The ratio of occurrence among those rated suspicious to the frequency among those rated negative was 16:1.

In the year that elapsed after the third Strang study, clinical signs of cancer developed in 48 cases which had a positive handwriting rating but were at that time clinically negative.

These cases provide an additional demonstration of the predictive nature of the handwriting test. This factor became particularly evident in the following two cases from the 48:

1) Male, aged 64: Test rating in 1969: 6 (maximum positive).
   Clinical findings at that time: peptic ulcer.
   Enema studies: negative.
   Clinical findings 1971: carcinoma of the sigmoid.
2) Female, aged 47: Test rating in 1968: 6.
   Clinical findings at that time: gastric ulcer.
   Clinical findings 1971: cancer of the stomach.

In both cases timely response to the test findings might have either detected the cancer earlier or even secured treatment to prevent it.

The third Strang Clinic study was carried out by two volunteers * working independently. This study has not yet been published. It can be stated, however, that (1) the two results agreed more than 95 percent with each other, thus proving the objectivity of the method. (2) The results agreed more than 90 percent with a three-year follow-up of clinical findings in non-malignant cases. (The importance of these findings is the fact that the majority of the group studied was above sixty years old, thus demonstrating that the handwriting criteria for detecting cancer are independent of the age factor.) (3) The results agreed 95 percent with clinical findings of cancer. (4) Both examiners were 100 percent correct in a second study of 33 cases which were negative at the time of the first clinical examination but developed clinical signs of cancer from 1 to 3 years later.

Within these findings the Kanfer test seems to be confirmed beyond reasonable doubt.

For this study a simplified technique was used as developed in a previous study by one of the examiners, Mrs. Naomi P. Roman.

One point further. One cannot learn to apply this test by looking at a few handwriting samples. It requires serious and controlled study. Nor is this test intended to provide a means of self-diagnosis. It can be put to good use only in cooperation with physicians who can combine the findings of the test with their own observations.

Here are a few case histories from the new and older studies to demonstrate the way the test would function in routine examinations:

From the Hospital for Joint Diseases:

150489, male, age 64:   Clinical finding 1952: internal and external hemorrhoids.
Handwriting test: positive.
Clinical finding 1953: carcinoma, sigmoid, metastatic to liver.

35963, female, age 48:   Clinical finding 1946: chronic cystic endocervitis with erosions.
Handwriting test: positive.
Clinical finding 1948: adenocarcinoma, uterus.

* Mrs. Irene Blaser and Mrs. Lillian Grebanier.

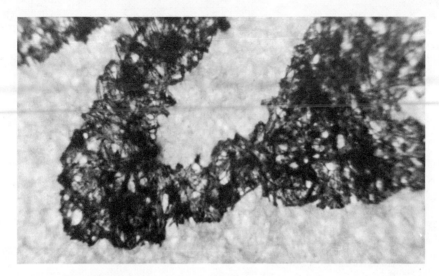

1) 1966

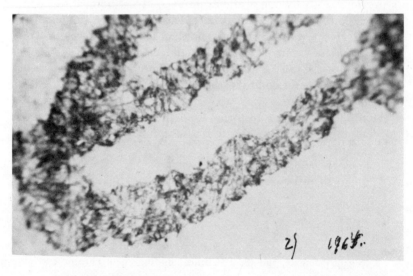

2) 1964

Preventive Medicine Institute—Strang Clinic:
1) female, age 57 (1966):

CASE HISTORY:
Clinical finding 1966: area in axis of left breast a little firmer, no axillary adenopathy.
Handwriting test: positive.
Clinical finding 1967: bilateral fibrocystic disease of breasts. *On left side cystic plaque, bilateral axillary nodes.*
Clinical finding 1968: intraductal cancer and infiltrating lobular cancer, left, metastatic to lymph nodes.

2) female, age 65 (1964):

Clinical finding 1964: breasts negative, with no dominant lumps or masses.
Handwriting test: positive.
Clinical finding 1970: breasts show minimum fibrocystic mastopathy, *left nipple slightly retracted.*
Clinical finding 1971: cancer, left breast.

From the Metropolitan Life Insurance Company Studies:
Signature of M.E., 1952, female, age 36, writing dated 1952.
Handwriting test: positive (rated by actuaries of the company). Clinical report of that time: nervous stomach. The insured person died one year later: cancer of the stomach.

In summary, the Kanfer Neuromuscular Test would divide a given population such as that found at the Strang Clinic into three groups: about 80 percent would be rated "negative." The percentage of cancer found in this group, present or developing within three years after the handwriting specimen was given, would be infinitesimally small; cancer would be practically absent.

Another group—about 10 percent—would be rated "doubtful." The incidence of cancer within this group would be higher than in the group rated "negative," but this category has for the time being to be regarded as unreliable.

Another 10 percent will be rated "positive." Among this group will be found most of the medically detectable cancer: between 80 percent and 90 percent of all cases. Furthermore there will be an equal percentage of cases which, although clinically negative at the time of examination, will develop cancer within three to five years afterward. There will also be a number of cases in which the trend to cancer may have been arrested or eliminated by timely medical intervention, such as removal of a polyp, a cystic condition, or a mole.

It should again be stressed very strongly that the rating "positive" does not constitute a diagnosis of cancer; it should be taken only as a warning to the physician for more intensive observation.*

The chief question one encounters in discussing Kanfer's work is the relationship between cancer and handwriting. These are the factors: it is widely accepted in medicine that with development of cancer certain neuromuscular disturbances of coordination take place. Since handwriting basically constitutes tracing of neuromuscular coordination, the microscopic characteristics of handwriting strokes become the foremost instrument for examining human neuromuscular development.

What the Kanfer Test does is to apply a neuromuscular tool to determine the presence or absence of such characteristic neuromuscular disorders. The Kanfer Test does not determine the presence or absence of cancer by itself—it determines only a factor which is associated with cancer.

---

* Further details of the tests outlined in this chapter may be found in Appendix E, page 344

Mental Disease

In no area of graphology is the potential more exciting and the status quo more frustrating than that of mental disease. Exciting, because handwriting, with its hypersensitive links to the brain, appears ideally suited to the exploration of the half-world of the mentally ill—and frustrating because little organized research is being done in this area by the medical profession, graphologists themselves often tend to bypass it, and the relationship between handwriting and mental illness is by no means an obvious one except in extreme cases. I don't know whether to take it as a compliment, but I would say that in my lifetime I have received almost as many letters from people with serious psychological problems as I have from so-called normal ones (a few on my birthday, and since I am becoming less and less anxious for the sane people to remember it, that's all right too!). I suppose many graphologists could have penetrated the abnormal writing at a glance, but not so me; and in the case of one great personal tragedy, I had considerably more warning from the text of letters I received than from the writing. Without any special interest

Mental disorder *

Mental disorder—the tangling of loops *

in graphology we all recognize the more blatant signs of mental disorder—the illegible script, the meandering of lines, the tangling of loops, the extremely muddy or tremulous pressure, the capitals in place of small letters, frequent touching-up and in fact omission of letters, omission even of words, sudden drastic changes in size, flamboyantly exaggerated rhythm, curlicues and designs and quotations, exclamation marks, parentheses, double "i" dots, doubly crossed "t"s which would shock us in the writing of eight-year-old children. But frequently I have studied pages and pages of writing I have received from my abnormal friends in search of even one clue to their condition with no success whatever. Sonnemann, who has written a most detailed chapter on this subject in his book *Handwriting Analysis*, appears to know all its answers, but even he warns us of the difficulties of putting the subtle gradations of mental disease into coherent categories. There are many dangers "to the left and right" of

* From the files of The Handwriting Institute, Inc., New York.

the investigator, he warns; no labels should be given to an individual case, no diagnoses made before ample graphic material has been studied and past and present samples produced by the same patient compared. And because of the conflicting theories within the field of psychopathology itself, the graphologist must be doubly careful before arriving at conclusions.

Irene Marcuse calls schizophrenia the collective name for various manifestations of the diseased mind, the most common being paranoia; Sonnemann lists paranoia under the general heading of schizophrenia, but manic-depression separately; and Lewinson speaks of the three forms of psychosis as dementia praecox (schizophrenia), paranoia, and manic depression. (If either of us is going into this any deeper, it's got to be you, dear reader!) In any case these labels which Sonnemann warns us against using loosely in attempting to analyze handwriting still exist, and rather than begging the question and simply listing the differing characteristics which graphologists ascribe to them (leaving the reader to sort them out for himself), I am going to see if Sonnemann and Lewinson in particular have arrived at any common ground. Let us start with mania and manic depression,

Manic depression *

* Reprinted by permission of Grune & Stratton, Inc., New York and Dr. Ulrich Sonnemann.

which Sonnemann describes under the heading of "Affective Disorders." In the case of the clinically manic, he tells us, "the more psychomotor pressure increases, the more will the handwriting tend to 'flee toward the right' . . . with a flighty handling . . . of single forms, with a tendency of lines to rise, and with other indications of a degree of 'absorption by the present moment' . . . [T]he graphic expression of manic psychosis tends to show an unusually high degree," he continues, ". . . of background involvement"—the filling up of space and a generally confusing manner.

Under the heading of hyperkinesis (exaggerated activity) Lewinson describes two phases of mania, the elated and the irritated, which correspond closely with Sonnemann's description. She sees the personality of the elated manic patient as presenting a picture of hyperactivity and restlessness which is driven outward to such an extent that conscious control may be more or less completely lost. Such writing, she says, is highly released, with strong acceleration, irregular distribution on the paper, and a tendency to move upward and outward: the writing of the former, the "irritated," is depicted as similar but with more tension, its size and speed reduced, and showing a tendency to move downward. She concludes her account of this type of writing by saying that that of the elated manic patient is the exaggerated expression of joy and that of the irritated manic patient of anger.

Hypomania *

* Reprinted by permission of Grune & Stratton, Inc., New York and Dr. Ulrich Sonnemann.

Somewhere between mania and depression are the "more stationary conditions of hypomania" which Sonnemann describes as follows:

> The layman, but also the graphologist, may be inclined to find the samples rather orderly . . . except that an impaired ability to keep line directions down and a disproportion between the reduced total height of the writing trail and its excessive wideness . . . will catch his attention. The patient's futile striving to resist his impulses, which thus is disclosed, can also manifest itself in an increased sharpness of the ductus and in an accentuation . . . of the pressure cycle, in brief, in attempts at *regulation,* and there may be no fancy curves at all: the impression conjured up in the observer is rather analogous to that which one might receive of a man on horseback who, seeing his animal go wild and anticipating a mad surge of uncertain direction and uncertain outcome, clings closely to his saddle, bending his head lower and tightening, along with the reins, every muscle in his body.

Sonnemann and Lewinson have very similar opinions of what they call "agitated depression." Sonnemann finds it marked by great inconsistencies in line or letter directions, frequently with extreme wideness and slant. Lewinson sees the inconsistency as due to a split between strong inhibitions on the one hand and strong releases and physical activity on the other. Constantly attempting without success to escape from their depressed moods, these patients cannot discover a true personality and are sensitive and irritable. Lewinson finds their writing, like that characteristic of most depression, small, with the letters more narrow than otherwise, but she finds the same irregularity in basic line and rhythm that Sonnemann does. (Werner Wolff, by the way, records a study in which 86 percent of the pictures drawn by depressive children were small in size, while 80 percent of those drawn by feeble-minded ones were large.)

Mania in general lies in the direction of pure psychosis; depression and hypokinesis, in that of neurosis. Lewinson describes

[handwritten text]

Agitated depression *

[handwritten text]

There is nothing one could do about

too will soon realize this your

all my heart I feel that the

not far when for you to write

and and I wonder about Bob

he then agree to own

Apathetic depression *

the apathetic depressive patients as unduly repressed, overcritical of themselves, with no fantasy life and with almost no interest except themselves and their troubles. They have anxieties, fears, and depressions and avoid all manner of contact. It is significant that Lewinson finds in this writing an extreme tendency toward slowness—characteristic of depression in general, according to Sonnemann—small-size descending or wavering basic lines, little

* Reprinted by permission of Grune & Stratton, Inc., New York and Dr. Ulrich Sonnemann.

rhythm, narrowness, weak pressure, and a tendency to reproduce school-copy with little ornamentation. As in all manic-depressive writing, she says, there is marked instability which affects in particular the height dimension—the intellectual processes in the upper zone—and the emotional and instinctive functioning in the lower. (I do not agree with equating the upper zone, however, with the mind.)

Reactive depression *

Whereas in pure cyclic depressions, characterized by low-saddled, drooping garlands, Sonnemann finds a continuous downward tendency of the trail or the basic line, in involutional and reactive depressions he discerns "a desperate attempt of the writer to resist a 'falling' tendency of the word endings." In involutional melancholia he sees "a marked inconsistency in the degree of doughiness, wavering between smeary excesses . . . and extreme sharpness" of the pen, as well as crippled and occasionally exaggerated lower forms. In reactive depressions, he says, "as more or less in all neuroses," the width of the writing greatly decreases, contraction is preeminent, and the height of the middle zone depends on the clinical involvement of traits of hysteria. In this regard, incidentally, he later comments that hysterics "are recognizable from the reduction of their middle zones, a marked propensity for threading, displacement of pressure into movements of release" and an inclination toward "artificial wideness, artificial fullness, peripheral inflations, and exaggerations." While a reduction of the middle zone, he tells us,

* Reprinted by permission of Grune & Stratton, Inc., New York and Dr. Ulrich Sonnemann.

Hysteric *

Hysteric *

"can . . . be defined as the decisive graphic tendency of the hysteric, *pure anxiety states* show a preeminent tendency toward horizontal shrinking." Sonnemann describes these anxiety states as characterized by "[a] great variation in total letter direction, rigidity of the ductus, slowness, extreme displays of pressure . . . particularly of the lower zone . . . unsteady line directions, general predominance of contractive qualities, yet occasional excesses of doughiness."

Coming to the subject of schizophrenia and the schizoid personality, we again discover a good deal of agreement between Sonnemann and Lewinson. Both find a dissonant character in the schizoid writing, or rather a lack of integrated character, not unexpected in a personality which alternates, in its extreme forms, between complete seclusion and uncontrolled outbreaks. Both find rigidity in the writing, a tendency toward angularity,

* Reprinted by permission of Grune & Stratton, Inc., New York and Dr. Ulrich Sonnemann.

[handwritten sample]

aden. Soon the trail led o
bund his load too much.
the of it for him, but th
'ed horse fell down under
then th man made th

Schizophrenia *

narrowness of letters, and undynamic and "flabby" rhythm. Both find a leftward tendency, with Sonnemann observing a displacement of lower extremities toward the left and angular intricacies of the leftward components. He tells us that "the specifically schizoid element in the realm of the forms of binding remains the arcade," and when Lewinson speaks of "the extreme egocentricity of the (schizoid) individual and the resulting cleavage between himself and his environment," it is understandable that such personalities build themselves archways in their writing beneath which to hide.

Under the general heading of "schizophrenic disorders" Sonnemann lists hebephrenia, paranoia, and catatonia. With my own research in mental disease affording such meager results, I take particular pleasure in the lucid description which Sonnemann gives, both verbally and pictorially, of hebephrenia—which, in spite of all my eloquence on this subject, is perhaps the only form of mental disease which I can now go out and be sure to

* Reprinted by permission of Grune & Stratton, Inc., New York and Dr. Ulrich Sonnemann.

Hebephrenia *

Hebephrenia *

identify through handwriting. The textbook characteristics of
hebephrenia are shallow, inappropriate affective reactions, silly
behavior, delusions, hallucinations, and retreats to simpler forms
of behavior. Sonnemann describes the handwriting of its victims
as having a high degree of inconsistency in all dimensions, appearing "torn" and "bizarre," contracted where release would
normally be called for, and vice versa. "Fragmentation is frequent," he tells us, "letter directions totally unruly"; its leftwardness is "excessive," it displays mannerisms of all kinds, and its
proportions are distorted, while sporadically a phase of "dead"
precision appears whose products "appear to 'float' in the trail
like foreign bodies in a liquid." Leftward curlicues are signs of

* Reprinted by permission of Grune & Stratton, Inc., New York and Dr.
Ulrich Sonnemann.

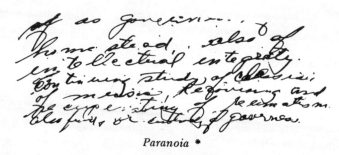

Paranoia *

narcissistic impulses further confirmed by rolling movements and secretive little enclosures, and the characteristic quality of "hairiness," says Sonnemann, the impressions of a multitude of little thorns or bristles, are due not to peculiarities of the pen but to "minute intricacies of the linear formation of the trail which in the typical hebephrenic's handwriting are as tiny as they are innumerable."

Let us now examine what Sonnemann and Lewinson have to say about paranoia. The paranoid's writing, according to Sonnemann, seems continuously to grow—"or else to combat a tendency to do so"—in the vertical; and "peripheral" expansion, he adds, tends to operate almost exclusively in the vertical. Lewinson verifies this conclusion by finding emphasis of the lower zone as to length, copiousness, and pressure and a great difference between long and short letters—meaning probably long upper and lower loops. Lewinson speaks of an irregular slant toward the right and all Sonnemann's examples slant in that direction; and both find angularity and a rigidity and sharpness of the stroke which, according to Sonnemann, makes diagnosis comparatively easy. Yet both graphologists find a tendency toward the left, and Sonnemann says that "the general qualities of curve applying here show a degree of accentuation not matched by any other syndrome." Sonnemann finds a "concavity toward the upper left" which in pure cases "looks as though a wind was blowing from behind the trail, swelling the 'sails' of the upper periphery and driving the whole structure on." Going on to

---

* Reprinted by permission of Grune & Stratton, Inc., New York and Dr. Ulrich Sonnemann.

examine "obsessional neuroses," both graphologists find a high degree of connectedness, an anxious attention to the school pattern, and a narrowness of the trail—less marked in paranoia.

Lewinson has a good deal to say on the subject of what she calls "the instinctive sphere," meaning, I suppose, pressure and the lower zone. She cites patients who are paranoid to the point of having dual personalities, who frequently possess two entirely different handwritings. In the schizophrenic personality, she explains, the emphasis of the split is on the "ego-you" relationship, in the paranoid personality it is on the instinctive-rational relationship. The severe dynamic disturbance in the instincts of the paranoid, with energy or libido blocked off, grave anxieties, and uncontrolled outbreaks, is exhibited by irregularity and rigidity in the area of pressure and the lower zone. At the same time, the full-blown upper loops show progress in what graphologists call the intellectual or rational upper zone. The paranoid patient thus learns but cannot assimilate; his experiences are vicarious only, and strive as he may to appear to exist normally by observing the conventions, he lives or rather vegetates, according to Lewinson, "in an empty, distorted, rationalized system which has no contact with reality." This constant effort to act a role causes him to be resentful, artful and cautious.

A final word on catatonics from Sonnemann: "Catatonic handwritings differ from the rest of the group," he says, "by their far greater genuine fullness and curvedness, high pressure, extreme slowness, and resulting extreme 'unslenderness' of the stroke [whatever that is!] and of the forms themselves which despite their emphasis on round movements seldom tend to show any smoothness of shape. Cracking, 'bumping,' and mending are in particular prominence. . . . The enormous rigidity of the movement," continues Sonnemann, "brings about the so-called long-wave tremor which can easily be distinguished from the tremulous effects both of intracranial and of alcoholic conditions, as well as of severe psychoneurotic anxiety."

I cannot conclude this chapter without taking one beautiful observation of Sonnemann's out of context and leaving it for us to mull over. "The schizophrenic's emotions," says he, "insofar *[handwritten specimen:]* Joseph F.

[handwritten specimen:] if you come here
I was born June 17. 1914 63 Huron St
P. 5 27 Cathedral St. ave

Catatonia *

[handwritten specimen:] I have spent enough time in
California, Washington north Carolina, Saint Albans
newton, + here. my belief is in being home I love to be home
I truly say that my belief is in being home. I love to be

Catatonia *

as they become articulate, are not 'shallow' as a body of water might be but their form of articulation conveys the image of shallowness; of course the schizophrenic does not 'withdraw' as an army might, but his behavior seems to have the gestural implication of withdrawing."

* Reprinted by permission of Grune & Stratton, Inc., New York and Dr. Ulrich Sonnemann.

Crime

Herry O. Teltscher writes in a recent book, *Handwriting—Revelation of Self,* that "the use of handwriting analysis in criminology is not new. The handwriting expert, familiar figure in American courts, is called upon to determine the authenticity of a document, to decide whether two signatures were written by the same person or whether a blackmail letter could possibly have been written by the accused. Since the Hauptmann trial the role of the handwriting expert in kidnapping cases is well known —his testimony was one of the deciding factors in the verdict of capital punishment."

But just as the handwriting expert who can identify a particular criminal tends to look down his nose at the emerging science of graphology (which is rarely even listed under that title in dictionaries and encyclopedias), so the graphologist knows and writes little about identification. Today crime is becoming more and more a problem for the psychiatrist and the hospitals— both general and psychiatric, with drug addiction rampant—and less and less for the old-fashioned prison. It is these psychological

Mr Lindbergh only wasting time with his search

Writing of Bruno Hauptmann *

and medical problems, rather than the legal ones, with which I am concerned in this book; and most of the characteristics of "dishonesty" listed by Pulver, Saudek, Sainte Colombe, and others and discussed here bear an ambivalence of meaning which is psychological as well as ethical in nature. The discussion of disguised writing, however, is such an intriguing one—few men and women will not claim to a graphologist that they can disguise their writing; we all have forgery as well as larceny in our hearts—that I will not leave it without providing a few clues about the pros and cons of passing a bad check.

Regarding the lists of characteristics which graphologists have designated as dishonest, I will discuss them in more or less the order in which they were made. Since they overlap a good deal, I have been tempted to reduce them to their common denominators and present one list instead of several, but in this case authenticity has prevailed over simplicity, and as Anthony Quinn puts it in *Zorba the Greek,* the reader will be presented with "the full catastrophe," or at least as much of it as I can make any sense of. The first list is that of Max Pulver, the Swiss psychologist, translated by Felix Klein (with an assist on my part from Sainte Colombe in interpreting it). Pulver claims that at least four of his characteristics must appear together to bear out a finding of dishonesty. The list includes "cover-strokes," as he calls them (up-and-down strokes written over each other), which appear to imply deceit and guilt varying with the "zone" in which they are found; arcades—always suspected by grapholo-

* From *Personality In Handwriting* by Alfred O. Mendel. Reprinted by permission of Frederick Ungar Publishing Co., Inc., New York.

Cover-strokes—Pulver *

Counter-strokes—Pulver *

Complicated loops †

* From *Symbolik Der Handschrift* by Dr. Max Pulver. Reprinted by permission of Orell Füssli Verlag, Zurich and Leipzig.

† From *The Language of Handwriting and How to Read It* by Oscar N. Myer. Reprinted by permission of Frederick Ungar Publishing Co., Inc., New York.

gists—particularly culpable when flattened out, denoting secrecy, and when combined with materialistic angularity; "thready" connections and a wavering basic line, the former having a sinuous agility which means "adapt at all costs," the latter signifying undependability; "counter-strokes," which appear to be the deliberate changing of a stroke or a letter to give it a false meaning; complicated loops, double loops, roll-ins, as Pulver calls them, with words and lines often tangled—"arising less from pedantic calligraphy than from evil cunning"; beginning letters too big or too small, expressing not so much untruthfulness as a lack of equilibrium "displacing the normal relationship of I to You" (I have a few words to say on the subject of my own research on "misplaced capitals" later in this chapter); unnecessary cross-strokes and lines indicating a protective concealment; broken-up letters: Pulver speaks of laziness and possibly feeblemindedness here, and Sainte Colombe quotes him as referring to ovals open at the base or traced in two parts as typical of the embezzler's script (almost every graphologist has something to say on this subject); slurring of letters, the avoidance of conflict and neglect shown arising either from laziness or a conscious intention to deceive; the touching-up of letters, which becomes a disquieting sign when the writing is deliberately slow and there are no mechanical or physiological handicaps; writing a letter in different ways—here Pulver gives as an example writing now in German and now in Latin, and I doubt if he is referring to the usual variations in such small letters as "s" and "r"; marked exaggerations in size, pressure, flourishes, spacing, slant, which blind the writer to objectivity; omission of letters; and finally discrepancy between writing and signature, which incidentally we often find in the scripts of important public figures from Dickens on down (as well as those of the bad guys). To this list Sainte Colombe adds—in the name of Pulver—weak "t" bars, which in spite of the fact that Eisenhower had them, have been the favorite target of all graphologists; smeary writing, with sensuous, ink-filled lower loops (sometimes a characteristic of murderers); and—the last item in Sainte Colombe's chapter on "how to determine dishonesty"—numerals voluntarily indistinct

Marked exaggerations in pressure *

Smeary writing †

* From *Character Reading From Handwriting* by Louise Rice. Copyright, 1927, by Frederick A. Stokes Company. Reprinted by courtesy of J. B. Lippincott Company.

† From *Graphology A Handbook* by Henry A. Rand. Reprinted by permission of Sci-Art Publishers, Cambridge, Massachusetts.

General instability of writing *

so they can be mistaken for other figures. Bank officials, beware!

The second list with which I shall deal is that of Robert Saudek, entitled "Signs of Honesty and Dishonesty." These are actually groups of signs, and since Saudek claims, as Pulver does, that at least four of them must occur to justify a diagnosis of dishonesty, it seems apparent that he must have been influenced by the Swiss graphologist in spite of the care he takes in avoiding the mention of his name. There are ten of them, and the first and principal one is slow writing with normal instruments and materials, although the writer has attained full graphic maturity and although no acute or chronic impediments are operative. The second arises as a result of aversion to the writer's own natural graphic expression and is characterized by adherence to the school-copy, the adoption of a reversed writing angle, and an inclination to arcades. The third is a general instability or "lability" of the writing, "a loose, decomposing, spineless structure— without pressure, firmness, or physiognomy." Such writing, Saudek tells us, represents an unstable, featureless character which can readily adapt itself to any role. The fourth comprises numerous signs of the touching up of letter formations, especially if the legibility or beauty of the writing is not improved thereby. Number five includes letters written as other letters, groups of letters replaced by other groups, with occasional covering strokes. This creates a guessing game popular with those writers who

* From the files of The Handwriting Institute, Inc., New York.

I am fascinated by your analysis of handwriting. This is a copy of my handwriting, so analyze accordingly.

Touching up the letter formations

Saudek's example of "blobbed handwriting" *

hesitate to commit themselves. Number six on Saudek's list is "blobbed or punctuated handwriting: . . . numerous 'resting-points,' and punctuations between words or syllables which are inconsistent with the spelling, or superfluous, or punctuations in the course of the stroke." Number seven reads: "The pen is frequently lifted from the paper, and individual words are written with three, four, or more separate strokes of the pen"—but I doubt that any modern graphologist would agree with Saudek's conclusion here, and Saudek himself gives no explanation for it. Number eight, the omission of important parts of letters, is considered decisive only if it occurs with the conjunction of slow

* From *Experiments with Handwriting* by Robert Saudek. Reprinted by permission of Dr. A. Saudek.

writing and complete graphic maturity. Number nine, marked initial emphasis of words, is dismissed lightly by Saudek as vanity but coincides with my own theory of misplaced capitals at the beginning of words of which I will speak later. Number ten, finally, is the notorious one noted (or at least echoed) by almost every graphologist—the letters "o," "a," "d," "g," and "q" being open at the base. Saudek comments—with typically German bluntness—that this feature is the only reliable one of the French school of graphology and also that in the files of the police it occurs in 30 percent even of the signatures of habitual thieves of both sexes. To Saudek—again apparently by way of Pulver—slow writing combined with full graphic maturity is by far the most significant of these ten groups, and it is this first characteristic on his list to which any three of the others must be added to confirm the imputed dishonesty. The absence of the features of group one essentially prejudices the reliability of the diagnosis, no matter how many other features may be included.

In case the reader is not yet sick and tired of lists, there is one more about which I probably ought to say a word since, unlike the others, it is strictly contemporary. Strangely enough, it differs little from the earlier ones. It comprises forty signs of unreliability—the modern word for dishonesty—and we are told by one of its authors, Louis P. Ciancio, that those who are weak, delinquent, or emotionally disturbed will possess a cluster of at least five or more of these. The number has risen—but the proportion has dropped! This list is the work of Dr. A. M. Muhl, a psychiatrist who specialized for years in handwriting analysis, and Mr. Ciancio, who established sixteen of the characteristics. Since this last list comprises details hard for the layman to grasp at first reading, is somewhat repetitive within itself and deals with subjects which I have already covered, I am not going to bore you with all forty characteristics. Instead, let us try to form some general picture of them. First, we have all the signs of withdrawal: small, tight loops, narrow in shape and concept, evasive, stencillike writing, compulsive leftward-tending half-ovals, the distrustful, rebellious leftward slant, arcades and secre-

Writing of Robespierre—distrustful and secretive *

tive centripetal movements, abrupt stops and covering strokes, weak "t" bars, and, of course, that ever-present villain, artificially slow writing, particularly if it is tremulous without apparent reason. Next, we have the signs of indecisiveness: letters eroded, illegible and thready, varying slant, varying pressure, varying size of letters, an undulating basic line, and generally poor and irregular spacing. Then we have the smeariness, the muddy writing, the heavy, brutal, downward diagonal strokes, characteristic of those with overpowering sensual and sensuous appetites, occasionally with those "eruptive" blotches which Mendel found in the writings of sixteen murderers which he studied. Finally we have the extremes, the exaggeration, the suspiciously *legible* writing versus the totally illegible, the unusually large writing, the excessive and overemotional slant to the right and spacing to the right, with its implied delusions of grandeur, and, complementary rather than contrasting, microscopic writing with its own complexes—all of this nearing the danger point of the loops within loops, the eccentric underscoring, the double "t" crossings, the misplacing of dots and dashes, and omission of letters, of those who have crossed the borderline of sanity.

I cannot conclude these lists of marks of "unreliability" without a comment about two graphological signs which may indeed be as revealing of the antisocial personality as the slow writing

---

* From *Robespierre* by J. M. Thompson. Reprinted by permission of Howard Fertig, Inc., New York.

which all three writers stress. The first is the little break at the bottom of "a," "d," "g," "o," and "q" because it is mentioned, as I have said, by almost every graphologist (including Ciancio and Dr. Muhl). It seems to be as much of a guarantee of deviousness and treachery as an opening at the top of these letters is of friendliness and candor. Lucas speaks of theft and falsehood in this connection, Sonnemann of concealment and "increasing self-intimacy"; and while Saudek finds it prevalent in the writing of "habitual thieves" in the police archives of two capitals, Louise Rice claims to have found endless examples in the writing of "big criminals" whose weakness is large sums of money.

The other sign is one which I have grown to call "misplaced capitals"—that is, capitals where small letters should properly be —usually at the beginning of words. It has been called a sign of

Errol Flynn. Notice the large capital "B" in, of all words, "Bloody"!

Misplaced capitals in homicide case *

* From the files of The Handwriting Institute, Inc., New York.

exhibitionism and mental disease, but I think Sonnemann describes it best when he claims that this characteristic reveals itself as relating to self-assertive impulses, asserting themselves with special force in situations not calling for them. The impulse can be specifically caused by the word to which the capital is incorrectly attached, sometimes favorably if the word suggests an object of love or respect, but more often unfavorably to the point of violence when the word has unpleasant associations. (One wonders if the capitalization of nouns peculiar to the German language might have any significance in this regard.) It has also been noted that the replacement of capitals by small letters—as in the case of Freud's signature, and what about e. e. cummings? —may represent the same rebellion from the norm as its opposite. John Morley—another Macmillan author!—caused a great sensation in 1870 when he published an article referring throughout to "god."

Many years ago, observing the misplaced capitals in the writing of some of my perfectly literate acquaintances, including Errol Flynn—who used to take great joy in forgetting to return the pens of his fans when they sought his autograph—I did a good deal of research on the subject. I sent a friend of mine named Irving Stoopack out to a prison in the Middle West, where we found an extraordinary percentage of misplaced capitals in the inmates' writings; the same held true when I made a similar survey at Sing Sing. The problem, however, was the degree of literacy of the subjects, for of course uneducated people, including children, are inclined to have this habit, and since I ran into difficulties in establishing the educational background of prisoners, I never completed my research. Contrary to most graphologists, however, I still feel that upper loops in general are more closely identified with aggression than with intelligence and the spirit and that a great deal of fascinating work remains to be done on misplaced capitals in the areas both of crime and of mental disease.

Is there a specifically "criminal" handwriting? If we consider that juvenile delinquents exemplify the criminal temperament in its early stages, then it should be interesting to examine a study in handwriting analysis published by Rose Wolfson in 1949. In this study she described delinquency as the behavior of an inadequate or deficiently integrated personality whose mode of adjustment to life lies in its disregard not only for other people's needs and satisfactions but also for the delinquent's own determinant needs as against subsidiary ones. The delinquent is in conflict, says Miss Wolfson, not only with society but also with his more personal environment, the family, and frequently with himself. He is hyperactive, abnormally restless, moody, subject to sudden outbursts, to feelings of insecurity and inferiority. He claims that he is not afraid of anything, apparently a defense mechanism. The delinquent generally comes from an unstable home. Lowry describes him as immature, egocentric, and unable to restrain present impulses to pleasurable activity in the face of imminent penalty or in favor of long-term goals.

In order to compare the writing of presumably normal boys with that of deliquents, Miss Wolfson made a study of thirty-three delinquents in the Warwick State Training School for Boys and thirty-three nondelinquent boys in the New York State public schools. The two groups were matched as closely as possible for race, nationality, age, IQ, and socio-economic level. The delinquent boys were placed in five categories: the situational or temporary, the personality, the pseudo-social or environmental, the asocial, and the medical. Of these boys about 50 percent suffered from deep-rooted conflicts and showed marked personality distortions and anxieties; 20 percent had temporary problems at home; and 14 percent had assumed no acceptable standards of behavior patterns due to inadequate home environment. Two were hard-core cases with apparently little hope of rehabilitation.

In analyzing the handwriting of these two groups by means of the Lewinson–Zubin scale of contraction and release, Miss Wolfson found that there was little difference in legibility and penmanship between them but that there was a tendency in the delinquents' writing toward filling up space horizontally; that letters inclined deeply to the right and swung out widely; that words followed closely upon one another and margins were pressed against the edge of the writing paper. Statistical analysis indicated that the Lewinson–Zubin scales succeeded in differentiating between the two groups in the expected direction—that is, in showing that the nondelinquent group, normally considered to be better adjusted, displayed more balanced and less extreme tendencies in the direction of either contraction or release of handwriting than the deviant group. As for the delinquent group, the significantly high recording at the release end of the continuum was to be expected; but the question remaining was the equally high recording for the delinquents at the contraction end, with the emphasis on carefully controlled pressure, narrow letters, and a low middle zone. After discussing this and quoting previous research, Miss Wolfson concluded that because of the continuous frustration felt by the delinquents, there are swings from normal behavior, or of abnormally controlled behavior to intermittent outbreaks, and that the recording of this was a graphic reflection of the dynamics of the delinquent's functioning. She added that the restriction of the State School, being an intensified form of the restrictions of society itself, could also have a strongly inhibitory effect upon the delinquents, showing up in the high recording at the contraction end of the scales; and this difference between the two groups could be due more to the external conditions under which they lived than to personality structuring. She completed her discussion of this topic by commenting that psychologists had pointed out that the delinquent differs from the nondelinquent not in kind but in degree; that whereas both groups generally tended in similar directions on the scale, the nondelinquents did not press on to such extremes.

I promised to say a word about disguise in handwriting. Saudek claims that experience in thousands of cases has proven that in nearly all forgeries those features of the writing were altered which graphologically were not relevant; that people are incapable of concealing their personalities for any length of time, and are invariably found out by a demand for more material. He points out that someone who, like most criminals, has not yet attained to graphic maturity can never imitate a completely mature hand. An individual's various scripts, he says, are fundamentally identical; handwriting is brainwriting; and hypnosis

Forgery *

offers further evidence of the fact. Allport and Vernon, agreeing with Saudek, declare that it is practically impossible either to disguise one's own handwriting completely or to copy the handwriting of another person beyond the range of detection.

In 1919 June Downey, professor of psychology at the University of Wyoming, published a study of graphology which included a chapter on disguised writing. The basis of the chapter was an experiment in which she asked twenty-four subjects, twelve of each sex and of different ages, to write a given verse, first in their usual manner and then disguising their writing as far as possible. The resultant writings were given to sixteen "reagents" for correct matching. Miss Downey then proceeded to explore

* From *Collecting Autographs and Manuscripts* by Charles Hamilton. Copyright 1961 by the University of Oklahoma Press. Reprinted by permission of the publisher.

what methods of disguise were employed by her subjects. They frequently changed the size of their writing, most often making it smaller. While the absolute size of writing was easily altered, the relative proportions of the parts remained fairly constant. "I" dots could be varied, but only with unusual care. But not all such change was voluntary: greater attention to the writing as a whole often led to smaller writing, and attention to individual letters—for the purpose of disguise—resulted in their becoming larger. A shift in slant was noticeable, usually in the direction of the vertical or backhand. Pressure was difficult to gauge, but the change was generally in the direction of a heavier line. Changes in small letters were difficult to achieve; changes in capitals were easier. To break continuity was found easier than to increase it. The results of this canvas of modes of disguise, observed Miss Downey, agreed closely with a scheme adopted by the Berlin police as part of their system of identification of criminals. The police found size, pressure, verticality, and slant at the top of their list of characteristics easy to change, and connecting strokes, proportions, and the shape of individual letters at the bottom of their list.

The second question Miss Downey explored was that of the success of a disguise as determined by the failure of the judges to penetrate it. Their successes ranged from only one correct pairing among the twenty-four specimens to an accurate pairing of eleven specimens. So far as the individual disguises were concerned, some were much more effective than others. Three hands could scarcely be called disguised since they were correctly paired by almost every judge. These three wrote very individual hands, and their attempts to mask their writing had little success. Of the four completely successful disguises, one was a semi-print style, another a clever imitation of a friend's hand included among the specimens. The other two showed great shifts in slant and size, effective in deceiving the ordinary observer. All four subjects whose disguises were not penetrated were women, and the best records on the test were made by the young women. But some of these successful disguises came from the older group and led Miss Downey to conclude that an effective disguise is

Methods Utilized in Disguise of Writing by 24 Subjects
Number of Times There Was a Noticeable Shift In

Size, 17	Slant, 16	Pressure, 15	Form, 16	Alignment 16	Continuity 11	Connecting-stroke, 17	Proportion, 16	i-dot, 5
Decreased 11	To backhand or vertical 15	Increased 12	Ornamented 8	Straightened 6	Decreased 8	More rounded 12	One space letter 7	Change in form 5
Increased 6	To right 1	Decreased 3	Fantastic 2	More serpentine 4	Increase 3	More angular 5	Increased down stroke 5	In localization ?
			Simplified 6	Rising 4			Decreased down stroke 2	
				Falling 2			Increased up stroke 2	

Tabulation from Downey's study *

much more a matter of the individual constitution than of age or even of sex. Generally those who were more adaptable, more pliable, showed most facility in the adoption of another chirographic individuality.

Miss Downey concludes by stating that a dramatic reaction to the instruction to disguise one's hand in which one yields confidently to a graphic-motor pattern different from his habitual one is more effective in disguise than an effortful disintegration of graphic details, with a constant attempt to suppress habit. The effortful disguise, she says, although it may conceal its source effectively, will give evidence of not being a natural hand by inconsistencies, by retouching, and "by the presence of fantastic forms." This type of disguise is most often found in the anonymous letter, while the dramatic type may relate to mental disturbance.

Since I have written to some length about disguise in writing, it is perhaps fitting for me to reinforce Miss Downey's report with one also written a number of years ago by Dr. Clarence

* From *Graphology and the Psychology of Handwriting* by June E. Downey. Reprinted by permission of the University of Wyoming.

Quinan of San Francisco, working from an experimental study of the difference between the writing of convicted forgers and convicted murderers. (The least physically dangerous criminals versus the most? Dr. Quinan gives no explanation for his comparison.) Preliminary tests, he tells us, had seemed to indicate that murderers are prone to make angular, spastic, or compressed letter forms, while forgers tend to write in a more rounded style and to pay greater attention to the diacritical marks—the "i" dots, "t" bars, etc. The rounded writing of the forgers would tend to suggest the "secretive" arcades of which we have spoken, and their writing incidentally appears to include more backhand specimens than that of the murderers. Dr. Quinan was particularly interested in the speed of the murderers' writing, timing each convict's performance in the course of his study with a stopwatch. He obtained specimens of writing from 100 murderers, 100 forgers, 100 unselected noncriminals of both sexes, and 6 abattoir "killers." (The latter were employees of the Swift Packing Company of San Francisco whose sole task was to slaughter animals in the various "kills.")

What were the final results of his study? First, he found no appreciable difference, attributable to age or race, among the murderers. Of the abattoir "killers," he says pointedly, "[Their] writings . . . were similar in every respect to those obtained from murderers." SPCA, take heed! In the handwriting of forgers he noted two peculiarities that appeared with unusual frequency: many specimens of script were "unmistakably calligraphic"—harking back again to the rigid roundness of arcades; secondly, "t" bars, the chief diacritical marks of which he speaks, were frequently made not at the usual horizontal but at an extreme downward slant. Almost 25 percent of the forgers produced this unusual "t" bar or some related eccentricity—perhaps a compulsion to disguise one's own writing leads to copying someone else's.

Dr. Quinan thus summarizes his results in regard to the factors of speed and angularity in murderers' scripts contrasted with forgers': "The average for the writing time of noncriminals, forgers, and murderers were, respectively, 48.6, 68.0, and 101.19

seconds. Hence bradygraphia [the hard way of saying "slow writing"] would appear to be characteristic of murderers. The total angularity figures [i.e., the number of angular loops] obtained for the same groups, in the same order, were 283, 286, and 469. For this reason the writings of murderers were unsightly and full of irregularities and wanting in roundness, the quality that distinguishes the writing of forgers." Differences in intelligence or social level, as Fluckiger, Tripp, and Weinberg have pointed out, could be contributing factors in these cases. But it is interesting to remember that slow writing on the part of those who have reached "full graphic maturity" was to Robert Saudek the first and principal sign of "dishonesty." (In the light of Dr. Quinan's results concerning the relatively normal speed of the writing of forgers, should Saudek's emphasis have been on violence in crime rather than dishonesty?) In regard to the finding of extreme angularity in the writing of murderers as contrasted with the rounded writing of forgers, we appear to have verification of Sonnemann's identification of angularity with violence and Anthony's—in "low form level script"—with "oppression, dogmatism, cynicism, or tyranny." In the roundness of forgers' scripts, we again find signs of the deceit which the arcade is so often held to signify.

One of the lectures of Felix Klein, the well-known New York graphologist born and trained in Vienna, is entitled "Rhythm, Groundrhythm and Beyond" and speaks of the work on criminality done by the German, Rhoda Wieser. Dr. Wieser discovered, according to Klein, that a lack of "elasticity" characterized the writings of known criminals which she studied, when compared to that of noncriminals. She found a definite relationship between the severity of the crime and a decrease in the "groundrhythm," as she called it (evoking, perhaps intentionally, an image of the ground swell of the ocean with its powerful but harmonious ebb and flow). Elasticity she compared to the swinging of a pendulum with a thrust-imparting center which regenerates it, like Antaeus when he touched the earth, at each movement forward and back. To Dr. Wieser the elasticity of the unrestricted momentum of the pendulum and of the pen and pencil in healthy, uninhibited writing characterizes the healthy mind and body; and the lack of it—the spastic, angular, neurotic stroke which we have encountered so often in this chapter on crime (and which we have noted in the writing of children, of cancer patients, and of the insane)—characterizes the physically and emotionally immature or ill. If graphology accomplishes no more than to add conclusive evidence to the link between physical and mental illness, how many unfortunate souls it will have saved in the process!

Business Use

In the Twenties, DeWitt Lucas wrote that many companies and other organizations in the United States used graphology as a method of selecting employees. He gave as examples steel companies, banks, automobile corporations, machinery manufacturers, government departments, colleges, but added that there was "great objection" on the part of some companies to having their names associated publicly with graphology, though they were often willing to give private testimonials. After half a century this situation has changed for the better, but not by a great deal. Miss Leslie W. King, editor-in-chief of the *Annals* of the American Association of Handwriting Analysts and also of their *News Letter*, writes in 1969 :

> In industry, the greatest strides have perhaps been taken in the past few years, where personnel selection by graphological conclusions has proved to be the most effective, accurate, time-saving, and economical means of psychological testing. More than six hundred major businesses in the United States use

the graphological evaluation. Few of them will readily allow
their names to be published, due to the poor image of graphology currently abroad in this nation. . . . Many, many insurance
companies have found that the best way for them to save money
on their training programs is to have the trainees' handwriting
analyzed before they are accepted into the program.

Though companies are increasingly intrigued with the search
for more scientific ways of evaluating personality than the traditional interview (just as inquiring people have been using the
handwriting computers displayed recently at railroad stations),
executives cannot but realize that to the average, well-informed
citizen graphology still ranks somewhere on a par with palmistry,
phrenology, astrology, and tea-leaf reading. Though of course it
gets much serious attention in Europe, and particularly in West
Germany, in the United States as recently as 1961 a standard
textbook on personnel psychology placed graphology among the
"Techniques of Doubtful Usefulness." It is not indeed an exact
study like chemistry or algebra, and the graphologist who suggests that his analysis of personality from script is not improved
by knowing the writer as well as the writing is misrepresenting
his profession. At the same time, I believe that when we use
handwriting analysis in conjunction with a résumé, letters of
recommendation, and a personal interview to help select someone for a job, we have invaluable insurance against wrong decisions. Many of the wrong decisions which I have made about
hiring people—I won't mention names—have been caused by not
paying enough attention to danger signals in the writing. The
art colony which I supported in California ran with idyllic
smoothness for fifteen years (with the invaluable help of its
director, Dr. John Vincent, and Charles Rogers and Betty Izant),
and though as a member of each admissions committee I was
only a small cog in the wheel of progress, I usually took great
pleasure in confirming the excellence of our committees' choice
of fellows by covert glances at the penmanship on their application forms.

An article was written several years ago describing a study by

May 23, 1962.

Mr. Huntington Hartford
Huntington Hartford Enterprises
420 Lexington Avenue
New York 17, N.Y.

Dear Mr. Hartford:

Dr. Vincent writes that you would like
to have a handwritten letter from me.
Here goes — What follows is a copy
of a typewritten letter I have just
mailed to Dr. Vincent:

"Dear Dr. Vincent:

"If nothing else, your excellent letter
has given me moral encouragement

Art colony—application letter

one of the largest manufacturing firms in the country. The article
was written jointly by Ulrich Sonnemann and John Kernan, a
personnel expert who was formerly with the company that spon-
sored the study and is presently with IBM. This study—"Handwriting Analysis—A Valid Selection Tool?"—and one other of
which I shall write later, are the only two I know that examine
the use of graphology in business, and I hope that the authors
of both will forgive me for finding their articles so excellently
written that a good deal of my paraphrasing simply degenerates
into quoting them verbatim. The company in which the first
study was made is a marketing-oriented corporation that has long
recognized the importance to its business of people with "idea
ability." Over the years, in its continuing quest for techniques

that might help to identify creative marketing talent, the company has made numerous studies of the subject, tried all sorts of tests, and consulted many psychologists. Some time ago it occurred to one of the company's executives that the possibilities of graphology as a selection tool were at least worth exploring. He accordingly submitted some samples of the handwriting of a small group of marketing trainees to a graphologist for analysis. When compared with management evaluations of the same trainees, the graphologist's ratings showed sufficient accuracy to warrant a further pilot study. The subjects selected for the study were a group of company executives. Samples of their handwriting at the time that they had been hired—anywhere from fifteen to twenty-five years before—were taken from their personnel jackets. This time, the graphologist's evaluations were cast in the form of predictions—that is to say, the executives were rated on their potential to rise to responsible management positions in this marketing-oriented company. These "time of hiring" ratings forecast the actual progress of the men quite successfully. In fact, said the executive who initiated the study, "the results astounded me because of their high degree of accuracy." Encouraged by the results of the pilot studies, management decided to carry out a larger, more systematic investigation.

The subjects of this final study were 37 executives at various levels in the organization. Their service with the company ranged from two years to over thirty, the average being close to fifteen years. These managers were rated by several senior managers who had many years of service with the company. Each assessor passed on only those managers whom he felt he "knew well enough to rate." The ratings encompassed five factors, of which the first four had long been used by the company for rating purposes and which had been carefully defined some years before. These were (1) "idea ability"; (2) executive ability; (3) ability to express oneself; and (4) achievement. The fifth factor on which the subjects were rated was their "overall value" to the company.

From the personnel jacket of each subject the company selected, wherever available, two samples of his handwriting—the first from material written by him at the time he was hired and the second written within the six months before the study began. The samples were coded by a company executive and transmitted to the graphologist in such a way as to insure that he did not have both writing samples from any one subject at the same time. The graphologist's evaluations were dictated on tape and returned to the company along with the samples; as these were received, additional samples were sent to him. The only information given to the graphologist was the subject's sex, his or her age at the time the sample was written, and whether the writing was done with the right or left hand. From his analysis of the handwriting alone, the graphologist submitted a brief verbal evaluation of each writer and a rating on the five factors, using the same descriptions and rating scale as the company assessors.

How did the ratings of the graphologist compare with those of the senior managers? For the sake of brevity, we will use only the fifth factor on which the subjects were rated—their "overall value" to the company. As the table shows, 17 of the 37 subjects were rated by the company *now* as "superior" or "very superior." The graphologist ranked 14 of these 17 people, or 82 percent, in the same category from handwriting *dating to the time of hiring* (on the average, some fifteen years earlier). At the other end of the spectrum, three of the subjects were now rated by the

AVERAGE COMPANY RATINGS NOW	GRAPHOLOGIST'S "TIME OF HIRE" RATINGS			
	Very Superior-Superior	Pros and Cons In Balance-Adequate	Inadequate-Inferior	Total
Very Superior-Superior	14	1	2	17
Pros and Cons In Balance-Adequate	7	4	6	17
Inadequate-Inferior	1	0	2	3
Total	22	5	10	37

Rating chart *

* Reprinted by permission of the publisher from *Personnel*, Nov.-Dec. 1962, © 1962 by the American Management Association, Inc.

company judges as "inadequate" or "inferior." Two of these three were likewise identified by the graphologist as falling into the same category at the time of hiring. In the middle category the agreement was admittedly rather less striking at first glance. But several of those men whom the graphologist considered "superior" and the company rated only "adequate" at the time of hiring had risen to divisional vice-presidents or better. And of all the others the graphologist had rated "superior" only one had failed to rise to, or hold, a senior executive position.

Here then, Sonnemann and Kernan tell us, we have a study in which independent graphological evaluations of two handwriting samples written many years apart were found to be highly consistent and certainly as reliable as the scores obtained in many tests usually deemed more scientific; and, even more important, these "blind" evaluations proved to be significantly related to actual performance and success on the job. The authors go on to point out some advantages of graphology as a research instrument over other psychological techniques. It makes it possible, they say, to carry out at any moment in time a predictive study after the fact, or that "ideal" validation study so many psychologists would like to be able to do. There is no need to wait for years, even decades, to see whether a prediction comes true or to validate the test results against later performance on the job. Further, every company has an ample supply of the raw material of graphological research—the handwriting of employees whose performance over the years is a matter of record. Samples of their handwriting at the time of hiring or at any other desired point in time can be analyzed and the analysis compared with present ratings. Thus, any number of years can be telescoped, and longitudinal studies can be carried out without prolonged lapses of time. Finally, graphology offers the advantage of being administratively simple and requiring no extensive facilities or testing time. Nor does it offer the threat or sense of being imposed on, which many experienced and highly qualified applicants feel at taking a battery of tests.

The second study to which I referred is written by George A. Mapp and entitled "A Multivariate Analysis of the Relationship between Handwriting and Sales Ability." The study is over a hundred pages long, and after spending two or three days trying to figure out how to summarize it, I decided that the best plan was to take a series of excerpts out of it with a minimum of paraphrasing. The various themes of this involved thesis keep repeating themselves, as in a musical composition, and it finally seemed easier to cut the knots than attempt to disentangle them.

The problems of identifying the attributes of a successful salesman, says Mapp, and the best methods for selecting salesmen are important concerns of industrial psychology. When sales managers are asked about the necessary attributes of a successful salesman the usual replies include, among other things, aggressiveness, high drive and energy level, responsibility, and an extroverted personality. Traditional techniques—psychological tests, biographical inventories and interviews—probe for these attributes with varying success. Let us examine two reports of the application of handwriting analysis to this endeavor.

The purpose of such an investigation is to establish whether any relationship exists between sales ability and handwriting. It is assumed that sales ability is distributed at random within a community in the same way as other capacities and is to be isolated by contrasting the successful salesmen who make up the experimental group with people of otherwise similar backgrounds and characteristics who make up a control group.

The basic hypothesis is that the handwriting of the experimental group will differ markedly in a number of respects from that of the control group.

The secondary hypothesis is that there will be a significant number of correlations between the presence of sales ability and the appearance of certain characteristics in handwriting.

The population used in this study consisted of 170 salesmen who, being considered "promotable," were allowed to attend a company-sponsored "personal development" program.

Over a period of approximately three years, the salesmen attended the personal development program, an intensive five-day session consisting of presentations, "in-basket games," leaderless group discussions, prepared talks, problem-solving, reading and writing exercises, psychological testing, and group exercises. During the program the salesmen were rated, by four corporate executives as well as by the program manager, on their potential promotability within the company. This potential is expressed on a five-point scale.

There were not adequate handwriting samples available for over half of the 170 attending salesmen, and many others printed instead of writing with a cursive style. As a result there were

From the salesmen group *

---

* Reprinted by permission of George A. Mapp.

only 57 adequate handwriting samples available. From these 57, 50 were selected as representing "successful salesmen" and constituted the experimental group in the present investigation. They were all American males; all had attended college, although four had not graduated; and two had advanced degrees. The mean age of the group was 30.

[handwritten sample]

From the salesmen group *

* Reprinted by permission of George A. Mapp.

Dear Sir,

My name is Ronald Teeter, a senior at the University of Dayton majoring in computer science. As part of a computer ~~science course~~ "operations research II" requirement, I am preparing a paper (some 40-50 pages in length) titled "The feasibility of the applications of a real time management information system to the personnel function". Of particular interest to me is ① system configuration - design, analysis, ② data gathering and storing techniques - the concept of a data bank?, ③ terminal connection and design, ④ cost analysis. In my readings I have had a difficult ~~time finding~~ detailed information, especially in the areas mentioned above. Could you assist me with any pertinent information? Any detailed information would be much appreciated.

From the control or nonsalesmen group *

In the control group were 50 American men. All had attended or were attending college—23 being graduate or undergraduate students at Baruch College—and four had doctoral degrees. The age of each subject in this group was not recorded. However, going by the ages of 41 of the subjects, the mean age of the control group was estimated at 28.

While attending the self-development program, the 50 "successful salesmen" were asked to write their self-development needs on a sheet of plain unlined 8½″ x 11″ bond paper. The setting was relaxed and informal and they were under no pressure to write. Thus we may assume that they wrote in their "natural" handwriting style.

* Reprinted by permission of George A. Mapp.

Twenty-three of the nonsalesmen were asked to fill out a mock questionnaire on a plain sheet of 8″ x 11″ bond paper. It is also assumed that they wrote in their natural writing style.

The other 27 "nonsales" samples were taken from handwritten messages and letters from associates who were of the same background as well as handwritten critiques of several businessmen who attended several management seminars. "Other pertinent

From the control or nonsalesmen group *

* Reprinted by permission of George A. Mapp.

biographical information was also available on most of the businessmen."

Using the 14 handwriting variables outlined in this report, the samples were independently scored by Mr. Mapp and by two students at Hunter College. The ratings were coded and subsequently key-punched at the City University of New York Graduate Center.

The primary hypothesis assumed that there would be a significant difference between the average of the scores of the successful salesmen as compared to that of the control group. This proved to be the case in the experiment; there was a less than one-in-a-thousand probability that such a correlation could have been obtained by pure chance. The secondary hypothesis stated that there should be a significant number of correlations between sales ability and certain handwriting characteristics. This was tested by "using a multiple correlation model computed by employing the Gauss–Jordan solution of normal equations, with an F-ratio for testing the significance of the coefficient of determination, R^2, of the regression," and was confirmed at the same high level of probability.

That both hypotheses tested out so strikingly strongly suggests that the average handwriting sample of a group of successful salesmen is different from the average handwriting sample of a group of nonsalesmen.

Mapp had drawn up the following hypothetical model of sales ability over a year before the data were analyzed and over six months before the 14 handwriting criteria had been formally decided upon (I have considerably abbreviated it):

> In developing a hypothetical model of sales ability as expressed in handwriting, the assumption will be made that aggressiveness, persistence, extroversion, ambition, emotional control, and stability are among the traits believed to be found in most successful salesmen.
>
> This hypothetical model will consist of handwriting variables which previous research suggests are reflective of the above-mentioned traits. For instance, aggressiveness is believed

to reflect itself in the degree of connection of the letters, degree of utilization of primary beginning strokes, and the size of letters. Persistence will be reflected negatively by the amount of fluctuation in the angle of slant and positively by lack of "i" dot deviation. Extroversion will be manifested in writing with a rightward tendency and reflected negatively by the number of loops used in the writing sample.

The results of this study are remarkably in agreement with the hypothetical model, says Mr. Mapp. For instance, the salesmen did show a higher degree of connection, variable 12; greater use of primary beginning strokes, variable 13; a larger letter size, variables 3, 5, and 6; a smaller fluctuation of slant, variable 10; a lower "i" dot deviation, variable 7; and more rightward tendency, variable 9. The predictions that did not hold true were a lower loop count, variable 1, and the breadth factor composed of distance between words, variable 11, and width of letters, variable 8.

I am surprised by Mr. Mapp's prediction that the more lower loops the less extroverted the character; if he had assumed, as graphologists generally do, that *lower* loops at least are signs of materialism and probably thus of a good salesman, he would have had one more correct prediction. That he finds a correlation between primary beginning strokes and aggressiveness is most interesting to me, since the terms "primary" and "secondary" beginning strokes are my invention and the study of the subject quoted by Mr. Mapp is by Larry Epstein and myself. It purports to identify beginning strokes in general with immaturity, and if we think of all the nonsense that the good salesman has to devote himself to with childlike enthusiasm, we might well consider a bit of immaturity essential to his functioning sanely.

The basic premise of the scientific study of graphology, concludes Mapp, is that writing is a form of expressive behavior. We are all taught standard school-copy scripts in elementary school, yet we all deviate from these forms in later life. The individuality in handwriting is believed to be an expression of the writer's personality.

Early research on the use of graphology as a psychodiagnostic technique suggested that the method was worthy of further consideration. But there has been little experimental research on the uses of graphology in personnel selection.

We may greatly regret that though many executives are increasingly interested in graphology, business as a whole has overlooked the insights of Sonnemann and Mapp, in the face of empirical evidence which shows them to be at least as accurate as the present folk arts of personnel management.

EXAMPLES

Biographies

Ingrid Bergman
Sarah Churchill
Salvador Dali
Bette Davis
Sammy Davis, Jr.
Joe Di Maggio
Ariel and Will Durant
Douglas Fairbanks, Jr.
Glen A. Fowler
Zsa Zsa Gabor
J. P. Getty
Barry Goldwater
Rex Harrison
Hugh Hefner
Alain Malraux

Archduchess Marta (Hapsburg-Bourbon)
William Masselos
Merle Oberon
Floyd B. Odlum
Wally Schirra and Jacqueline Susann
Dick Smothers
Tom Smothers
Leopold Stokowski
Edward Durell Stone
Terry-Thomas
Tiny Tim
Valentina
Jack Warner

I am walking down the street to get the horse and carriage out of the old garage

Ingrid Bergman

Ingrid Bergman

A great deal of pride (the inflated capital "I"), a temper (the misplaced capital "S" in street), and a critical disposition (the numerous figure-9 "g"s). Otherwise, a highly creative writing, with an unexpectedly conventional streak seen in the copybook "t" bars.

I am walking down the street to get the horse and carriage out of the old garage —

Sarah Churchill.

Sarah Churchill

Churchill re-created in his daughter, with all the resulting frustrations. (To one who knows her, the likeness of personality can be uncanny.) With the heavy, almost muddy pressure, the anti-social misplaced capital "S" in "street," the impatient "t"s and slightly descending basic line, the poetess and actress with Greek "d"s and figure-8 "g"s is almost crushed. I was amazed the first time I saw the same misplaced capitals in Churchill's small and intellectual script. But I would have been more amazed if I had not found some evidence of rebellion—and might have given up graphology!

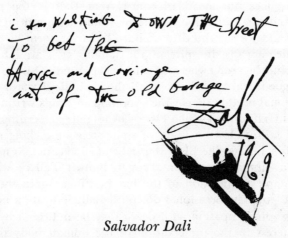

Salvador Dali

In analyzing handwriting, it is always helpful to know something about the writer and to be able to correlate one with the other. With some of the celebrities whose handwriting I have obtained, my acquaintance is mostly hearsay; in the case of Dali it is firsthand. I have constantly heard all the wild stories, of course, about his eccentricities, and some of them I have observed. But to me, Dali has always been primarily a charming, considerate person, and a good friend, and I have known him too long to believe, as I once did, that the polite, responsible side of his nature he shows me is mostly for effect. The dynamic rhythm of his writing, the lack of unnecessary beginning strokes, and the persistent "t" bars betray the hard worker, the businessman, and in fact the good salesman whose worldly characteristics are usually blamed on Gala, his wife. Nothing could be better evidence of this responsible side of Dali's nature than the manner in which he slaves away every summer in his house at Port Lligat (without guest rooms, as I learned to my regret last year when I slept on the floor in his studio). Nor the fact that it was only the strikers on the New York docks, not Dali, who prevented my receiving the great *Discovery of America by Columbus* (which I commissioned him to do) on time, in spite of the size and complexity of the subject.

All this does not mean, of course, that Dali is 100 percent normal, and if it did I don't think he would let me print it! On the one hand we see the tiny capital "I" in the form of a small letter which means, in spite of the famous ego, an inferiority complex lurking somewhere in the background. On the other, we see a good deal of violence in all the capitalized words and in the occasional muddy spots which you find in Dali's writing. The stories of his childhood which Fleur Cowles tells concerning his deliberately falling down a flight of stone steps or nicking himself with a razor because he liked the sight of blood (not to mention the famous jump, years later, through Bonwit Teller's window) provide ample verification of the handwriting. Again the small capital "I" and the occasional downhill slant indicate a negative side whose preoccupation with death may be indicated by Dali's recent interest in the preservation of the human body through freezing. And finally, one could not analyze Dali's writing without observing one of the most infallible signs of the highly creative person, the Greek "d." It is shown only once, and there partially, in this specimen (in the case of the first letter of the word "down"), but it is prevalent throughout Dali's writing. Whether he makes the figure-8 "g" which usually accompanies the "d" I am not sure, but to the extent that he does not there is perhaps a partial explanation of why Dali so often strives for the sensational and the exotic rather than being satisfied with the philosophy that the most sensitive is often the simplest.

I am walking down the street to get the horse and — carriage! (out of the old garage — B D

Bette Davis

It is probably safe to say that Bette Davis was the most famous movie actress in the world during the Thirties. Winning an Academy Award and crowning her great performances at Warner Bros. with that of the Southern belle in *Jezebel,* she was on everyone's tongue as a candidate for the part of Scarlett O'Hara in *Gone with the Wind.* When she failed to get it she did get the great part of the dying girl in *Dark Victory,* and it was only because she was competing with Vivien Leigh as Scarlett that she did not get a third Oscar.

Did all this success have a happy ending? Bette Davis wrote an autobiography and it is interesting to observe that the title is *The Lonely Life.* After reading it I am not quite sure whether she meant her own life, an actress', or anyone's! In any case she meant, I am sure, that material success often brings spiritual malaise, as she indicated at the conclusion of her book when she calls her three marriages "a farce" and sees no lasting reward in human relations. What she believes in finally is hard work, and perhaps the battle which always accompanies it is the real key to her character. In her handwriting it is shown by the large and stubborn capital "I," the slightly backhand slant (like a fisherman, if you will excuse the unfeminine analogy, standing firm while he tries to haul in a big catch), the unusually long and ambitious "t" bars, the meticulous small "e"s made like capitals. Bette Davis always had to support a family—a mother whom she adored, and later, various husbands—and success in the theater did not come easily. Turned down by Eva Le Gallienne in New York for not being "serious" about acting, laughed at in one of her first classes for her high, thin voice and her Boston accent, when she finally went to Hollywood with a contract she was considered an ugly duckling until a great stage actor, George Arliss, decided to accept her for one of his pictures. She then rose quickly to the top, but even at the height of her career she was not free from having to struggle, as her famous bout with Warner Bros. testified. Attempting to break her seven-year contract and make two pictures in Europe, she was sent back from England by the courts with the admonition from the opposing lawyer to the judge, "I think, m'lud, this is the action of a very naughty young lady."

One of the lustiest battles that Bette Davis ever had was one which few people ever knew about—on the set of *Elizabeth and Essex* with Errol Flynn, her co-star. I am sure that Miss Davis was the victim of very mixed feelings regarding Flynn. She found him on the one hand "utterly enchanting," as she admitted in her book, but on the other hand rather bitterly termed him "the stud of the Warner stables" (which was of course an understatement) and was perhaps unhappy, to hear Flynn's side of it, because this brash young newcomer was already making more money than she. He did not improve the situation by likening the relationship of Davis and Flynn to that of the Queen and Essex, since the thirty-year-old Bette Davis was depicting a sixty-year-old Elizabeth. Finally, Laurence Olivier, who had always been an idol of Miss Davis's, was in Hollywood at the time the picture was about to be made, but in spite of her efforts to have him cast opposite her she only succeeded in dreaming about him every night in the part. (Getting back to handwriting, the figure-8 "g"s and the wide-spaced letters betray a romantic side which was quite contradictory to the image presented to Flynn.)

Errol tells the story of the battle at length in his own auto-biography, *My Wicked, Wicked Ways* (in which, incidentally, he characterizes me as one with whom he "never fell out over the sight of a figure 35-23-34, or some other even more vital statistic"). Suffice it to say that when Bette Davis as Elizabeth struck him violently across the ear in rehearsal, her hand heavy with Tudor rings, he felt he had been hit by a railroad locomotive and was so dazed and flabbergasted that he went back to his dressing room and threw up. When he went to her in private and she refused twice to consider another way of acting the part, Errol made his decision. Scandal or not, if she did it again he would, in his words, "whack her and drop her . . . and I might break her jaw." (He did not have that revealing sign of the anti-social, misplaced capitals, scattered through an otherwise cultured handwriting, for nothing.) Whether or not she could see the anger in his eyes when the actual scene was played, I do not know—"just give it to me, Bette, and you will be as flat as a sardine in a can," as he put it in his book. In any case, discretion was finally the better part of valor, and Women's Lib lost out; she missed his face totally with technical perfection. And Flynn? He went back to his dressing room and threw up for a third time.

Sammy Davis, Jr.

As you can plainly see, Sammy Davis neither wrote exactly what I requested nor in fact wrote at all. He printed. Herein lies a tale. In the summer of 1969 he was performing at a night club in London and he asked me to sit at a table with his friends and come back to a lounge adjoining his dressing room after the show. The small lounge was crowded with friends and so stifling —the English, like the French, are still unfamiliar with air-conditioning—that my friends and I were on the verge of de-

I'M

WALKING DOWN THE
STREET, GOING TO THE
GARAGE TO GET MY
CARRIAGE

parting when Sammy appeared. He was gracious as always; he still remembers the time when he called me from Hollywood to ask for Saturday night off from his performance at the Huntington Hartford Theatre in Hollywood—to get married!—and I of course agreed. But when I brought up the subject of handwriting he got very uptight, as the phrase is, and protested with something approaching panic that he had not done any writing for years. I told him that didn't make any difference. He then said that if I would speak to him about it in two or three years he would have had a chance to practice a bit, and the handwriting would look a lot better. I explained that writing which he had practiced to look a certain way would be intolerably dull and that purely spontaneous writing was the most interesting. Finally he reluctantly disappeared into the dressing room with a friend, closed the door, and was gone for ages. When he eventually reappeared he presented me with the specimen shown here.

I think that he and his friend had gotten into some kind of a huddle about how to handle the dilemma, and I guess they decided that the safest way out was to print.

But of course there is a great deal of Sammy Davis revealed in this specimen in spite of the printing. The simple capital "I" means instinctive good taste; the absence of unnecessary strokes, maturity; the forward-leaning slant, emotion and a relating to others; the strong, high "t" bars, determination and imagination, respectively; the very high third stroke of the first "m," an innate stubbornness (diplomats do it the opposite way, with the letters trailing off at the end of the word); and finally, ambition shown in the upward slant of the "t"s and particularly in the rising stroke at the end of the word "down."

The signature is wild, but signatures often are, for as the capital "I" is the innermost part of the personality, the signature is the outmost, the side of the personality which extroverts in particular wish to exhibit. The extravagant loop of the capital "D" shows exhibitionism and persistence. The ties or knots in the capital "S" and in the following "a" and the loop of the "y" again indicate persistence, and the unusually high points of the capital "S" and the small "s" at the end of the name indicate a vaulting ambition which rarely takes "no" for an answer. Sammy, please let me see the rest of your writing one of these days. It ain't fair to tease us like that. How many years do we have to wait?

Joe Di Maggio

Highly physical writing—with the long "t" bars and lower loops—which might well be the writing of an outstanding enter-

tainer. Look at the ego in that capital "I" and that ambitious
upstroke at the end of the word "down."

*I am walking down the street
to get the horse + carriage
out of the old garage.*

Ariel Durant

*I am walking down the street —
& get the horse & carriage out
of the old garage.*

Will Durant

Ariel and Will Durant

I was so lucky to be able to get the writing of these great
people (and good friends of mine). In both cases, the complete
scholar—with the small writing, the figure-8 "g"s, and, in the
case of Will, the intuitive broken letters. The practical side which
has insured worldly success is seen in the occasional lower loops
of Ariel and the stubborn, persistent "t"s of Will.

*I am walking down the street to get
the horse and carriage out of the old
garage.*

Douglas Fairbanks, Jr.

I ought to know Doug Fairbanks, Jr. better than I do, because
our paths have crossed many times since we both cringed before
the iron-willed Miss Bovee at her school on Fifth Avenue a few
hundred years ago. One time we will not forget was before
World War II, when he met my wife Mary Lee at Merle Oberon's house in Santa Monica (in the company of the beautiful
Norma Shearer, who recently reminded me) and married her a
year later, two weeks after our divorce. Perhaps one reason that
I do not feel that I know Doug as well as I ought is that in a
sense he is a little like myself, a jack-of-all-trades who does not
fall easily into a conventional category. *Unlike* myself (who was
plodding along in a Coast Guard cargo ship), he was a hero
during the war and was decorated for his bravery in an early
raid on Normandy. He started off as a movie star, of course, inspired by his world-famous father, but in later years has turned
to business interests, most recently threatening to give our Para-
dise Island competition with a new resort down in the Bahamas.

If I were asked about Doug's handwriting without knowing to
whom it belonged, I might well say that with the simplicity and
elimination shown, the sensitivity of the figure-8 "g"'s, the small
size, it might well belong to a writer. As a matter of fact, writing
has always been a great interest of Doug's, as I remember from

our school days, and perhaps his career might have turned out otherwise (as John Barrymore's might with his interest in art) except for the famous name. Doug *had* to start off as an actor, and the flamboyant signature may indicate rather his efforts to fit the role than innate desire and ambition. The fact is, however, that we cannot be too dogmatic about what an actor's writing should look like. The extreme loops and flourishes which we find in the writing of an entertainer like Bob Hope, however great, are usually equated with the writing of actors and actresses. But the fact is that the more highly creative a performer is, the closer he approaches the simple writing of the artist in any profession—and believe me, I'm not trying to downgrade Bob Hope; I just wish I had his money!

Doug has indeed had a few great roles in motion pictures. But not enough, in my opinion, for the talent shown in his writing. Perhaps for him, like myself, life has been too easy. I am sure Mary Lee, to whom I was married for eight years and to whom he has been married over a quarter of a century, has helped to make it that way. She has been a wonderful wife, and certainly it has been partially through her efforts that they have been the favorites of everyone from royalty on down in England, where they have spent so much time. But then, Doug has been a good husband and father, too. That's pretty creative in itself.

"I'm walking down the street to get the horse and carriage out of the garage."

Glen A. Fowler

Glen A. Fowler

Written entirely by a man without arms holding the pen between the teeth, this highly mature script is proof positive that handwriting is primarily a product of the brain rather than of the muscles.

I am walking down the street to get the horse and carriage out of the old garage — *Zsa Zsa*

Zsa Zsa Gabor

Like everyone else in the United States, I always felt that I knew Zsa Zsa Gabor like a long-lost sister, though in fact I first got to know her when we shared an appearance on TV a few years ago and her serene presence comforted me greatly in my usual hour of stage fright. How has this Hungarian immigrant —and a female at that—become one of the greatest celebrities in our country, where celebrity is more earnestly pursued than anywhere else in the world? And without really doing anything that most people can remember except marrying the owner of the Hilton hotels and having a beautiful daughter by him and possessing a sister, Eva, and a mother, Jolie, who somehow always seem to share the spotlight with her?

Let us look at the writing. Though not mercenary, for we search in vain for the long lower loops of materialism, it is a supreme example of the worldly and the practical, with a strong emphasis on showmanship. Zsa Zsa, of whom I have seen quite a lot lately, likes to think of herself as the reticent idealist and talks, like Scarlett O'Hara, of retreating to a plantation in the Deep South. She emphasizes her point by mildly lamenting the fact that her vivacious mother fails to appreciate fully the potentials of a dignified old age as the grand dame of the Gabor dynasty and often prefers the night life of New York and Hollywood. But when we look at that heavy pressure, the dominating size of the capital "I," the height of all the upper loops (mean-

ing, as I have said, not spirituality, as graphologists have assumed since the early days of European graphology, but ambition
and a desire for power), and the vertical slant of the writing, it
is the woman of the world which emerges. It is the woman who
is always at her best when she has to think on her feet with
lightning rapidity, who is at her wittiest in front of TV cameras,
who has Johnny Carson and Merv Griffin sending flowers to the
Waldorf on the same day in competition for her appearances,
who knows just about everyone in the public eye from the President down.

But what has made Zsa Zsa so famous, in my opinion, is the
fact that, no matter how often she "walks with kings," she never
loses the common touch—or her sense of humor. In spite of the
reticence of the slightly backhand writing, it would be difficult
to write the long stroke at the end of the word "carriage" as she
does without a real love of people—and, in Zsa Zsa's case, of
animals! When I asked why she wrote such a large "c"—almost
a capital—in the word "carriage," she replied that she had always
wanted to live in the days of horses and carriages, and I am not
quite sure whether it was the elegant carriages or the horses with
which she was more impressed. The other day she was telling
me that her mother was most annoyed at her for all the "veteran"
bills she accumulated for taking care of her dogs and claimed
that for the money she spent on them she could have bought a
house!

The sense of humor—graphologists like to relate it to the way
small "i"s are dotted, but I will stick with the figure-8 "g," the
great symbol of *sense*—is world-famous; it is usually at its best
when Zsa Zsa gets a bit riled up or disturbed. When she was
robbed at gunpoint in the Waldorf elevator of her half-million-
dollar diamond and had to replace it with a magnificent copy
produced in a factory, she exclaimed (before threatening to sue
her ex-husband, Mr. Hilton, as some people suggested), "Oh,
it's all right. I love anything man-made!" When we were sitting
in Sardi's the other day and a young girl at the table, apparently
trying to flatter Zsa Zsa, commented that she reminded her of
her mother, Zsa Zsa flew into a rage for twenty minutes and

later as we were all about to leave turned to me with a stage whisper and said, "I hate that girl, I never want to see her again. Thank God I can't remember her name!"

Some time ago I met a young international traveler with a rather lurid reputation, and it turned out that when I mentioned him to Zsa Zsa she already knew him and was most reluctant to have anything to do with him. Though he was handsome and smooth, he was an adventurer that I should beware of. She then proceeded to explain how he had maneuvered himself into sitting next to her on a plane and spent hours trying to get into her good graces—to little avail, for as she was leaving the plane she bade him a fond goodbye but refused to give her address or phone number. Whereupon he took the gold crucifix from around his neck and handed it to her as a parting token. "I was terribly angry at his giving it to me," said Zsa Zsa, "but I am a good Catholic and I had to take it. Don't ever have anything to do with him; he's a very dangerous man." She paused for a moment, and then added, "I might have liked him, but he came on much too strong."

J. P. Getty

A suggestion of ill health. The ideal writing for a great businessman still comes through. The dynamic rhythm, the emotionally

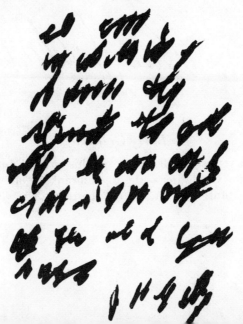

forward slant, the spacing, the broken letters signify the creator, while the fierce angularity (with the third stroke of that first "m" stubbornly uppermost), and the persistent and ambitious "t" bars show the aggressive nature which rarely takes no for an answer!

Barry Goldwater

I have not yet asked Mr. Nixon for his writing, but now that I have Senator Goldwater's—the highest-ranking one so far!—I am starting to think about it. To tell the truth, I was a little afraid to bother Senator Goldwater, whom I had never met, when I saw him having dinner at the Twenty-One Club in London. My publisher had requested that I send out letters asking for celebrities' writing, but I was aware of what happened to such "form" letters when they reached me, and I had decided that the best approach was the frontal attack. (So far the only person who has turned me down is Sol Hurok.) After introducing myself to Senator Goldwater (whom I don't believe knew my name but was perfectly friendly), to his wife, who didn't seem too happy with me, and to some Army man who was sitting with them, I sat down at the table, which consisted of ten or twelve people. The Army man, who I think associated me with the A & P, kept up a running barrage of conversation in trying to prevent me from talking to the Senator, but to no avail. The latter was most courteous—a bit more in writing the silly sentence I had asked for than I had been in requesting it.

Goldwater's image at the time he ran for President against Johnson, of course, was extremely right-wing and conservative, and this fact is somewhat borne out by the highness and narrowness of the small letters. On the other hand, President Kennedy had frequently said that although he disagreed with the Senator politically he was a good friend personally, and it is not hard to see why from the writing. With the sensitive figure-8 "g"s, the lack of beginning strokes, and the absence of long materialistic lower loops (which may be reflected in occasional lapses of diplomacy), it is certainly the writing of a creative person. At the same time it is also true that if there are no long lower loops, there are certainly some high upper ones, which is of course a sign of an ambitious nature desirous of dominating. Here again, though, the aggressiveness is blunted by the rather conventional "t" bars placed very low on the "t"s, by a slight drooping off of the basic line, and by the pressure on vertical, downward strokes rather than horizontal ones.

The total picture is one of a complex nature whose inner battles are not entirely resolved.

I'm walking down the street, to get the horse & carriage — out of the old garage

Rex Harrison

With the backhand writing and impatient "t" bars, more of an introvert than we would expect. Only the large capitals and the occasional long lower loops betray the actor. He might have been a writer.

Hugh Hefner

My acquaintance with Hugh Hefner began around the time he merged his ill-fated entertainment magazine, *Show Business Illustrated,* with the original version of my magazine *Show* in 1962. I was not particularly conscious of any intense reactions to Hef at that time except pure jealousy, of course, at his success

I'm walking down the street to get the horse + carriage out of the old garage.   Hugh M Hefner

with *Playboy*. Gradually, as I got to know him and to read about the "wild parties" around and about the indoor swimming pool at the Playboy Mansion in Chicago, an image began to form in my mind of Hefner as a diabolical *metteur en scène* who slept all day—as indeed he often does—and appeared only in the black of night as a grinning satyr with horns instead of Bunny ears. This image was reinforced by rumors that Hefner was somewhat of a hermit, and the fact that I could never get him on the phone—if at all!—before six in the afternoon.

However, after two or three visits to the Playboy Mansion I began to become terribly disillusioned. The girls that one saw around seemed to be only window dressing for VIPs, and they reminded me of flocks of geese which disappeared at the slightest movement in their direction. Hefner in particular had eyes only for his fiancée. If you sat down and talked with him in the great paneled living room, of course, as I did recently, he talked very big. He was an atheist; he believed in free love and legalized marijuana. All this had overtones of the party line of *Playboy* magazine. But when you pinned Hef down you got a different story. It wasn't that he didn't want to introduce you to some particular Bunny, he didn't even remember her name. He may be an atheist in theory, but in practice he goes to church regularly. And in regard to pot, grass, a joint, or what have you, an acquaintance of mine got a jolt when he told Hefner how outraged some friends of his had been at being thrown out of the New York Playboy Club for indulging. "Why, naturally, what else do you expect?" exclaimed Hefner. "Self-preservation!" The real Hefner, ladies and gentlemen (even if I blow the entire Playboy image in telling you), is a square!

A square, perhaps, but by no means a patsy. The conventional "g"s and the slightly immature rhythm do not reveal, perhaps, a highly creative personality, but one searches in vain for any real weakness in the writing. The concentration of the small writing and the lack of waste motion are balanced by the ambitious lower and upper loops and the strong "t" bars, and in seeing Hefner's writing I am reminded of a character from Conrad's *Heart of Darkness,* the ivory trader Kurtz, the power of whose black magic out there in the jungle was the fact that he had a genius for the commonplace and the unexpected in an arena where the theorist and the specialist could never have survived. If such is the talent of Hefner, it is also that, I suppose, of 50 percent of American business—but on the other hand, who but Hefner can claim to have built an entire empire out of forty-two-inch bosoms and bunny tails?

I am walking down the streets to get the horse and carriage out of the old garage

Alain Malraux

Alain Malraux

Gentle, sensitive, creative but unworldly. It is not surprising that the son of André Malraux's brother by the lady who was married to both brothers should be embarking on a musical career. (And note the broken letters.)

I am walking down the street to get the and house and carriage out of the old garage

Archduchess Marta Hapsburgo Bourbon

Archduchess Marta (Hapsburg-Bourbon)

The Rock of Gibraltar—and a pillar of "society." Domineering, highly opinionated, but never dull if those long high "t" bars and outgoing strokes mean anything—and they do!

I am walking down the street to get the horse and carriage out of the old garage.

William Masselos.

William Masselos

Numerous signs of the great artist, including the fast and brilliant rhythm, the Greek "d"s and the figure-8 "g"s. The heavy pressure betrays the physical nature of the art—and the marathon concerts!

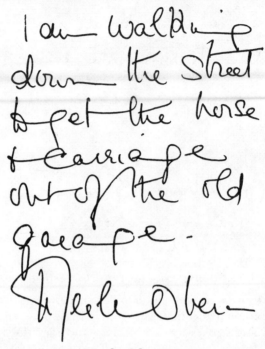

Merle Oberon

Combination of the business-oriented (the vertical slant, the upward "t" bars, and the stubborn capital "M" in Merle) with taste and warmth, shown by the simple capital "I," the figure-8 "g"'s and the outgoing strokes.

Floyd B. Odlum

Parkinson's disease, but the absolutely brilliant rhythm (reminiscent of Shaw's) cannot be suppressed.

I was walking down the street to get my car out of the old garage.

Wally Schirra

Im walking down the street To get the horse and Carriage out of the old garage —

Jacqueline Susann

Wally Schirra
and
Jacqueline Susann

The astronaut and the writer have similar scripts. The astronaut's is more physical and more persistent, with the heavier pressure and knotted "t" bars, and the writer's is more impatient ("t"s) and more interested in the window dressing of minor detail (the Greek "e"s). The astronaut is more stubborn and the writer more critical. But both have simple, philosophical capital "I"s, a slightly withdrawn left-hand slant, and show little evidence of diplomacy in the short strokes of the lower zone.

Dick Smothers

Of the two Smothers brothers, Dick is the racing-car driver and
yet probably the more sensitive of the two. There is plenty of
violence in all the lassoed "t" bars and the inflated upper loops,
and yet a gentle and creative bent in the many figure-8 "g"s.

Tom Smothers

The first time Tom Smothers met me he plunged right in and
asked me if I wasn't the fellow with the bad reputation. The
domineering "t" bars, the critical figure-9 "g"s, and the high
upper loops show little patience, as the TV networks found out.

[handwritten text] I am walking down the street to interview the horse & carriage in the old garage —

[handwritten signature]

Leopold Stokowski

As in the case of Masselos, the writing of a great artist is here exhibited by the rhythm, the Greek "d"s, and the figure-8 "g"s. The stability yet near-violence characteristic of many conductors (remember Toscanini?) is seen in the vertical writing with those huge capitals of "carriage" and "garage."

Edward Durell Stone

If I were looking for a specimen of handwriting with clear-cut characteristics easy to analyze, it would be hard to find a better example than that of Edward Durell Stone, the architect of the Kennedy Center in Washington, the General Motors Building in New York, and a host of other famous buildings throughout

[handwritten text] I am walking down the street to get the horse and carriage out of the old garage.

Edward D. Stone

the world. Since Ed was the architect of my museum on Columbus Circle, now turned over to Fairleigh Dickinson University, I have known him for many years; such long acquaintance is also of great help to the graphologist, in spite of the fact that writing is frequently analyzed by professionals without knowing the writers. In general I would say that Ed's writing is an equitable mixture of the idealistic on the one hand and the materialistic and physical on the other. Idealism is indicated by the single figure-8 "g"—which I will discuss later—the wide, generous spacing between letters, the outgoing stroke at the end of the signature. The practical or materialistic signs are the vertical slope, the large lower loops, the heavy pressure of the pen (indicated by Ed's automatic choice of a "magic marker"), the strong "t" bars, and finally that tie-in, as shown in the signature, between the "t" bar and the capital "S," which some graphologists might consider a subconscious dollar sign! Upon my visiting Ed recently at his new office after a hiatus of several years, one of his first comments to me was not about the architectural drawings of Adolf Hitler which we were showing in our museum but whether I got rid of the entire burden of the mortgage when I turned the building over to Fairleigh Dickinson. And when I asked him to write the sentence exhibited here, he remarked to his beautiful English secretary, "Oh, I've seen Hunt's handwriting before—on checks!" In fairness to Ed, however, he has always been sincerely concerned with my financial welfare, which sometimes needs it.

For all his worldly success, however, Ed Stone has never been the typical pillar of the Establishment like his fellow architect Luckman, who was willing to replace that masterpiece of his predecessor, Stanford White, the Pennsylvania Station, with a purely commercial structure. Ed has always preferred arches and textures and fountains to the cold abstractions of much contemporary architecture—take, for instance, the charming sidewalk café which he and I and Bob Moses tried so hard to give to the New York public at the south-east corner of Central Park, over the continuous protests of the Fifth Avenue Association. The physical side of the personality of Ed Stone, indicated by the lower loops and the heavy pressure, has given a feeling of warmth to his architecture. At the same time it has afforded a lustiness and love of life which at one time gave Ed quite a reputation as a hell-raiser and drinker. As a reaction to this Ed in recent years—apart from rarely touching liquor—has accentuated his characteristic old-world formality to the point where, for example, when I asked him to sit down and write for me he wrote almost no figure-8 "g"s (typical of informality and humor) in spite of the fact that he frequently makes them. This pose of formality might be interpreted as a façade characteristic of many great artists. It is not surprising in Ed's case to detect a lurking inferiority complex in the backhand slant and the small, abbreviated capital "I."

Terry-Thomas

Brilliant script in which the connections between words are reminiscent of Somerset Maugham's. The exhibitionism of the actor and comedian is betrayed in the misplaced capitals of "street" and "carriage" and the wide spacing.

I am walking down the street to get the horse and carriage out of the old garage Tiny Tim

Tiny Tim

With the squatty-looking capital "I" and the leftward "t" bars, a possible inferiority complex manifests itself, and the "t" bars suggest Tiny Tim's love for the music of the Twenties and of earlier times. But the Greek "d"s show the perfectionist and the artist.

Valentina

A strong, dramatic personality, stubborn (the backward slant, the Greek "e"s), with an obvious flair for design.

I walking on the street to get the horse and that is all Valentina

*I am Walking down the street
To get the horse and Carriage out
Of the Old Garage.*

Jack Warner.
C. B. E.

Jack Warner

The extrovert—the inflated "I," the wide spacing, the forward slant, the long lower zone. But creative and a man of action.

Blind Analysis

During an interview, David Frost invited me to analyze unlabeled samples of the handwriting of various prominent people. These sketches are based on notes made before the writers were identified to me on Frost's show.

Joan Baez
William Buckley
David Frost
Allen Ginsberg
Hubert Humphrey

Hedy Lamarr
Burt Lancaster
Gordon MacRae
Edmund Muskie
Sugar Ray Robinson

I am going down town to get the horse & carriage out of the garage .

Joan Baez

Stubborn, opinionated, secretive (narrow writing with prominent arcades). The audience got a big laugh on the David Frost show when I called her conservative—they knew to whom the writing belonged but I didn't—but perhaps my comment only goes to remind us that if one person walks to the right and the other to the left, if they go far enough they will eventually meet!

I am going down to get th horse & carriage out f th garage.

William Buckley

With the very small letters and narrow spacing, the Greek "d"s and figure-8 "g"s, the handwriting of a sensitive intellectual. All the ego in the world—and it's there in that large capital "I"— will never turn this conservative, slightly backward writing into that of a good politician.

David Frost

Surprisingly like Humphrey's writing, with the heavy pressure, the good rhythm, and the circle "i" dot. The frequent figure-8 "g"s and the Greek "d" in "and" make David Frost, as I said in

I am going downtown to take the horse and wagon out of the garage.

my analysis before identifying him, a highly creative person—
with a suggestion of physical or sensual excess in the accompanying heavy pressure.

am going down the street get the horse and carriage out of the garage

Allen Ginsberg

Before the writer was identified to me I jotted down the following analysis: emotionally unstable, sensitive, depressed, procrasti-
nating yet persistent, and not much of a politician.

I am going downtown to take the horse and Wagon out of the Garage.

Hubert Humphrey

With the heavy pressure and full lower loops, a politician, and
a man physically oriented with much enthusiasm and energy.
The large capital "W" in "wagon" betrays an attachment to
force, however controlled. But the whole picture is softened by
the prominent figure-8 "g" and by a circle "i" dot (seen in another specimen of HHH's writing) by which I referred to him—
before his identity was revealed to me—as a possible "adapter
of art."

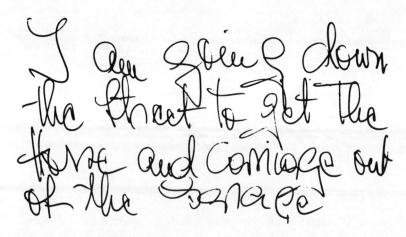

Hedy Lamarr

My analysis of the unidentified script: probably an actor or actress, sensitive, emotional, dramatic, with definite anti-social tendencies (the numerous and prominent misplaced capitals), and a stubborn follow-through which could indicate business ability.

Burt Lancaster

Easygoing, idealistic, with an anti-social or violent streak seen in the capital "S" of "street."

I am going down the street to get the horse and carriage out of the garage.

Gordon MacRae

My analysis started off with two words, "showmanship and exhibitionism." The handwriting of a supersalesman. The extraordinary length of the looped "t" bars might make an interesting study for some future team of grapho-psychologists!

I am going down the street to get the horse and carriage out of the garage.

Edmund Muskie

My analysis: very intelligent, well balanced, persistent, generous but critical, physically and mentally active (the rhythm and heavy pressure). But I might now add that the comparative absence of figure-8 "g"'s, the high "t" bars and the leftward slant could give strong but a bit dogmatic overtones to the whole.

I am going down town to get the horse and carriage out of the garage

Sugar Ray Robinson

A strong, overpowering personality in which a bent toward the physical predominates. Though I did not express it in so many words in my analysis, the fact that this is the handwriting of a fighter sticks out all over it—the heavy, almost muddy pressure, the extreme forward slant, the long, upward and downward "t" bars, and, finally, the huge "C" in the word "carriage."

APPENDICES

Appendix A

Which One Would You Trust?

L da Vinci

LEONARDO DA VINCI *   vs   **CESARE BORGIA** †

G. Washington

GEORGE WASHINGTON   vs   **BENEDICT ARNOLD** ‡

---

* From *Collecting Autographs and Manuscripts* by Charles Hamilton. Copyright 1961 by the University of Oklahoma Press. Reprinted by permission of the publisher.

† From *Handbook of Facsimiles of Famous Personages*, Karl Geigy (ed.). (Rudolf Geigy Pub., Basle, Switzerland).

‡ Reprinted by permission of Massachusetts Historical Society.

LORD NELSON *   vs   NAPOLEON †

THOMAS JEFFERSON *   vs   KARL MARX *

ABRAHAM LINCOLN ** vs JOHN WILKES BOOTH *

MARIE CURIE ‡   vs   MATA HARI ‡

* From *Collecting Autographs and Manuscripts* by Charles Hamilton. Copyright 1961 by the University of Oklahoma Press. Reprinted by permission of the publisher.

† From *Handwriting Tells,* copyright © 1936, 1959, 1969 by Nadya Olyanova, reprinted by permission of the publishers, The Bobbs-Merrill Company, Inc. and Peter Owen Ltd.

** From *Autographic Mirror* Volume 1.

‡ Manuscript Division; The New York Public Library; Astor, Lenox, and Tilden Foundations.

‡ From *Self-Knowledge Through Handwriting* by H. J. Jacoby. Reprinted by permission of J. M. Dent & Sons, Ltd., London.

[signatures]

COUNT LEO TOLSTOY* vs JOSEF STALIN**

SIMON BOLIVAR‡ vs FIDEL CASTRO †

†MARTIN LUTHER KING, JR. vs HENRI CHRISTOPHE*

ALBERT EINSTEIN vs ADOLF HITLER ‡

* From *Collecting Autographs and Manuscripts* by Charles Hamilton. Copyright 1961 by the University of Oklahoma Press. Reprinted by permission of the publisher.

** From *Handwriting—Revelation of Self* by Herry O. Teltscher. Reprinted by permission of the author.

‡ Specimen submitted by the Embassy of Venezuela, Washington, D.C.

‡ From *Diagrams of the Unconscious* by Werner Wolff, Ph.D. Reprinted by permission of Grune & Stratton, Inc., New York and Mrs. Kate A. Wolff.

† From *Handwriting Tells*, copyright © 1936, 1959, 1969 by Nadya Olyanova, reprinted by permission of the publishers, The Bobbs-Merrill Company, Inc. and Peter Owen Ltd.

Appendix B

Authentic and Forged Signatures of Howard Hughes

The tremulousness of pressure of the writing of an older man, as was pointed out by Captain Joseph McNally of the New York Police Department, is seen in the authentic signatures. Secondly, the figure-8 "g"s with no interruption whatever in the downward stroke—a basic sign of intelligence—appear much more clearly and frequently in the authentic signatures than in the forged ones. If the document-examining firm of Osborn Associates had taken the broader science of graphology (in addition to their own specialized knowledge) a bit more seriously, they might not have erred as they did.

Authentic signatures

Forged signatures

Appendix C

Three Studies of Beginning Strokes

The following three tests were conducted by myself and two associates, Lawrence Epstein and Harriet B. Linton. Though reported here in somewhat abbreviated form, they are still couched in a formal and technical style. I feel that those interested in exploring the implications of graphology for the experimental sciences should find them of great interest. The authors are indebted to William Berenson for his assistance in this study.

Introduction

The beginning strokes in handwriting which were of concern in this study are of two types. One type, which we shall call the primary beginning stroke, is the initial upstroke sometimes found on words beginning with the small letters "a," "c," "d," "g," and "q" (see Fig. 1, Column A). The other type, which we shall call the secondary beginning stroke, is the initial upstroke frequently found on words beginning with the small letters "u," "v," "w," and "y" (see Fig. 1, Column B).

Fig 1. Examples of the primary and secondary beginning strokes. The broken line in Column A exemplifies the primary beginning stroke. The broken line in Column B exemplifies the secondary beginning stroke.

Although the primary beginning stroke is still being taught in other countries (1) [1], it has probably not been taught to children anywhere in the United States during the past twenty years. Thus, its appearance in the handwritings of people up to the age of twenty-five who have been educated here is usually an individual embellishment—in other words, its appearance in a given handwriting in this age group represents something *elaborated* rather than retained. When present within a given sample of writing, primary beginning strokes are almost always accompanied by secondary beginning strokes.

[1] The figures in parentheses refer to the references on page 327.

The secondary beginning stroke continues to be taught in nearly every modern system of cursive writing (3, 7, 14). However, we have observed that a tendency to eliminate the secondary beginning stroke often develops with age and with writing experience.

Both types of beginning stroke constitute additions to the "essential letter form" (8, p. 18)—*i.e.,* they are superfluous for purpose of legibility. The American graphologist Rice has called the beginning stroke "an unnecessary gesture," and she has written, ". . . the presence of the beginning-stroke in people who are past the first stages of education is a sure indication of the fact that they are not progressing very fast" (14, p. 97).

One of the investigators in the present study has long felt, on the basis of his observations, that there may be an inverse relationship between a person's tendency to use beginning strokes and the level of his emotional maturity. We wished to pursue this possibility further and began by reflecting on the possible meaning of the tendency to make primary beginning strokes.

The presence of primary beginning strokes in the handwriting of an educated person, we thought, may signify a lack of confidence in one's ability to negotiate a sustained, smoothly flowing motoric pattern. The primary beginning stroke is an awkward elaboration. In making it, the writer may be gaining for himself a momentary foothold at or near the base line of the writing. Figuratively, he may be gaining a home base from which he can more securely find his way to the more ambiguous point in space which is the origin of the essential downstroke. It occurred to us that the writer of primary strokes may be expressing a mistrust of his motor impulses and the need to guard against their going astray. The same reasoning would also apply to the retention of secondary beginning strokes, although educational experience probably plays a part as well.

Reflecting further on the possible meaning of the tendency to retain the secondary beginning stroke, we thought it might evidence the retention of childish patterns of behavior, a passive acceptance of past teachings, and perhaps a general acceptance of heteronomous norms and standards. Accordingly, the tendency to eliminate secondary beginning strokes from the handwriting suggested the growth of an individual's ability to differentiate the essential from the nonessential; it suggested a greater drive in the individual to free himself from the bonds of the arbitrary conventions and standards of his past. In general, it suggested the development of greater self-individuation.

TEST NUMBER ONE

"SOME RELATIONSHIPS OF THE BEGINNING STROKES IN HANDWRITING TO THE HUMAN FIGURE DRAWING TEST" [1]

Hypotheses and Sample

The purpose of the study was to test our hypotheses by investigating some psychological correlates of beginning-stroke tendencies in a sample of 116 male medical students, relatively homogeneous in age, intelligence, and educational level.

Two hypotheses were tested: (a) Whether the strength of a subject's tendency to write with beginning strokes is directly related to the number of signs of immaturity appearing in his figure drawings. (b) Whether the number of immaturity signs is greater in the figure drawings of subjects who write with primary beginning strokes than in the figure drawings of subjects who write with only secondary beginning strokes.

Test Instruments

The instrument we thought suitable for our purposes was the Short Scale of Figure-Drawing Items (6, pp. 517–24). The scale was developed by K. Machover in an effort to use the figure-drawing technique to differentiate the personality characteristics of field-

[1] Material is extracted from Epstein, L. and Hartford, H. "Some Relationships of Beginning Strokes in Handwriting to the Human Figure Drawing Test." *Perceptual and Motor Skills,* 1959, 9, 55-62. Reprinted by permission of the Publisher.

dependent and field-independent perceivers. The scale for male subjects consists of 40 items, each of which was found to predict field-dependent perception with a high degree of accuracy.[2] The items have the virtue of being more or less objectively scorable by nonexpert judges.

The chief reason for choosing this instrument was that the personality correlates of field-dependent perception, as reflected in the items of this scale, seemed closely related to those features of personality we would expect to correlate with beginning strokes. Each item had been interpreted by Machover as signifying a lack of some aspect of emotional maturity, or a presence of some aspect of immaturity. Some of the traits signified by different items are: lack of self-differentiation, lack of self- or body-confidence, lack of drive or drive-modification, fear of one's own impulses, poor control over impulses, passivity in dealing with the environment and dependence upon the environment. Thus, the 40-item scale yields total score which may be viewed as an index of immaturity.[3] One purpose of the experiment was to relate this index to beginning-stroke performance. A second purpose was to relate the individual items on the figure-drawing scale to the beginning-stroke scores in order to learn something more about the specific psychological correlates of beginning strokes.

Discussion

Our expectation that subjects with primary beginning strokes would have a higher index of immaturity than subjects who made only secondary beginning strokes was not fulfilled. Whether

[2] For male subjects the correlation between the total number of signs present in the drawings and the general index of field-dependent perception was .70. For female subjects the relationship between the figure drawings and perception was not as strong.

[3] It should be kept in mind that the figure-drawing scale cannot in itself provide a test of the relationship between field dependence and the use of beginning strokes. That relationship is being investigated in test number two, page 316 of Appendix C.

there is any psychological difference between these two beginning-stroke tendencies, further studies may tell.

Because our subjects were so homogeneous in intellectual and educational level, the variability among subjects both in beginning-stroke tendencies and in human figure-drawing scores was probably minimized. The relationship in a more heterogeneous population may well be more marked.

Assuming that the total number of figure-drawing signs was a valid indication of emotional or psychological maturity, one may conclude that the group of subjects who made beginning strokes was found to be more immature than the group that made no beginning strokes. For subjects who used beginning strokes at all, the frequency with which they were made was not found to be related to the figure-drawing index of immaturity in any consistent manner.

In the investigation of the individual figure-drawing items, however, the contrast between the nonbeginning-stroke writers and subjects who used many beginning strokes was found to be more marked than the contrast between the nonbeginning-stroke group and the total group of beginning-stroke writers. The non-beginning-stroke group was not distinguished by any particular figure-drawing characteristic signifying a trait of immaturity. By comparison, a greater proportion of the figure drawings made by the high-frequency beginning-stroke writers contained certain Gestalt-like qualities reflecting a passive mode of behavior, feelings of weakness, and a disharmony both in self-image and in ego functions. The figure-drawing items reflecting passive behavior and feelings of weakness did not discriminate the total group of subjects who made beginning strokes from those who made none.

It might be argued that the relationships found in this study between beginning-stroke scores and figure-drawing scores may reflect nothing more than a consistency in the quality of two different graphomotor performances. In order to check the validity of our interpretations and to make a more extensive investigation of the psychological correlates of beginning strokes, we undertook a second study with male college subjects. (See Test Two which follows.)

Summary of Test Number One

The purpose of the present investigation was twofold: to determine whether the incidence and type of beginning stroke in the handwritings of a male population (N = 116) homogeneous in age, intelligence, and educational level would be related to the degree of psychological immaturity as expressed in the human-figure drawing and to learn something about the specific psychological correlates of different beginning-stroke tendencies. The total score on the K. Machover Short Scale of Figure-Drawing Items was used as a general index of immaturity. We found the figure drawing of the 18 nonbeginning-stroke subjects to yield a significantly lower mean index than did those of the group of 98 subjects with one or more beginning strokes. The frequency with which beginning strokes were used was not found to have a linear relationship to the figure-drawing index, and the figure-drawing index did not differentiate between two different types of beginning strokes. Both the total group of subjects which wrote with one or more beginning strokes and that part of the total group which wrote with 50 percent to 100 percent beginning strokes were compared with the nonbeginning-stroke writers on each of the 40 figure-drawing items. The chi-square test showed only four items to be associated with the presence of beginning strokes, but eight items to be associated with frequent usage of beginning strokes. The psychological implications of the discriminating items were discussed.

TEST NUMBER TWO

"PERSONALITY AND PERCEPTUAL CORRELATES OF SECONDARY BEGINNING STROKES IN HANDWRITING" [4]

[4] Material is extracted from Linton, H. B., Epstein L., and Hartford, H. "Personality and Perceptual Correlates of Secondary Beginning Strokes in Handwriting." *Perceptual and Motor Skills,* 1961, 12, 271-281. Reprinted by permission of the Publisher.

Hypotheses and Sample

A second test was undertaken with a sample of 53, 17-year-old college freshman students to establish the relationship of beginning strokes to perceptual, cognitive, and nongraphic projective test variables. This study particularly concerned itself with the psychological correlates of the secondary beginning strokes.

Discussion

Those subjects who, in the present sample, use many secondary beginning strokes tend to be more passive and constricted than those who use few secondary beginning strokes, and they are less adequate in coping with the environment. They can be characterized as "passive," however, only in certain senses of the word and clearly not in others.

The most significant single finding is that subjects who use many secondary beginning strokes do more poorly on the ACE test. Since all subjects had been admitted to a municipal college on a highly competitive basis, there is no question of low intelligence in this group. The distinction is rather between bright and very bright students. Within this range, however, subjects using many secondary beginning strokes are clearly less adequate in coping with intellectual tasks.

There is some tendency for these subjects to be more field-dependent in Witkin's perceptual tasks. They differ significantly, however, only in *series 1b*, which requires that they alter the environment—that is, adjust the room to verticality.[5] The fact that they report less autokinetic movement suggests, in the light of other evidence about the correlates of autokinetic movement (Sexton, 1945; Voth, 1941), that they are less able, when in a

[5] *Series 1a* is also a room-adjustment series, but analysis of the nature of the tasks shows that it is a less pure measure of this tendency than *1b* (*cf.* Witkins, *et al.*, 1954). High users of secondary beginning strokes are also more field-dependent on *series 1a*, but the difference is not significant.

completely dark room, to give up the cues provided by the room, the framework provided by the environment.

These findings, in conjunction with the lower ACE scores, suggest that they are passive in the sense of not actively controlling the environment. They tend to accept the room as it is in the TRTC; in the autokinetic situation they tend to hold onto their image of the environment (thus inhibiting the movement), and their intellectual functioning is generally less adequate.

Some of the personality data add to the conception of these subjects being less active in dealing with the environment. The less assertive nature of their human movement responses in the Rorschach test suggests that they have a passive self-image. In the personality questionnaire they describe themselves as less likely to assert themselves, so that this image is at least partly conscious. In the authoritarian questionnaire, they are more likely to accept clichés, which indicates that they are less likely to think for themselves but rather accept stereotyped views of issues. Their anti-intraceptiveness, indicating a lack of intellectual interests, also suggests that they do not think for themselves as much as the other subjects. The total picture is one of comparatively little intellectual curiosity and activity, combined with a low degree of self-assertion. It is noteworthy that four of the five authoritarian sub-scales that do not relate to the use of secondary beginning strokes involve hostility and aggressiveness; these subjects are not really authoritarian in that sense, but resemble the authoritarian personality primarily in their tendencies toward intellectual stereotype.

Their inability to report a predominant direction for the autokinetic movement is difficult to interpret because differences in perception cannot be separated from differences in recall and manner of reporting. The more conservative interpretation would be that the difference does not lie in the actual perception of movement, but rather represents difficulty in remembering the movement after the experimental session is over or difficulty in deciding which direction predominated when the movement varied in its directions. If this is so, it could be considered a further indication of poorer intellectual functioning and, more specifically, an inability to deal effectively with an unstructured mass of impressions.

The lack of certainty about their plans for the future and their avoidance of unconventional fields suggest difficulty in coming to grips with the demands of maturity. Choosing a field because one "does well" in it seems more passive than making a positive choice based on any feeling for the work itself or its potential gains to themselves or to society.

Since the picture so far is one of comparative inadequacy and passivity, it is noteworthy that subjects using many secondary beginning strokes [6] are not especially influenced by external pressure—i.e., they do not particularly alter their behavior to conform to outside stimuli as represented in the autokinetic situation, the opinion-change test, the ID-OD questionnaire or, in a more derived form, the syllogisms test. Correspondingly, the chair-adjustment series of the TRTC (2a and 2b), where the structure of the external visual field influences the person's perception of his own bodily position, are unrelated to the use of secondary beginning strokes. This is particularly striking because passivity in the sense of inadequate ability to cope with tasks alone is associated, in this sample and in others, with a tendency to use outside stimuli as guides for behavior.

The projective data provide some clues to the solution of this apparent paradox. The figure drawings of subjects using many beginning strokes suggest they have greater anxiety, as well as more problems in the control of impulses that tend to be solved by overcontrol. Specifically, the long necks on the figures suggest a repressive overcontrol, while the greater use of margins and

---

[6] The beginning-stroke scores utilized by Epstein and Hartford included the primary beginning stroke in addition to the secondary beginning stroke. In comparing their findings with those of the present study (i.e., Test One with Test Two), it is important to note that Epstein and Hartford would have obtained virtually identical results if they had used secondary beginning strokes exclusively, since only two of their ninety-eight beginning-stroke writers used primary beginning strokes exclusively. The remaining ninety-six used one or more secondary beginning strokes.

encasements suggests defensiveness, barriers between the self and the environment that might mean greater ego strength in some contexts but hardly seem to in the present context. The larger eyes in their drawings suggest that they need the environment, but it appears that they are also afraid of it and so defend themselves against it.

In the Rorschach test, their longer reaction times on the earlier cards suggest that they experience initial difficulty in dealing with a new, unstructured task. The low use of color indicates that, when they do finally respond, it is in a constricted manner and, furthermore, that their lack of responsiveness is particularly marked when the stimulation has emotional connotations. They are less able to make use of color stimuli in an adaptive way, as shown by the fact that they are notably lacking in FC; they produce about equal amounts of FC and CF + C, while subjects using few secondary beginning strokes produce about twice as many FC responses as CF +C.

These findings indicate that they do not respond as adaptively to the environment and that such stimuli tend to disrupt their performance rather than to serve as a guide for effective behavior. In this context, the use of margins and encasements in their figure drawings suggests that they defend themselves against external stimuli.

We can now return to the problem of why subjects who use many secondary beginning strokes are no more responsive to the influence situations than subjects who use few. Two kinds of personality variables found in subjects who use many secondary beginning strokes have been described, and they relate in opposite directions to the response to external influence. These subjects are relatively passive and inadequate in coping with tasks on their own and this, in itself, should make them more likely to accept outside sources of help and thus be influenced. They are also, however, rather constricted and not only exhibit difficulty in making productive use of cues from the environment but actually seem to defend themselves against such stimulation; these tendencies would make them less likely to accept outside sources of help. It may be suggested that these two trends cancel each other out, leading to the lack of relationship between secondary beginning strokes and the influence measures.

The use of secondary beginning strokes is, then, associated with relative inadequacy and lack of energy in intellectual functioning and other forms of coping with the environment, with a tendency to accept things as they are rather than actively trying to control or alter them, and with constriction that applies particularly to emotional interaction.

The secondary beginning strokes themselves are taught in school, although they are not essential parts of the letters in which they occur. Using them, then, means that a pattern learned early in life has been retained, while not using them means that the person has improved his efficiency by dropping an unessential part of the letter. The retention of a pattern learned in childhood that is not really efficient is in keeping with the kinds of performance found in this study to be associated with high use of the secondary beginning stroke. It should be kept in mind that in the present sample of seventeen-year-old boys only three subjects have abandoned its use completely and that the comparisons that have been made are primarily between low users and high users.

Summary of Test Number Two

The purpose of Test Number Two was to explore the psychological correlates of the secondary beginning stroke in the handwritings of a sample of 53 male college freshmen, using a variety of tests and experimental situations dealing with perception, intellectual ability, personality, social values, and conformity to social influence. As predicted, subjects using many beginning strokes showed less intellectual ability, a less active approach in dealing with a new, unstructured task, were more likely to accept clichés and have anti-intellectual values, responded to emotional stimulation with avoidance, and experienced anxiety and difficulty in impulse control which they tended to handle by repressive overcontrol. However, predictions that they would be influenced by external pressure either in the social conformity situations, on a test of other-directed values, or in the tests of perceptual field-dependence, were not fulfilled. An interpretation is advanced for this seeming inconsistency.

TEST NUMBER THREE

"PERSONALITY AND PERCEPTUAL CORRELATES OF PRIMARY
BEGINNING STROKES IN HANDWRITING" [7]

Hypothesis and Sample

The purpose of the present study was to investigate more thoroughly the personality correlates of the two kinds of beginning strokes. As the findings in relation to the use of secondary beginning strokes were reported in Test Two, Test Three will deal with the correlates of the primary beginning strokes in the same sample of 53 college freshmen.

Discussion

The most striking characteristics of those who use primary beginning strokes, in terms of statistical significance, have to do with social conformity in values and in behavior. Their authoritarian attitudes consist primarily in their acceptance of clichés and other conventional statements, expressions of deference to parents and parental authority, a rejection of intraceptive values together with a high valuation placed on power and ethnocentrism. It is of interest, in this connection, to consider the authoritarian scales that do *not* characterize these subjects. Three of the four scales that are unrelated to the use of the primary beginning stroke express hostility and bitterness—namely, cynicism, projectivity, and punitiveness toward social deviates. The latter is noteworthy because it is clear that they disapprove of social deviation.

[7] Material is extracted from Linton, H. B., Epstein, L., and Hartford, H. "Personality and Perceptual Correlates of Primary Beginning Strokes in Handwriting." *Perceptual and Motor Skills*, 1962, 15, 159-170. Reprinted by permission of the Publisher.

These subjects are quite other-directed in their values, feeling that the wishes of the individual should be subordinated to both the pressures of the peer group and to the norms of the larger society. Their change of judgments in the autokinetic situation may be viewed as a behavioral expression of these values, since the confederate was presented as a peer. Their great readiness to admit that they were influenced is understandable in the light of their other-directed values, which express the feeling that one should be so influenced. Their behavior in the autokinetic situation may be compared with their response to the other measure of social influence, the opinion change test, on which they were not influenced more than other subjects. The sources of influence in the two situations differ in two ways: (a) the influence comes from an authority in the opinion change test and from a peer in the autokinetic situation and (b) the influence is exerted through written communication in the opinion change test and by the statements of a person who is physically present in the autokinetic situation. While both these factors are undoubtedly important, the latter is probably more important in view of the Rorschach findings discussed below. That is, we may hypothesize that it is the direct personal contact that makes these subjects more likely to be influenced in the autokinetic situation.

As striking as these relationships is the fact that these subjects do not appear to be generally dependent or passive. The use of the primary beginning stroke is unrelated to the perceptual measures of field-dependence, or to the projective test measures (Rorschach and figure drawing) previously found to be associated with field-dependence. This is particularly noteworthy because of the fact that influence in the autokinetic situation *is* related to all of these measures of dependence in the very same sample (Linton, 1954, 1955). The relationship between use of primary beginning strokes and autokinetic influence, then, is apparently on a different basis and cannot, in itself, be taken as an indication of passivity or dependence.

Other Rorschach measures may throw some light on the dynamics underlying the pattern of measures that relate to the primary beginning strokes. If we consider that the outstanding feature of Card IV is that it is the first appearance of strong shading, the longer reaction time and poorer form level on this card may be considered as a shading disturbance. An examination of the content of their responses to this card reveals even more differences between users and nonusers. Users of primary beginning strokes are more likely to react in a way that indicates a withdrawal from life and a fear of destruction (i.e., rejection of the card, something killed, anatomy, icicles; $x^2 = 4.86$, .05 level). They are also more likely to describe the card as "weird, distorted" ($x^2 = 6.12$, .05 level). Either or both of these reactions are shown by 86 percent of users, vs. 30 percent of nonusers ($x^2 = 10.62$, .01 level). Card IV, then, causes them real trouble, and they cannot integrate it effectively but tend to see it as unreal, damaged or dead.

Their reaction to color, on the other hand, is complex but much more positive. Although they are somewhat disoriented by color, especially in its first full appearance on Card VIII, they become stimulated by it to increased activity and better performance, reflected in improved form level. Klopfer distinguishes interpretively between the implications of shading and of color (Klopfer, *et al.*, Vol. I, 1954) by conceiving of the reaction to shading as indicative of the inner affectional life of the person, while the reaction to color is considered more indicative of his reaction to external stimulation and the way in which his affectional needs are acted out. The shading disturbance shown by users of primary beginning strokes would, in these terms, reflect a frustration or deprivation of affectional needs that is apprehended, on some level, by the person himself and, in view of the content of their Card IV responses, is partly felt as an inner deadness. Their handling of color, however, suggests that they are mobilized by external stimulation, almost in the sense of seeking an external object for playing out their emotional needs. With this external stimulation they seem, as it were, to come to life.

An additional interpretation of Card IV, which supplements rather than contradicts the interpretation offered above, is that it represents unconscious attitudes toward the father and toward authority in general. If we may speculate that these subjects feel deprived and deadened in their affectional relationships to their own fathers, their authoritarian views may be seen, in a sense, as a search for a more adequate father. This throws an interesting sidelight on their ethnocentrism, which is very striking in a sample where ethnocentrism is, in general, very low and where two-thirds of the subjects (users of primary beginning strokes as well as nonusers) have at least one foreign-born parent. When asked where their parents were born, however, more users than nonusers failed to answer the question ($p = .047$, Fisher's exact test). Their ethnocentrism seems, then, to be a rejection of their own backgrounds and, in view of their other values, it may indicate a desire to be accepted by what they conceive of as the standard American culture.

Their handling of shading is also in keeping with their higher scores on both the anti-intraceptive scale and the scale of denial of irrational feelings. They seem to deny feelings of sensitivity and of inner disturbance. In keeping with these tendencies also is their opinionation. This is reflected directly in their difficulty in accepting syllogisms when they don't like the conclusions. It is also shown in the greater self-assertion that they report on the personality questionnaire, since many of the items in that scale have to do with "telling someone off."

The remaining significant finding that must be considered is their poor coping in the autokinetic situation before the confederate's judgments are introduced. It is of particular interest since they do not cope poorly in general and do not show the signs of field-dependency generally associated with poor coping. It may be suggested that it is the almost total lack of stimulation that is responsible, since the only stimulus is a single point of light in an otherwise dark room. The Rorschach findings suggest that their resources are best mobilized by a wealth of stimulation, and it may be that in other situations as well a clear external stimulus is necessary for them to be productive. Their poor coping with the judgment task, as well as their desire to be accepted by peers, both play a part in causing them to be influenced in this situation.

What does this pattern tell us about the primary beginning stroke itself and the ways in which it differs from the secondary beginning stroke? Use of the secondary beginning stroke represents the retention of a pattern learned in childhood and, as was predicted, the subjects who use it most tend to be passive, inadequate and generally immature (Linton, Epstein, and Hartford, 1961). The primary beginning stroke, in contrast, is not something that the person was taught to use. It is something that he adds himself, but it detracts from the efficiency of his performance. It is, then, a personal embellishment, an expression of "individuality," but it is neither efficient nor really creative. It has the added feature that it represents a way of holding on to the base line of the writing for support and so may serve as a help in control.

The subjects who use the primary beginning stroke seem to be ambitious, but within a framework of conforming values. They show a deficit in inner life, particularly in the emotions, but a good deal of response to external stimuli, which they utilize comparatively well. We may hypothesize that they would like to make their mark, not by originality or creative achievement, but by greater-than-average utilization of the resources provided by the environment. They would like to "be somebody" and are probably somewhat opinionated and exhibitionistic.

Within this framework, the primary beginning stroke seems to represent a kind of assertion of self, an extra flourish added by the writer and an expression of extra energy, but it is at the same time a safe kind of self-expression that does not challenge convention or endanger the writer's acceptance by others. Furthermore, it actually helps him to control his impulses. In a safe kind of way, he is "making his mark."

Summary of Test Number Three

The purpose of Test Number Three was to explore psychological correlates of primary beginning strokes in the handwriting of a sample of 53 male college freshmen and to contrast them with the correlates of secondary beginning strokes presented in Test Number Two. Primary beginning strokes were defined as voluntary elaborations of the essential letter form, while secondary beginning strokes were described as the retention of patterns learned in the first years of school. Subjects using many primary beginning strokes were similar to subjects using many secondary beginning strokes in their tendency toward authoritarian attitudes. But while users of secondary beginning strokes had been found to be passive, inadequate and generally immature, users of primary beginning strokes were found to be actively seeking external stimulation and ways of asserting themselves in a framework of other-directedness and conformity.

References

1. Adorno, T. W., Frenkel-Brunswik, E., Levinson, D. J., and Sanford, R. H. *The Authoritarian Personality.* New York: Harper, 1950.
2. Bell, E. G. Inner-directed and other-directed attitudes. Unpublished doctoral dissertation, Yale University, 1955.
3. Blumenthal, E. *Schulschriften der verschiedenen Laender.* Bern and Stuttgart: Huber, 1957.
4. Epstein, L., and Hartford, H. "Some Relationships of Beginning Strokes in Handwriting to the Human Figure-Drawing Test." *Perceptual and Motor Skills,* 1959, 9, 55–62.
5. Handwriting Research Institute. *Handwriting Made Easy.* New York: Noble & Noble, 1957.
6. Klopfer, B. *The Rorschach Technique: A Manual for a Projective Method of Personality Diagnosis.* Yonkers-on-Hudson: World Book, 1946.
7. Klopfer, B., Ainsworth, M. D., Klopfer, W., and Holt, R. *Developments in the Rorschach Technique. Vol I: Technique and Theory.* Yonkers-on-Hudson, World Book, 1954.
8. Lewinson, T. S., and Zubin, J. *Handwriting Analysis.* New York: King's Crown Press, 1942.

9. Linton, H. B. Relations between mode of perception and the tendency to conform. Unpublished doctoral dissertation, Yale University, 1952.

10. ———. "Rorschach Correlates of Response to Suggestion." *Journal of Abnormal and Social Psychology*, 1954, 49, 75–83.

11. ———. "Dependence on External Influence: Correlates in Perception, Attitudes, and Judgment." *Journal of Abnormal and Social Psychology*, 1955, 51, 502–507.

12. Linton, H. B., and Graham, E. "Personality Correlates of Persuasibility." In *Yale Studies in Attitude and Communication Vol. 2*, by C. I. Hovland and I. L. Janis (eds.), *Personality and Persuasibility*. New Haven: Yale University Press, 1959.

13. Linton, H. B., Epstein, L., and Hartford, H. "Personality and Perceptual Correlates of Secondary Beginning Strokes in Handwriting," *Perceptual and Motor Skills*, 1961, 12, 271–281.

14. Palmer, A. N. *The Palmer System of American Arm Movement Writing*. New York, 1909.

15. Rice, L. *Character Reading from Handwriting*. New York: Frederick A. Stokes, 1927.

16. Sexton, M. C. "The Autokinetic Test: Its Value in Psychiatric Diagnosis and Prognosis." *American Journal of Psychiatry*, 1945, 102, 339, 402.

17. Voth, A. C. "Individual Differences in the Autokinetic Phenomenon." *Journal of Experimental Psychology*, 1941, 29, 306–322.

18. Witkin, H. A. "Individual Differences in Ease of Perception of Embedded Figures." *Journal of Personality*, 1950, 19, 1–15.

19. Witkin, H. A., Bretnall-Meissner, P., Hertzman, M., Lewis, H. B., Machover, K., and Wapner, S. *Personality Through Perception*. New York: Harper, 1954.

Columbia University, College of Physicians and Surgeons
The Handwriting Institute, Inc.
New York University

Appendix D

*A Study of the Small "g," "d," and "f"**

The model of good penmanship has remained the same throughout the United States for many years, despite the fact that the methods used to teach handwriting have undergone considerable change. As a result, this basic handwriting model, which has been called the "school-copy" model by Lewinson and Zubin (6),† may be used as a yardstick to evaluate the tendency of individuals to deviate from what they first learned.

Everyone who writes has deviated somewhat from the "school-copy" form by altering the forms and size ratios of his letters

* This appendix was originally published in an article entitled "The Relationship of Certain Letter Form Variants in the Handwriting of Female Subjects to Their Education, IQ, and Age," by Epstein, L., Hartford, H., and Tumarkin, I. in the *Journal of Experimental Education,* Vol. 29, No. 4, June 1961. It is now reproduced by permission of the authors and the publisher.

† Numbers in brackets refer to the bibliographical reference at the end of this appendix.

in an idiosyncratic way. It is for this reason that signatures can be accepted as legal identification all over the world. Furthermore, it is the fact that each individual learns to write in a unique but consistent way which underlies the science of graphology.

Two essential reasons that each individual departs from the "school-copy" form are to achieve efficiency and speed. Naturally, the demand for legibility remains even after the demand for rigid reconstruction of the school-copy form is relaxed. Typically, handwriting is not taught to students over fourteen years of age and thus it is then that the tendency to vary accelerates. Many students crystallize their own writing styles in high school or, perhaps, in college when they are called upon to take lecture notes at high speeds.

If handwriting typically departs from the school-copy model, what then is reflected in those adult handwritings which closely adhere to, rather than depart from, the school-copy model? If we regard such samples as cases of arrested handwriting development it would seem to follow that such handwritings may also reflect an arrested intellectual and/or emotional development.

In a recent study, Epstein and Hartford (4) found that in a group of male medical students the retention of the superfluous initial upstrokes on the letters "u," "v," "w," and "y" [1] ‡ was, in fact, related to emotional immaturity. In another recent unpublished study, Linton, Epstein and Hartford found the use of these initial upstrokes to be associated "with relative inadequacy and lack of energy in intellectual functioning and other forms of coping with the environment. . . ."

In our survey of earlier graphological studies, we can find but few studies dealing with the relationship between handwriting and intelligence in adult subjects.

Thorndike (11) and Omwake (7) have reported virtually zero correlations between scales of handwriting quality [2] and adult intelligence. These results, in effect, indicate the lack of relationship between adult intelligence and conformity to such school-copy values as legibility, aesthetic appearance and neatness. In children, however, since they learn to write while under strong

‡ Notes will be found at the end of this appendix.

external pressure to conform to the school-copy model, correlations of about .30 have been found by Gesell (5) and Starch (10) between ratings of handwriting quality and general scholarship.

The Thorndike and Omwake studies, in having established that adherence to school-copy values in adult handwritings is not positively related to intelligence, raised the further question of what departures, if any, from the school-copy might be associated with intelligence in adult subjects. A study performed by Castelnuovo-Tedesco (3) points the way. He instructed six untrained judges to rate 100 adult handwritings for intelligence and originality, separately, and then correlated these ratings with IQ scores. As criteria for intelligence, the judges were told to use aesthetic spacing, handwriting speed, and the simplification (and/or) deviations of the letter forms. They were told to use as the main criteria for judging originality "the extent to which the writer of a given script has followed, in the process of writing a specific letter, a different writing pattern from that which he was probably taught in school." These correlations were all at

TABLE I

g, d, AND f VARIANTS AND THE FREQUENCY AT WHICH THEY OCCUR AT LEAST ONCE IN A WRITING SAMPLE
(N = 150)

g		d		f	
Variant	f	Variant	f	Variant	f
	13		6		21
	19		7		21
	34		25		31
	50		66		43
	60		129		66
	74		136		95
*	143			*	137

*School copy

least .50, and since 100 samples were rated it is extremely unlikely that the obtained relationships came about as a result of sampling errors.

The only other study in which judges were successful in predicting handwriting from intelligence is that reported by Binet (2). He used professional graphologists. Unfortunately, however, the handwriting criteria upon which these graphologists based their predictions have not been indicated.

In the present study, our purpose was to explore the relationship of particular deviations from the school-copy letter forms to the educational level, the IQ and the age of a group of female writers.

Method

Samples of the writing of 150 female clients were selected from the files of the New York University Testing and Advisement Center. An examination of them suggested three letters as worthy objects of investigation because they permitted wide graphological variations within the three handwriting zones—upper, middle and lower—without loss of identity. These letters were "g," "d," and "f." The more predominant script variations of these letters within our sample were then noted.

In addition to the school-copy form, there were five form variants of the letter "d," six form variants of the letter "g," and six of the letter "f." For purposes of analysis, the appearance of at least one instance of a particular letter variant in a writing sample was considered sufficient to describe that variant as present in this sample. For each variant of the letter "g," "d" and "f," the number of samples in which it was present was determined. For instance, the school-copy "g" appeared at least once in 143 of the 150 writing samples. Table I presents the form variants for each of the letters and the number of subjects who used each variant at least once.

The experimenters also were struck by an additional handwriting phenomenon. Some subjects economized in a special way in writing the word "of." They would convert the upstroke normally used to round off the letter "o" directly into the initial upstroke of the following "f." We selected this phenomenon for separate study and it is shown in Table II, which also presents the number of samples in which it was present at least once.

The ages, IQs and the highest grades attained by the subjects were recorded. The ages ranged from fifteen to fifty-five and the median age was nineteen years. The IQ scores, which were either scores on the Wechsler Bellevue Intelligence Scale or the Wechsler Adult Intelligence Scale, ranged from 80 to 145. The median IQ score was between 124 and 125. It was decided to use 125 as a cut-off point for various statistical tests.

As for educational level, the subjects at the lowest level had completed the eleventh grade, and the subjects at the highest level had completed more than four years of college (Table III). The subjects were divided into two groups on the basis of grade completed; one group consisted of those who had gone no further than the twelfth grade (the first two groups on Table III), and the other consisted of those who had gone to college for at least some period.

In sum, the distributions of scores on three variables, age, IQ and grade completed were dichotomized for purposes of doing statistical tests. The best approximation of the median was used as the cut-off point in each case.

TABLE II

"Of" CONNECTIVE AND THE FREQUENCY AT WHICH IT OCCURS AT LEAST ONCE IN A WRITING SAMPLE
(N = 150)

Variant	f
	45

TABLE III

DISTRIBUTION OF THE HIGHEST GRADES COMPLETED BY THE 150 FEMALE SUBJECTS

Highest Grade Attained	Number of Subjects
Eleventh grade or lower	26
Twelfth grade	59
Some college	35
Four years of college or more	30

Characteristics of the Sample

A preliminary analysis of the criterion variable was made to throw light on the nature of the sample. The correlation between age and education was .42. The vast majority of subjects were still in school, so that this correlation was to be expected, since educational level depends upon age among subjects who are of school age.

The correlation between age and IQ was .27. The older subjects in the sample were predominantly those who had continued their education beyond the period of compulsory attendance. Undoubtedly such subjects are mainly from the upper intelligence range, so there was a selective factor in favor of high IQ scores at the upper age levels. The correlation between education and IQ was .34 for the same reason.

Results and Discussion

The relationships of the "d" variant to age, education and IQ are presented in Tables IVa and IVb. Table IVa, containing

TABLE IVa

CORRELATION COEFFICIENTS OF d VARIANTS WITH
EDUCATION, I. Q., AND AGE

Variant	Education	I. Q.	Age
d	.12	.03	-.05
d	.04	-.12	.10
d	.09	.05	-.19*
d	.08	.04	-.13

*Significant at .05 or above.

TABLE IVb

CHANCE PROBABILITY FOR RELATIONSHIPS BE-
TWEEN GREEK d, MODIFIED GREEK d, AND
EDUCATION, I. Q., AND AGE*

Variant	Education	I. Q.	Age
d	.007	.181	.10
d	.005	.356	.220

*The one-tailed level of significance is read directly
from the table.

the phi coefficients for the more frequently appearing "d" variants, shows only one significant negative relationship, a negative one between age and the third "d" variant. (Significance is considered established at the .05 level unless otherwise indicated.) Table IVb, containing the exact probability ratios for the two infrequently appearing "d" variants, shows each of these variants to be positively associated with educational level at better than the .01 level on a one-tailed test of significance. A one-tailed test was used because of the suggestion in the literature of the relationship between these "d" forms and intellectual ability (8). (The exact probability ratios for age and IQ showed a positive relationship between these "d" forms though this relationship did not reach significance.) Because of its resemblance to the Greek alphabet delta, graphologists have traditionally referred to the "d" variant presented first in Table IVb as the Greek "d." We shall refer to both of these variants as the Greek "d" types.

The phi coefficients for the "f" and "g" variants are presented in Table V. The variants are ordered so that the one having the most positive correlation with educational level is listed first and the variant having the strongest negative correlation is listed last. Table V also shows the phi coefficients with IQ and age. Incidentally, the phi coefficient reflects the frequency of appearance

TABLE V

CORRELATION COEFFICIENTS OF g AND f VARIANTS WITH EDUCATION, I.Q., AND AGE

| Variant | f | | | Variant | g | | |
	Education	I.Q.	Age		Education	I.Q.	Age
d	.19*	.01	.13	*g*	.33**	.23**	.19*
f	.19*	.16	.10	*p*	.23**	.19*	.10
f	.17*	.13	.08	*q*	.05	.05	.13
l	.15	.00	.06	*g*	-.04	.02	-.04
f	.14	-.06	.05	*g*	-.09	-.08	-.06
f	-.03	-.14	-.15	*q*	-.13	.00	.10
f	-.11	-.09	-.19*	*g*	-.22**	-.10	-.18*

* Significant at .05 level.
**Significant at .01 level.

of the variants as well as the strength of their relationships to other variables, so that comparisons should be made with caution.

Table V shows that there are three "f" variants which have significant positive associations with educational level, although none are significantly associated with IQ. Among the "g" variants, two have significant positive associations both with educational level and IQ. These are identified as the figure-8 and half-figure-8 "g." The figure-8 "g" also has a significant positive association with age. One "g" variant is significantly and negatively associated both with age and educational level.

Considerable deviation from the school-copy model is reflected in those "d," "f," and "g" variants which were found to be associated with higher educational level, IQ or age. The question arises how these variants deviate from the school-copy model. We shall consider these variants, first, with respect to the relative degree of simplification which they have undergone and, second, with respect to the relative degree of motoric economy with which they are written.

Simplification is rated roughly in terms of how much graphite or ink is used to make a particular variant, as compared with the amount used in the school-copy form. Among the variants positively associated with educational level, the Greek-type "d"s, first and second "f" variants in Table V and the half-figure-8 "g" all involve a considerable degree of simplification. Yet, the third "f" in Table V is among the least simplified "f" variant, and the figure-8 "g," which correlates more highly with educational level, IQ and age than any other single variant, is less simplified than the last "g" in Table V which is negatively associated with age and educational level. It is apparent that simplification alone cannot account for the obtained relationships.

Turning now to economy: in graphology, economy usually refers to the amount of energy and time which is involved in the writing. Hence, a letter form is judged more economical if less time elapses and less energy is utilized between the termination of the preceding letter and the beginning of the following letter. An emphasis on rightward tending strokes, an avoidance of leftward tending strokes, and a minimum of breaks and stoppages are therefore the key criteria.

The "d," "f," and "g" variants, with the exception of the second "f" on Table V, that were found to be significantly associated with higher educational level, IQ or age all show a high degree of economy. However, the second "d" in Table IVa, the fourth and fifth "f" variants in Table V, and the third and sixth "g" variants in Table V are also very economical forms but not significantly associated with age, IQ or education. Therefore, economy alone also cannot account for the relationships which were obtained.

Beyond having undergone simplification and economization, those "d," "f," and "g" variants which were positively associated with higher educational level, IQ or age, also represent the most original deviations from the school-copy form. Considering the "f" variants from this viewpoint, we can see that nothing original has been evolved in any of the three variants following the school-copy one in Table V. The transformations from the school-copy have been mainly in the direction of simple omission—of either, or both upper and lower loops. In each of the three "f" variants which were positively associated with educational level we see the emergence of a new form relative to the school-copy model.

In the case of the figure-8 and the half-figure-8 forms, the transformation when compared with other "g" forms seems even greater than in the case of the "f." It is interesting to note what the American graphologist Louise Rice (8) has said concerning the figure-8 "g": "People who use this formation. . . have a certain amount of intuition and instinct; they are the people who innately judge literature and art fairly well, even though not trained for such judgments. . . . This "g" also shows innate understanding of humanity."

The upper and middle zones of the Greek "d" did not differ in as specific a fashion from their school-copy counterparts as did the zonal elements of the higher "f" and "g" forms. Yet, the Greek-"d" types taken as *Gestalten*, seem to embody an aesthetic simplicity not found in the other "d" variants. Of the Greek "d," Louise Rice (8) has said, "It is not surprising to find stylists among writers and poets using this "d" exclusively, nor to find that college professors and scientists innately take to it. When found in ordinary writing, this formation is the 'straw in the wind' which tells of the intellectual possibilities of the writer. . . ."

Turning now to the "d" and "f" variants which were negatively associated with age, and to the "g" variant which was negatively associated both with age and educational level, we note that none of the three shows any evidence of originality. The "f," of course, is the school-copy model; the "g" variant may be described as an "unfinished" school-copy "g," and the "d" variant is a somewhat deteriorated or inept school-copy "d."

Table VI reveals the "of-connective" to have a significant positive association to educational level, IQ, and age. The direct conversion of the upstroke of the "o" into the initial upstroke of the "f" is a radically economical measure which transforms the separate letters into a unified, simplified Gestalt.

Among the twenty letter-form variants which we have studied, only the figure-8 "g" and the half-figure-8 "g" were found to have a significant, positive association with higher IQ. The "of-connective"—the only connective form which we included in this study—was also found to be associated with higher IQ. At this point, we might wonder whether a comparably extensive study of other connective-form variants might yield a greater number of significant positive correlations with IQ than we have found

TABLE VI

CORRELATION COEFFICIENT OF "of" CONNECTIVE WITH EDUCATION, I. Q., AND AGE

Variant	Education	I. Q.	Age
	. 31*	. 23*	. 35*

*Significant at . 01 level.

among letter-form variants. To the extent that the need to produce a more or less legible script limits one's freedom to forge new pathways, the limitation may be greater on the individual letter forms than on the modes of combining letter forms.

Summary and Conclusions

Each of the small-letter forms selected for study were written at least once in the school-copy manner by about 90 percent of our group of 150 late adolescent and adult female subjects. In addition to the school-copy forms, we were able to classify five variants of letter "d," six variants of letter "f," and six variants of letter "g." These variants appeared in far fewer handwritings than did the school-copy form. Also selected for separate study was a highly economical variation of the word "of."

Among the "d," "f," and "g" variants, some adhered rather closely to the school-copy form and some deviated to a much greater extent. We found the school-copy "f" and one "d" variant to be significantly associated with lower age and one "g" variant to be significantly associated with both lower age and lower educational level. Both the "d" and "f" variants departed only slightly from their school-copy counterparts.

Among the seven letter-form variants which were shown to be associated with higher educational level, there were two "d" variants, three "f" variants and two "g" variants. Both "g" variants were also associated with higher IQ and one with higher age. All seven of these variants are clearly set off from the remaining eleven variants in that they combine a high degree of motoric economy with the most radical and original departures from the school-copy form. They combine efficiency with creativity and can be considered the most highly evolved of all the variants we have studied. The special case of the of-connective, which is graphologically also a highly developed variation, was also found to be associated with higher educational level, higher IQ and higher age.

In effect, our results suggest that the female adult who continues to write in the fashion that would have pleased her elementary-school teacher is less likely to be as well educated, as bright or as mature as the adult who has worked her way out of the school-copy rut and has evolved a more efficient and original way of writing.

The results of the present study, in revealing that there is an evolutionary trend away from the school-copy model, have led us to wonder whether the values underlying the teaching of handwriting should be revamped. Instead of attempting to cast all children in the school-copy mold, perhaps the teacher should be taught to evaluate handwriting progress in the child with respect to the efficiency and legibility of his letter forms as they appear in the context of cursive writing. With this orientation, the teacher may be less likely to make the error of diagnosing spontaneous, creative and economical deviations from the school-copy as an expression of poor progress. Why shouldn't the child who, for one reason or another, can never be a facile copyist, be encouraged to persist in whatever unique modes of writing he discovers, so long as they are no less efficient or legible than the school-copy? It would seem that an early acceptance by teachers of unique styles of writing would make writing more of a pleasure than a chore for the child who is learning to write. More important is the likelihood that many children might be spared repeated experiences of failure to write "correctly." Such experiences might be the predominant cause of the immature, inept handwritings that are seen in later years—handwritings which persist as foci of self-consciousness, embarrassment and shame.

Notes

The authors wish to express their appreciation to Dr. Wallace Gobetz of the New York University Testing and Advisement Center, whose cooperation made this study possible.

[1] In learning the school-copy model, we are all taught, when we write words beginning with any one of these four letters, that our first stroke

should be an upstroke, originating at the base line. Since this beginning stroke is completely superfluous to the essential letter form, and since it tends to reduce the efficiency and the fluency of the writing, people tend to omit it as they mature.

[2] Scales of handwriting quality such as those of Ayres[1], Thorndike[12], Rosenhaus[9] are commonly used in the elementary schools to evaluate the individual child's progress in cursive writing. The scales all typically consist of a graded series of handwriting samples, from worse to better, the best and highest grade sample always being an ideal school-copy model.

References

1. Ayres, L. P. *A Scale for Measuring the Quality of Handwriting of Children.* New York: Russell Sage Foundation, Division of Education, 1917.

2. Binet, A. *Les Révélations de l'Ecriture d'après un Controle Scientifique.* Paris: Alcan, 1906.

3. Castelnuovo-Tedesco, P. "A Study of the Relationship Between Handwriting and Personality Variables." *Genetic Psychological Monographs,* XXXVII (1948), pp. 167–220.

4. Epstein, L., and Hartford, H. "Some Relationships of Beginning Strokes in Handwriting to the Human Figure Drawing Test." *Perceptual and Motor Skills,* IX (1959), pp. 55–62.

5. Gesell, A. "Accuracy in Handwriting as Related to School Intelligence and Sex." *American Journal of Psychology,* XVII (1906), pp. 394–405.

6. Lewinson, T., and Zubin, J. *Handwriting Analysis.* New York: King's Crown Press, 1944.

7. Omwake, K. T. "The Value of Photographs and Handwriting in Estimating Intelligence." *Public Personnel Studies,* III (1925), pp. 2–15.

8. Rice, L. *Character Reading from Handwriting.* New York: Frederick A. Stokes Co., 1927.

9. Rosenhaus, M., and others. *Survey Chart for Cursive Handwriting.* New York: Board of Education of City of New York, 1949.

10. Starch, D. "The Measurement of Handwriting." *Journal of Educational Psychology,* IV (1913), pp. 445–64.

11. Thorndike, E. L. "Handwriting." *Teachers College Record,* XI, No. 2 (1910).

12. Thorndike, E. L. *Handwriting Scale.* New York: Bureau of Publications, Teachers College, Columbia University, 1910.

Columbia University.

College of Physicians and Surgeons.

The Handwriting Institute, Inc.

Appendix E

The Role of Handwriting Analysis in Cancer Detection
Condensed Résumés of Research Undertaken
Between 1950 and 1971

CONDENSED RÉSUMÉ OF NEUROMUSCULAR TEST RESEARCH (ALFRED KANFER) 1950–1959

I. HOSPITAL FOR JOINT DISEASES

OVERALL CONTROL OF STUDIES: Dr. Henry L. Jaffe, Director of Laboratories.

INVESTIGATORS: Research Committee of hospital staff members, Dr. Daniel Casten as chairman and Drs. Martin Clyman, Louis Kagen, Ralph Mishkin, and Gustave Steinberg as members.

VERIFICATION OF HOSPITAL FINDINGS: Dr. J. J. Golub, Director, Dr. Henry L. Jaffe, Mr. Rosenberg, Administrator.

VERIFICATION OF FINDINGS ON EQUITABLE LIFE ASSURANCE SOCIETY SAMPLES: Dr. Richard Gubner and Mr. John Mills, who submitted the results to Dr. Jaffe.

OBJECT: Validation study of the Neuromuscular Test for Separation of High-risk from Low-risk Groups for Cancer.

1) Findings 1950–52

1. SOURCE: patients' signatures on consent forms of old and new hospital charts. All six members of the Research Committee examined independently the same signatures.

Overall No. of cases:	*clinical cancer.*	*corr. rat.*	*clinical negat.*	*correct:*
1. 1,361	489	90%	872	73%

2. Additional study, as above.

175	60	96%	115	84%

3. Signatures on insurance forms of persons of a similar age group disabled either from cancer or from a chronic degenerative disease:

198	125	89%	73	85%

4 and 5. Predictive study in retrospect, same examiners as above.
a). Hospital:

213	108	91%	105	91.5%

b). Insurance:

66	21	90%	45	92%

In all studies above findings were considered as correct when four of the six examiners agreed with the medical findings.

II. STUDIES ARRANGED AND CONTROLLED BY THE AMERICAN CANCER SOCIETY (1950–1954)

1) Handwriting samples gathered from five different hospitals and findings verified by the American Cancer Society. Examiner: Alfred Kanfer.

935	88	84%	847	79%

The findings showed no significant difference between sex and age groups. Twenty-three samples were from cancer patients classified as stage 1. Of those twenty-two were rated positive—i.e., 95.6 percent.

2) *Yates Memorial Study, Detroit*

A number of handwriting samples were gathered by the American Cancer Society from the Detroit Cancer Detection Center and submitted first to Kanfer and then to Mr. Gordon Shellard, an associate actuary, at that time with the Metropolitan Life Insurance Company, who was trained in the technique of the neuromuscular test. No detailed data on this study were made available besides the following statement made by Dr. Cuyler Hammond: "Mr. Kanfer fell down badly on this study, Mr. Shellard fell down on one batch, and on another batch Mr. Shellard did very well."

It turned out that errors in the technical arrangements for this study were made and later on corrected, leading then to Mr. Shellard's positive results.

3) *Metropolitan Life Insurance Company Study,* also arranged

by the American Cancer Society, but carried out at the premises of the company and on samples provided by the company. Also the two examiners who carried out this study were appointed by the company—one, the aforementioned Mr. Gordon Shellard, and a second one, Mr. Tap Taves, who was assigned subsequently for a control study of Mr. Shellard's findings.

This was also a predictive study in retrospect, the handwriting samples being taken from the files of deceased insurance holders of whom some have died within one to ten years after the date of the writing from cancer, others from various other conditions. For the examiners, not knowing time and cause of death, it was a blind and predictive study.

a) Mr. Gordon Shellard

interval between signature and death	No. of cases: cause cancer	Rating: neg.	doubtf.	posit.	No. of cases: cause not malignant	Rating: neg.	doubtf.	posit.
up to three years	252	0.8	0.8	98.4%	323	89.4	8.7	1.9%
four to ten years	44	6.8	77.3	15.9%	243	99.2	0.8	0. %
ten plus	17	94.1	0.	5.9%	203	100.	0.	0. %
Total	313				769			1,082

b) Mr. Tap Taves

Repeat study on 294 old samples
Study on a new batch of 157 cases

(Similar results) Cause of death:	No. of cases	Rating posit.	neg.	No. of cases	Rating posit.	neg.
cancer	140	100%	0%	51	96%	4%
not malignant	143	8%	92%	106	0%	100%

eleven cases were excluded.

Follow-up time from date of signature to death for both studies: one to five years.

III.   Memorial-Tower-Strang Clinic Study
(arranged by Dr. Emerson Day, 1959–61)

Examiner: *Alfred Kanfer.* Number of cases: 708

Type of cases:	No. of cases:	Rating:	
		positive	negative
non-neoplastic	92	13%	87%
benign tumors	442	40%	60%
cancer	174	72%	27%

Re-examination: John Donahue, Joyce Farro, Naomi P. Roman, Strang Clinic, 1967.

nonmalignant	277	10.5%	89.5%	Total:	466
cancer	189	94.1%	5.9%		

THIRD STUDY, P.M.I.–STRANG CLINIC
NEUROMUSCULAR TEST DATA, REPORTED 7/28/71
(FINDINGS OF EXAMINERS A & B COMBINED)
NUMBER OF CASES RATED

	Positive	%	Doubtful	%	Negative	%	All Cases
Present Developed during three years of observation	53	100	0	0	0	0	53
Present at initial examination	119	85	14	10	7	5	140
All cases with cancer	172	89	14	7.3	7	3.6	193
Absent	52	7.7	80	12.3	537	80	669
All cases	224		94		544		862

Percentage of cancer in cases rated negative: 7:669   1%
Percentage of cancer in cases rated positive: 172:224 76.8%

Minimum period of follow-up for negatives three years: 62 percent of the negatives and 36 percent of the cancer patients are above age sixty.

Probability for each of the examiners less than one in a million (determined by Mr. Gordon Shellard, associate actuary, Metropolitan Life Insurance Company).

Examiners: Mrs. Irene Blaser and Mrs. Lillian Grebanier.

Criteria modified by Mrs. Naomi P. Roman.

Appendix F

Relationship of Secondary Beginning Strokes in Handwriting
to Reading Skills[1]

Linton, Epstein, and Hartford (1961) have used the term "secondary beginning-stroke, to identify the initial upstroke in handwriting that is frequently found on words beginning with the small letters "u," "v," "w," and "y." Their study, designed to investigate psychological correlates of secondary beginning strokes, led to the conclusion that "The use of secondary beginning strokes is . . . associated with relative inadequacy and lack of energy in intellectual functioning and other forms of coping with the environment with a tendency to accept things as they are rather than actively trying to control or alter them, and with constriction that applies particularly to emotional interaction." [2] It appeared to the present writers that poor readers often possess

[1] Material extracted from Otto, W., and Lasswell, A. "Relationship of Secondary Beginning Strokes in Handwriting to Reading Ability." *Perceptual and Motor Skills*, 1962, 14, 530. Reprinted by permission of the authors and the Publisher.

[2] Please refer to Test Number Two, Appendix C, page 316 of this volume; "Personality and Perceptual Correlates of Secondary Beginning Strokes in Handwriting" by Linton, H. B., Epstein, L., and Hartford, H., originally published in *Perceptual and Motor Skills*, 1961, 12, 271-281; and the University of Oregon.

350

these same psychological attributes and that, therefore, it might be expected that poor readers would tend to use more secondary beginning strokes than would good readers.

Subjects were fifty seventh- and eighth-grade students with group test IQ scores between 90 and 110. Twenty-five subjects were poor readers (reading six months or more below grade level) and twenty-five subjects were good readers (reading six months or more above grade level) according to standardized reading tests corroborated by teacher judgment. Informal English themes and spelling exercises were examined to find ten words beginning with the small letters "u," "v," "w," or "y" for each subject. The number of secondary beginning strokes found in the ten words was then determined.

The poor readers used a significantly greater number of secondary beginning strokes than did good readers ($x^2 = 19.68$; 6.635 required for .01 level with 1 df), as was expected. It was observed that seventh-graders tended to use secondary beginning strokes more frequently than eighth-graders. When the numbers for thirty-nine eighth-graders only were compared x^2 became 24.741.

The data imply that the psychological attributes which make for retention of the use of secondary beginning strokes in handwriting may also make for poor performance in reading. That seventh-grade subjects tend to use more secondary beginning strokes is logical because seventh-graders are less far removed from formal handwriting instruction, in which the letter-form models almost invariably include the secondary beginning strokes. Further study might profitably be devoted to the relationship of grade placement and reading level and interactions of these variables to tendency to use secondary beginning strokes.

Appendix G

Effects of Alcohol on the Graphomotor Performances of Normals and Chronic Alcoholics[1]

The effect of alcohol [2] on the behavior and functioning of individuals is of much theoretical and practical concern. Studies of the motoric changes arising from alcohol seem especially appropriate: the more obvious consequences of alcohol are predominantly motoric—slurred speech, unsteady gait, depressed or exaggerated motor reactions, and other phenomena suggesting that the musculature is affected sharply by this drug. Therefore, it is appropriate to search the motor system for reflections of imbalances induced by alcohol.

Studies of motor functioning were most popular in the early stages of research on alcoholism (Jellinek and McFarland, 1940). Most investigators used a variety of motor coordination tests; some included complex performances such as driving (Goldberg, 1943; Forbes, 1947; Bjerver and Goldberg, 1950; McCleary and Johnson, 1954; Mueller, 1954). Handwriting has sometimes been used as the test of motor functioning (Rabin, 1953; De Trey, 1954; Schweiter, 1955).

[1] Material reprinted from Tripp, C. A., Fluckiger, F. A., and Weinberg, G. H. "Effects of Alcohol on the Graphomotor Performances of Normals and Chronic Alcoholics." *Perceptual and Motor Skills,* 1959, 9, 227-236. Published in this book by permission of the authors and the Publisher.

[2] We are indebted to Dr. Benjamin Kissin, Director of the Alcohol Clinic, for his extensive participation and cooperation in this study.

The choice of handwriting as an appropriate medium for motor study is supported by numerous considerations. Handwriting is easily and quickly taken. It is a task which has been seasoned by previous practice and familiarity. It may be used to record performances under various degrees of strain; for instance, signature writing is a thoroughly habituated task, whereas the writing of unfamiliar sentence material is more strenuous. Handwriting is a logical sequence of movements which emphasizes rhythm and flow, discouraging any overemphasis on atomistic detail. In reasonable quantities, it does not become boring, nor otherwise invite arbitrary variety. Though held within certain formal limits by its communicative obligation, it is sensitive to intrusions, abbreviations and performance peculiarities which have arisen from individuation. And when peculiarities do occur, their relative distance from conventionally established norms can be recognized.

These advantages and sources of great promise in the use of handwriting as an experimental variable do not exist without penalty, of course. Some features of handwriting are affected by differences in socio-cultural level and by the degree of literacy, factors which must be considered in the selection of subjects. Sometimes, easily visible differences in letter forms or space usage prove virtually impossible to quantify. On the other hand, numerous variables in the written performance can be quite precisely quantified.

Most previous experiments have dealt merely with the immediate effect of alcohol on normal subjects. To our knowledge, only two investigations (Kates and Schmolke, 1953; Curnutt, 1953) compared the motor performance of normals with that of chronic alcoholics.

The present study was designed to compare motor functioning in normals and in alcoholics both when sober and when inebriated. Specifically, two questions were asked: (a) Is there a characteristic difference in motor functioning between normals and alcoholics? and, (b) How does alcohol affect graphomotor functioning and are the effects different on normals and alcoholics?

Method

SUBJECTS

Subjects consisted of an experimental group of 68 alcoholics and a control group of 18 normals. The patients were taken from the alcoholic ward of Kings County Hospital, where they had been diagnosed as chronic alcoholics. The normals were volunteers from the community. They were selected after psychiatric interviews, so that the group did not include individuals with serious personality disturbances. They had also been cleared regarding their use of alcohol. At most they were in the category of "social drinkers."

All subjects were male and ranged in age from twenty to fifty, the mean age being 29.9 for the control group and 40.5 for the alcoholic group.

The testing procedure, which will be described below, was administered individually to each subject.

TESTING THE SUBJECTS WHEN SOBER

The normals came to the hospital at 8:30 A.M. without having had breakfast. They were tested by 9:00 A.M.

The alcoholics had been under hospital care for at least five days. They were transferred to the testing ward at least twenty-four hours before experimental procedures began. They were tested by 9:00 A.M. without having had breakfast.

TESTING THE SUBJECTS UNDER ALCOHOL

Each subject was given 1.0 gr. of ethanol per kg. of body weight as a 25 percent solution in fruit juice. This quantity was sufficient to obtain a blood alcohol level of 100 mg. percent within one hour. The tests were then administered to the subjects again, usually by 10:30 A.M. No food was taken during the whole experiment.

APPARATUS AND DATA

Subjects performed three kinds of tasks, and graphodyne records were taken.

The graphodyne used in our research for the measurement of

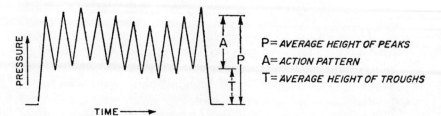

P = *AVERAGE HEIGHT OF PEAKS*
A = *ACTION PATTERN*
T = *AVERAGE HEIGHT OF TROUGHS*

Fig. 1. Diagram of a graphodyne wave showing component parts

pressure variables and speed has been described in detail elsewhere (Tripp, Fluckiger and Weinberg, 1957). This instrument yields a graph of subject's pressure recorded along the vertical axis, and time along the horizontal. A diagram of a graphodyne wave appears in Fig. 1.

After writing his name three times as a warm-up, each subject was asked to write the following: (a) A sequence of "garland" (u-shaped) loops. This is called the spontaneously written *garland* sequence. (b) Another sequence of such loops under the instruction to write "as lightly as possible." This is called the *low garland* sequence. (c) The sentence (copied from a printed form), "I am walking down the street to get the horse and buggy."

Finally, each subject was asked to operate the dynamometer in order to obtain a measure of gross muscular strength. For this, subjects stood erect, elbows straight, and left-hand measures were taken first.

MEASURES

The focus of this study was on the measures taken from the garland and the low garland tasks. Since the garland task is repetitive, stable scores could be obtained from small samples, thus increasing our power to make a variety of comparisons. Variations in subjects' performances when writing garlands could, for the most part, be ascribed to the subjects themselves. Note that the garland is a spontaneous writing task, whereas the low garland requires considerable control.

The writing of a sentence was added because it calls for the negotiation of complex forms. Such a task is maximally sensitive to differences in writing speed.

The measures were obtained from two sources: the graphodyne wave and the written products themselves. Irregularities and coordinational difficulties appear in the graphodyne wave as variations in the heights of corresponding parts of the wave, or as variations in the shapes of the wave.

The following measures were obtained for the garland and for the low garland tasks. (a) The average maximum pressure exerted in writing. This value was obtained by tabulating and averaging the heights of all the peaks for each subject. (b) The action pattern—i.e., the difference between the average maximum pressure and the average minimum pressure. (c) The variability of the peaks. The absolute differences between the heights of adjacent peaks were obtained and the standard deviation of these differences was found for each subject. (d) The degree of ataxia. We counted each of the interferences in the smoothness of the graphodyne wave, provided their magnitude was at least one-half mm. The total of these deviations divided by the number of garland loops in the wave provided the measure of ataxia. (e) The width of the loops. This measure was taken directly from the writing samples. (f) The size or average vertical extension of the loops. This measure was taken directly from the writing samples. (g) The speed of loop writing. This measure was computed as the average number of loops written per second.

A speed measure was also obtained for the writing of the sentence. Here, the gross time spent by each subject was used as the score.

Results

The results will be presented in three separate sections. In the first section we shall compare the performances of the normals and the alcoholics under the control condition (i.e., when both groups were sober). In the second section we shall compare the *effects* of the ethanol on the performances of the two groups. That is, we shall compare the "change" scores of the normals with the "change" scores of the alcoholics. In the third section, we shall compare the performances of the two groups under the experimental condition (i.e., when the members of both groups were under the effect of ethanol).

Note that the analysis of the change scores is statistically the most powerful. The reason is that subjects serve as their own controls when the change scores are computed, whereas, in the pre and post comparisons, the two independent groups are compared with each other. To put it another way, it was easier to detect a significant change in either group than a significant difference between the two groups. Thus it sometimes happened that the two groups did not differ significantly from each other either before or after ingestion of alcohol, even though one or both groups changed significantly.

COMPARISON OF THE TWO GROUPS WHEN SOBER

The tendency was for the alcoholics to be higher than the normals on the three pressure variables, whether writing spontaneously or as lightly as possible. The two groups, when writing spontaneously, did not differ in average maximum pressure exerted. However, the alcoholics showed a significantly higher action pattern and wrote with significantly more variability of pressure than did the normals.

Under the instruction to write garlands as lightly as possible, the alcoholics exerted significantly more maximum pressure, showed a significantly higher action pattern, and wrote with significantly more variability of pressure than did the normals.

The alcoholics showed considerably (and significantly) more ataxic disturbance than did the normals when writing both

TABLE 1

MEAN SCORES AND t RATIOS FOR 18 NORMALS AND
68 ALCOHOLICS WHEN SOBER

Measures	Spontaneous Pressure			Low Pressure		
	Normals	Alcoholics	t	Normals	Alcoholics	t
I. Garland Writing						
Average Maximum Pressure (mm.)	15.36	16.45	.83	5.09	9.50	5.12*
Action Pattern (mm.)	6.62	8.40	2.68*	2.13	4.75	5.55*
Variability of Pressure (mm.)	.82	1.05	1.96	.40	1.19	7.23*
Ataxia (N disturbances per 100 loops)	5.28	46.46	6.04*	5.46	63.26	5.96*
Width of Loops (mm.)	5.39	5.99	1.40	5.46	5.68	.16
Size of Loops (mm.)	2.70	3.53	2.95*	2.25	3.27	3.37*
Speed (N loops per sec.)	3.86	3.74	.52	3.84	3.59	.74
II. Sentence Writing Gross Time (sec.)	20.67	35.45	7.35*			

* Significant at 5 percent level or better

spontaneously and as lightly as possible. For the normals, the constraint to write as lightly as possible did not lead to a change in the degree of ataxic disturbance present. However, the alcoholics, trying to write as lightly as possible, showed even more ataxic disturbance than when writing freely. Thus the disparity between the two groups was magnified during the "low" garland task.

The average width of the garlands drawn by the two groups did not differ significantly under either the spontaneous or the constrained condition. However, the alcoholics drew garlands of a larger size (or average vertical extension) under both conditions than did the normals.

The two groups did not differ significantly in speed of writing the garlands either spontaneously or under constraint. However, the normals wrote the assigned sentence (a more complex task than writing garlands) considerably and significantly more quickly than did the alcoholics.

COMPARISON OF THE CHANGES DUE TO ETHANOL IN THE TWO GROUPS

The effects of ethanol on the spontaneous garland writing of the two groups is noteworthy. Ethanol pushed the two groups in opposite directions on all three pressure variables. For the normals, the average maximum pressure, the action pattern and the variability of pressure increased. For the alcoholics, the scores on these variables decreased. On all three measures: average maximum pressure, action pattern and variability of pressure, the difference between the "change" scores of the two groups was significant.

When writing as lightly as possible, the normals did not change significantly on the same three variables. However, even under the low garland constraint, the alcoholics significantly reduced their scores on all three variables.

For the normals, ethanol did not significantly affect the degree of ataxic disturbance present in their writing. But for the alcoholics, ethanol significantly reduced the degree of ataxic disturbance present in both their spontaneous and low garland samples.

Ethanol significantly increased the width of the loops done by members of both groups, both when writing spontaneously and when writing as lightly as possible. Ethanol increased the size of the loops done by the normals. However, it did not affect the size of the loops done by the alcoholics (which were originally quite large).

TABLE 2

MEAN "CHANGE" SCORES FOR 18 NORMALS AND 68 ALCOHOLICS RESULTING
FROM ETHANOL; AND *t* RATIOS OF DIFFERENCES BETWEEN
"CHANGE" SCORES

Measures	Spontaneous Pressure			Low Pressure		
	Normals	Alcoholics	t	Normals	Alcoholics	t
I. Garland Writing						
Average Maxi-mum Pressure (mm.)	2.91	−1.46†	3.07*	−.15	−1.46†	2.22*
Action Pattern (mm.)	2.71†	− .76†	3.41*	.31	− .88†	3.97*
Variability of pressure (mm.)	.23	− .23†	3.28*	.02	− .25†	5.53*
Ataxia (*N* dis-turbances per 100 loops)	2.10	−22.56†	4.38*	3.53	−32.46†	3.72*
Width of Loops (mm.)	1.52†	.85†	1.86	1.37†	.49†	2.12*
Size of Loops (mm.)	.93†	.12	3.25*	.95†	.18	.20
Speed (*N* loops per sec.)	.16	.04	.67	−.07	− .08	.06
II. Sentence Writing						
Gross time (sec.)	1.37†	− .35	1.50			

† Change with group significant at 5 percent level or better
* *t* ratio significant at 5 percent level or better

COMPARISON OF THE TWO GROUPS UNDER THE INFLUENCE OF ETHANOL

First, we shall consider the three pressure variables: average maximum pressure, action pattern, and variability of pressure. The two groups did not differ significantly when writing spontaneously with respect to these three variables. However, the normals managed to write with significantly lower pressure when both groups were asked to write as lightly as possible.

The alcoholics showed significantly (and vastly) more ataxia in both the spontaneous and constrained writing. Incidentally, the effect of the ethanol had been to cut ataxia almost exactly in half for both groups writing under either condition.

TABLE 3

MEAN SCORES AND *t* RATIOS FOR 18 NORMALS AND 68 ALCOHOLICS
UNDER ETHANOL

Measures	Spontaneous Pressure			Low Pressure		
	Normals	Alcoholics	t	Normals	Alcoholics	t
I. Garland Writing						
Average Maximum Pressure (mm.)	18.27	15.00	1.57	4.94	8.04	4.23*
Action Pattern (mm.)	9.36	7.64	1.50	2.44	3.87	3.14*
Variability of Pressure (mm.)	1.04	.82	1.66	.42	.94	4.91*
Ataxia (*N* disturbances per 100 loops)	3.18	23.90	4.73*	2.11	30.80	5.80*
Width of Loops (mm.)	6.91	6.83	.13	6.84	6.17	.90
Size of Loops (mm.)	3.63	3.66	.08	3.20	3.45	.59
Speed (*N* loops per sec.)	4.02	3.78	1.09	3.77	3.51	.84
II. Sentence Writing						
Gross Time (sec.)	22.04	35.10	6.62*			

* Significant at 5 percent level or better

Under the alcoholic condition, no significant differences between groups were found in either the width or size of the loops. No significant speed differences between the groups were found on the repetitive garland tasks. However, the normals wrote the assigned sentence significantly faster.

It was necessary to ascertain whether any of the results found were merely a function of the age, body weight, or gross physical strength of the subjects. Age and weight were correlated with the scores obtained on the writing tasks in each experimental state, but no significant correlation was found.

Dynamometer readings were used as a measure of gross muscular strength. No significant correlation with the scores obtained on the writing tasks in either experimental state was found.

Discussion

Four general statements serve to pull together the findings in this study. (a) The normals turned in a performance generally superior to that of the alcoholics. (b) In general, ethanol seemed to have a disturbing effect on the performances of the normals, whereas it actually had a steadying effect on the performances of the alcoholics. (c) The performances of the normals "under the influence" became like those of the chronic alcoholics. In general, the resemblance was in kind but usually not in degree. (d) The measures taken from the graphodyne do not have strong commonalities with obvious anatomical variables, such as subjects' weight or their strength. Instead, some of the graphodyne variables which relate to alcoholism and the intake of ethanol evidently have more subtle psychological associations.

We shall consider the first three statements in order and elaborate somewhat upon them.

1. The normals' performance was generally superior. The normals wrote with markedly less ataxia than did the alcoholics under both conditions. As a matter of fact, the normals even when inebriated showed less tremor than the alcoholics performing with maximum efficiency. The comparison of the two groups when sober reveals the most drastic differences. The normals wrote with less variability than the alcoholics; they were also able to reduce their pressure considerably more than the alcoholics when instructed to do so.

The greater the demand of the task, the greater was the superiority of the normals in carrying it out. For instance, the two groups did not differ in the speed of writing garlands, but when it came to writing the sentence, the normals were faster under both conditions. Similarly, spontaneous garland writing is easier than low garland writing, so that the pressure difference between the two groups appeared mainly on the low garland. The garland loops drawn by the two groups were equal in width. Width is basically a horizontal dimension, and thus relatively insensitive to motor discoordinations.[3] When dry, the alcoholics drew loops of a considerably larger size. Size is a vertical and therefore more demanding dimension; consequently the alcoholic's increase is best seen as a primitivization due to loss of motor control.

How are we to account for the superiority of the normals? One possibility is that the *effects* of chronic alcoholism are to decrease efficiency of functioning. Another possibility is that the deficiencies antedated the alcoholism—i.e., physiological factors may have interacted with psychological and/or social ones to *cause* alcoholism. The implication would be that we have picked up true functional differences between the alcoholics and the normals which might even have been present at birth. The crucial experiment to test this hypothesis would entail comparing the performances of pre-alcoholics with those of normals.

2. An important finding is that, in general, ethanol seemed to have a disturbing effect on the performances of normals, whereas it had a steadying effect on the performances of alcoholics. The alcoholics were induced by drink to write with less pressure and less variability. They became less ataxic and were better able to carry out the low garland task. The effect of the same relative dose of ethanol on the normals was to increase their scores on the pressure variables. Ethanol did not help them on the low

---

[3] Horizontal movements are believed to be fundamentally simpler and easier than vertical ones. This has been demonstrated by drawing tests and in the Bender-Gestalt Test, Design #6 (Tripp, 1957, p. 79). Horizontal movement is predominantly simple extensor activity, phylogenetically ancient; vertical movement—i.e., adductive flexor activity—requires integrated motor action more closely related to cortical processes (Goldstein, 1939, p. 482).

garland task and did not reduce significantly the degree of ataxic disturbance in their writing.

There are several possible explanations of the finding that ethanol has opposite effects upon the two groups. One possibility is that the alcoholic has adapted to a state of partial inebriation. His body "demands" a drink to restore it to equilibrium, whereas the normal becomes disrupted by the alien influence of ethanol. It might also be that ethanol is reinforcing to the alcoholic for psychological reasons and that the ego-enhancement produced by ethanol enables him to perform more efficiently.

3. The normal who is given ethanol performs in various ways like the chronic alcoholic. His motor control becomes poor. He becomes overly expansive and gives the general impression of blundering into the field without his usual focus. The various changes effected by ethanol on the writing of the normals include an increase in pressure and variability and an increase in both the width and size of the garlands.

These changes are not so great that their writing may be considered equivalent with that of chronic alcoholics. For one thing, the writing of the normals "under the influence" of alcohol is not nearly as ataxic as that of the alcoholics. The normal is still able to conform to a specific demand and to maintain a high degree of control when he exerts conscious effort. Even "under the influence" he is able to carry out the low garland task far better than the chronic alcoholic. In sum, ethanol induces in the normals, spontaneous motor behavior which is a small-scale version of behavior that characterizes the chronic alcoholic.

Summary

The present study was designed to compare the graphomotor functioning of 68 alcoholics with that of 18 normals who were given a variety of handwriting tasks to perform both when sober and after ingestion of ethanol. These tasks included the writing of a standard sentence and a sequence of u-shaped loops (garlands), both spontaneously and under the constraint to write as lightly as possible. Measures of pressure, variability, ataxia, and speed were recorded on the graphodyne. Subjects' age, weight, and physical strength were also recorded. The normals turned in a performance generally superior to that of the alcoholics. The higher the demands of the task, the larger was the difference between the two groups. Ethanol had the effect of pushing the two groups in opposite directions: while the performances of the normals were impaired, those of the alcoholics showed marked improvement. Ethanol induced the normals to write in ways ordinarily characteristic for the alcoholics. However, when asked to maintain control in a difficult task, they were able to do as well as when sober. The handwriting measures did not correlate with the measures of subjects' age, weight, or physical strength. Some physiological and psychological conditions and processes which are most likely to account for the findings were suggested.

References

Bjerver, K., and Goldberg, L. "Effect of Alchohol Ingestion on Driving Ability: Results of Practical Road Tests and Laboratory Experiments. *Quarterly Journal of Studies on Alcohol,* 1950, 11, pp. 1–30.

Curnutt, R. H. "The Use of the Bender-Gestalt With an Alcoholic and Non-alcoholic Population." *Journal of Clinical Psychology,* 1953, 9, pp. 287–290.

De Trey, M. *"Handschriftveraenderungen unter Alkoholeinfluss."* *Ausdruckskunde,* 1954, 1, pp. 9–12.

Forbes, G. "The Effect of Alcohol on the Psychomotor Reactions as a Possible Index of Alcoholic Intoxication. *Medico Legal Journal,* 1947, 15, pp. 23–38.

Goldberg, L. "Quantitative Studies on Alcohol Tolerance in Men; the Influence of Ethyl Alcohol on Sensory, Motor and Psychological Functions Referred to Blood Alcohol in Normal and Habituated Individuals. *Acta Physiologica Scandinavica,* 1943, 5 (Suppl. 16), pp. 1–128.

Goldstein, K. *The Organism.* New York: American Book, 1939.

Jellinek, E. M., and McFarland, R. A. "Analyses of Psychological Experiments on the Effect of Alcohol." *Quarterly Journal of Studies on Alcohol,* 1940, 1, pp. 272–371.

Kates, S. L., and Schmolke, M. F. "Self-related and Parent-related Verbalizations and Bender-Gestalt Performance of Alcoholics." *Quarterly Journal of Studies on Alcohol,* 1953, 14, pp. 38–48.

McCleary, R. A., and Johnson, R. H. *Psychophysiological Effects of Cold, 2. The Role of Alcohol Ingestion and Complexion in Manual Performance Decrement.* U.S. Air Force, School of Aviation Medicine. Project #21-1202-0004, Report #2, 1954, pp. 1–9.

Mueller, B. "*Alkoholgenuss und Fahrfaehigkeit; Bericht ueber Modellversuche.*" *Hefte z. Unfallheilkunde,* 1954, 47, pp. 188–193.

Rabin, A., and Blair, H. "The Effects of Alcohol on Handwriting." *Journal of Clinical Psychology,* 1953, 9, pp. 284–87.

Schweiter, H. "*Graphologische, klinische und psychologische Untersuchungen unter Alkoholwirkung.*" *Oeffentl. Gesundheitsdienst,* 1955, 16, pp. 361–372.

Tripp, C. A. "Some Graphomotor Features of the Bender Visual-Motor Gestalt Test in Relation to Delinquent and Non-delinquent White Adolescent Males." Unpublished doctoral dissertation, New York University, 1957.

Tripp, C. A., Fluckiger, F. A., and Weinberg, G. H. "Measurement of Handwriting Variables." *Perceptual and Motor Skills,* 1957, 7, pp. 279–94.

The Handwriting Institute, Inc., New York.

Alcohol Clinic, the State University of New York, College of Medicine at New York City.

Bibliography

Allport, Gordon W., and Vernon, Philip E. *Studies in Expressive Movement*. New York: Macmillan, 1933.

Anthony, Daniel S. "The Graphological Psychogram Psychological Meaning of its Sectors and Symbolic Interpretation of Its Graphic Indicators." Newark, New Jersey, privately published 1964.

Booth, Mary H. *How to Read Character in Handwriting*. Philadelphia: The John C. Winston Company, 1910.

Brook, Lyn. *Your Personality in Handwriting*. Westport, Connecticut: Associated Booksellers, 1960.

Brooks, Harry C. *Your Character from Your Handwriting*. London: George Allen and Unwin Ltd., 1930.

Bunker, M. N. *Handwriting Analysis*. Chicago: Nelson-Hall, Co., 1966.

Crépieux-Jamin, J. *Handwriting and Expression* (Translated by John Holt Schooling). London: Kegan Paul, Trench, Trübner & Co., Ltd., 1892.

———. *The Psychology of the Movements of Handwriting*. Translated and arranged by L. K. Given-Wilson. London: George Routledge & Sons, Ltd., 1926.

De Sainte Colombe, Paul. *Grapho-Therapeutics Pen and Pencil Therapy.* Hollywood, California: Laurida Books Publishing Company, 1966.

Doremus, Laura. *Character in Handwriting.* New York: The Charles Renard Company, 1925.

Downey, June E. *Graphology and The Psychology of Handwriting.* Baltimore: Warwick & York, Inc., 1919.

————. "Preliminary Study of Family Resemblance in Handwriting." Department of Psychology *Bulletin,* No. I, 1910. Laramie, Wyoming: University of Wyoming.

Eliasberg, W. G. "Graphology and Medicine," *Journal of Nervous and Mental Disease,* Vol. 100, No. 4, October 1944.

————. "Pen Paper and Parkinsonism," *Geriatrics.* Vol. 14 (November 1959): 705–708.

Eliasberg, W. G., Teltscher, H. O., and Trautman, E. C. "Neuropsychiatry and Graphodiagnostics in Parkinson Research," *Acta Psychiatrica et Neurologica Scandinavica.* Vol. 36, Fasc. 3, 1961.

Epstein, L., and Hartford, H. "Some Relationships of Beginning Strokes in Handwriting to the Human Figure Drawing Test." *Perceptual and Motor Skills* 9 (1959) : 55–57, 61–62.

Epstein, L. Hartford, H., and Tumarkin, I. "The Relationship of Certain Letter Form Variants in the Handwriting of Female Subjects to Their Education, I.Q. and Age," *Journal of Experimental Education.* Vol. 29, No. 4, June 1961.

Fasulo, Joseph C. How to Read Character in Handwriting. Privately published, 1954.

Fluckiger, Fritz A., Tripp, Clarence A., and Weinberg, George H. "A Review of Experimental Research in Graphology 1933–1960," *Perceptual and Motor Skills,* Monograph Supplement I–V, 12 (1961) : 12, 67–90.

French, William Leslie. *The Psychology of Handwriting.* New York and London: G. P. Putnam's Sons, 1922.

Getzels, Jacob W., and Jackson, Philip W. *Creativity and Intelligence.* London and New York: John Wiley & Sons, Inc., 1962

Goldberger, Leo. "Personality correlates of handwriting: an exploratory study." New York: New York University unpublished manuscript, 1967.

Hamilton, Charles. *Collecting Autographs and Manuscripts.* Norman, Oklahoma: University of Oklahoma Press, 1961.

Holder, Robert. *You Can Analyze Handwriting.* Englewood Cliffs, New Jersey: Prentice Hall, Inc., 1958.

Jacoby, H. J. *Analysis of Handwriting.* London: George Allen and Unwin Ltd., 1939.

————. *Self-Knowledge Through Handwriting.* London: J. M. Dent and Sons, Ltd., 1941.

King, Leslie W. "In Regard to Bias: An Open Letter," *Annals,* No. 1 (August 1969), Chicago, Illinois: The American Association of Handwriting Analysts.

Klages, Dr. Ludwig. *Handschrift und Charakter.* Leipzig: Verlag Von Johann Ambrosius Barth, 1921.

Klein, Felix. "Rhythm, Groundrhythm and Beyond," Lecture Delivered at the Fifth Annual Convention of The American Association of Handwriting Analysts, August 1970.

Land, Adelle, M.A. "Graphology: A Psychological Analysis." University of Buffalo Studies, Vol. III, No. 4, (May 1924).

Lewinson, Thea Stein. "Expression of Crisis in Handwriting" *("Der Ausdruck der Krise in her Handschrift"), Zeitschrift Für Menschenkunde,* 3 (1961): 127–137. Translated by Seymour W. Beardsley and Ilse P. Fritsch.

————. "The Use of Handwriting Analysis as a Psychodiagnostic Technique," *Journal of Projective Techniques,* Vol. 25, No. 3 (1961).

Lewinson, Thea Stein, and Zubin, Joseph. *Handwriting Analysis.* New York: Kings Crown Press, 1942.

Linton, H. B., Epstein, L., and Hartford, H. "Personality and Perceptual Correlates of Primary Beginning Strokes in Handwriting," *Perceptual and Motor Skills,* 15 (1962) : 159, 166–170.

————. "Personality and Perceptual Correlates of Secondary Beginning Strokes in Handwriting," *Perceptual and Motor Skills,* 12 (1961) :

Lucas, De Witt B. *Handwriting and Character.* Philadelphia: David McKay Company, 1923.

Mapp, George A. "A Multivariate Analysis of the Relationship Between Handwriting and Sales Ability," an unpublished paper (April 1970).

Marcuse, Irene, Ph.D. *Guide to Personality Through Your Handwriting.* New York: ARC Books, Inc., Second Edition, 1967.

———. *The Key to Handwriting Analysis.* New York: The McBride Company, 1955.

Marley, John. *Handwriting Analysis Made Easy.* North Hollywood, California: Wilshire Book Company, 1967.

Mendel, Alfred O. *Personality in Handwriting.* New York: Stephen Daye Press, 1947.

Michon, Jean-Hippolyte. *Système de Graphologie.* Paris: Librairie Marpon et Flammarion, 1893.

Moretti, Girolamo. *The Saints Through Their Handwriting,* translated by Serge Hughes. New York: Macmillan, 1964.

Myer, Oscar N. *The Language of Handwriting and How to Read It.* New York: Stephen Daye Press, 1951.

Olyanova, Nadya. *Handwriting Tells.* Indianapolis: The Bobbs-Merrill Company, 1936, latest revised edition 1969.

———. *The Psychology of Handwriting.* New York: Sterling Publishing Company, Inc., 1960.

Otto, W., and Lasswell, A. "Relationship of Secondary Beginning Strokes in Handwriting to Reading Ability," *Perceptual and Motor Skills.* 14 (1962): 530.

Pulver, Dr. Max. *Symbolik Der Handschrift.* Zurich and Leipzig: Orell Füssli Verlag, 1931.

Quinan, C., M.D. "Handwriting of Criminals: An Experimental Study." *Archives of Neurology and Psychiatry,* 32 (1934): 350–358.

Rand, Henry A. *Graphology A Handbook.* Cambridge, Massachusetts: Sci-Art Publishers, 1947.

Rice, Louise. *Character Reading From Handwriting.* New York: Frederick A. Stokes, Company, 1927.

Roman, Klara G. *Handwriting A Key to Personality.* New York: Pantheon Books, Inc., 1952.

———. *Encyclopedia of The Written Word.* New York: Frederick Ungar Publishing Company, 1968.

———. "Tension and Release: Studies of Handwriting with the Use of the Graphodyne." Personality-Symposium, No. 2, New York: (1950).

Sara, Dorothy. *Handwriting A New, Improved Method of Personality Analysis.* New York, Bantam Books, Inc., 1968.

―――. *Handwriting Analysis for the Millions.* New York: Bell Publishing Company, Inc., 1967.

Saudek, Robert. *Experiments With Handwriting.* London: George Allen and Unwin Ltd., 1928.

―――. *The Psychology of Handwriting.* London: George Allen and Unwin Ltd., 1925.

Schermann, Rafael. *Secrets of Handwriting,* translated by Prince S. Lubomirski. London: Rider & Company.

Schwab, Robert S., and McLennan, James E. "Micrographia Found Early Symptom in 5% of Parkinson's Disease Cases." *Medical Tribune,* October 9, 1967.

Singer, Eric. *Personality in Handwriting The Guiding Image in Graphology.* London: Gerald Duckworth & Co., Ltd., 1954.

Smith, Albert J. *Applied Graphology.* New York: The Gregg Publishing Company, 1920.

Sonnemann, Ulrich, Ph.D. *Handwriting Analysis as a Psychodiagnostic Tool.* New York: Grune & Stratton, 1950.

Sonnemann, Ulrich, and Kernan, John P. "Handwriting Analysis—A Valid Selection Tool?" *Personnel* (Journal American Management Association) Vol. 39, No. 6, November/December 1962.

Stafford, Muriel. *You and Your Handwriting.* New York: Dell Publishing Company, Inc., 1963.

Starch, Daniel. "The Similarity of Brothers and Sisters in Mental Traits." *Psychol. Rev.,* Vol. 24 (1917): 235–238.

Teltscher, Herry O. *Handwriting—Revelation of Self.* New York: Hawthorne Books, Inc., 1971.

Thewlis, Malford, W., M.D., and Swezy, Isabelle Clark. *Handwriting and the Emotions.* New York: American Graphological Society, Inc., 1954.

Trillat, Raymond. *Graphologie Pratique.* Paris: Vigot Frères, 1953.

Trillat, Raymond, and Masson, Huguette. *Expérience de Graphothérapie en Psychopédagogie.* Paris: Vigot Frères, 1957.

Tripp, Clarence A., Fluckiger, Fritz A., and Weinberg, George H. "Effects of Alcohol on the Graphomotor Performance of Normals and Chronic Alcoholics," *Perceptual and Motor Skills,* 9 (1959): 227–236.

Victor, Frank, Ph.D. *Handwriting A Personality Projection.* Springfield, Illinois: Charles C. Thomas, 1952.

Wolff, Werner, Ph.D. *Diagrams of the Unconscious.* New York: Grune & Stratton, 1948.

Wolfson, Rose. *A Study in Handwriting Analysis.* Privately published, New York, 1949.

Index